# PEARSON
# myspanishlab ¡Hola!

Save Time, Improve Results! Over 200,000 students use the award-winning MyLanguageLabs online learning and assessment system to succeed in their basic language courses. If your instructor has required use of MySpanishLab, you will have online access to an eText, an interactive Student Activities Manual, audio and video materials, and many more resources to help you succeed. For more information, visit us online at http://www.mylanguagelabs.com/books.html.

| A GUIDE TO *GENTE* ICONS | | |
|---|---|---|
| ACTIVITY TYPES | | |
| ✔ | Readiness Check for MySpanishLab | This icon, located in each chapter opener, reminds students to take the Readiness Check in MySpanishLab to test their understanding of the English grammar related to the Spanish grammar concepts in the chapter. |
| 🔊 | Text Audio Program | This icon indicates that recorded material to accompany *Gente* is available in MySpanishLab, on audio CD, or the Companion Website. |
| 👥 | Pair Activity | This icon indicates that the activity is designed to be done by students working in pairs. |
| 👥 | Group Activity | This icon indicates that the activity is designed to be done by students working in small groups or as a whole class. |
| 📖 | Student Activities Manual | This icon indicates that there are practice activities available in the *Gente* Student Activities Manual. The activities may be found either in the printed version of the manual or in the interactive version available through MySpanishLab. Activity numbers are indicated in the text for ease of reference. |
| 🎬 | Video Program | This icon indicates that a video episode is available on the video program that accompanies the *Gente* text. The video is available on DVD and in MySpanishLab. |

D1314561

# PEARSON

ALWAYS LEARNING

María José de la Fuente • Ernesto Martín Peris • Nues Sans Baulenas

# Gente, Volume 2

Third Custom Edition for Southern Connecticut State University

Taken from:
*Gente*, Third Edition
by María José de la Fuente, Ernesto Martín Peris, and Nues Sans Baulenas

Cover Art: Courtesy of FatSprat, clodio, Vanish_Point, Emeraldchik, fazon1/iStockphoto.

Taken from:

*Gente*, Third Edition
by María José de la Fuente, Ernesto Martín Peris, and Neus Sans Baulenas
Copyright © 2012, 2007, 2003 by Pearson Education, Inc.
Published by Prentice Hall
Upper Saddle River, New Jersey 07458

This special edition published in cooperation with Pearson Learning Solutions.

Pearson Learning Solutions, 501 Boylston Street, Suite 900, Boston, MA 02116
A Pearson Education Company
www.pearsoned.com

Printed in the United States of America

1 2 3 4 5 6 7 8 9 10 V092 16 15 14 13

000200010271799071

JL

ISBN 10: 1-269-41739-8
ISBN 13: 978-1-269-41739-6

# BRIEF CONTENTS

| | TASK | OBJECTIVES |
|---|---|---|

Organize a trip to the Dominican Republic

**Communicative**
- Talking about trips, routes and itineraries
- Requesting and giving time and date
- Situating actions in time
- Talking about the future

**Cultural**
- Dominican Republic
- Hispanics in the United States

Write a cooking recipe

**Communicative**
- Talking about food/dishes
- Interacting in a restaurant or bar
- Talking about quantities
- Giving instructions

**Cultural**
- Cuba
- Hispanics in the United States

Identify the main problems on campus and propose solutions

**Communicative**
- Describing and comparing cities and places
- Expressing opinions and wishes
- Expressing agreement and disagreement
- Making and defending proposals

**Cultural**
- Perú
- Hispanics in the United States

Write a biography of a famous person using given information.

**Communicative**
- Relating biographical and historical data
- Talking about past events occurred in specific time frames
- Talking about dates

**Cultural**
- Chile
- Hispanics in the United States

| GRAMMATICAL/ FUNCTIONAL GOALS | VOCABULARY GOALS | STRATEGIES |
|---|---|---|
| ■ Spatial references<br>■ Time references (dates and months, periods of time, parts of the day)<br>■ The time<br>■ Talking about the future (*ir a +* infinitive)<br>■ *Estar a punto de...*, *acabar de...* | ■ Trips<br>■ Transportation<br>■ Activities related to travel | **Oral communication**<br>■ Beyond *sí* and *no*: emphasizing affirmative or negative replies<br><br>**Reading**<br>■ Skimming and scanning texts<br><br>**Writing**<br>■ Using a bilingual dictionary when writing<br>■ Using spatial references when writing descriptions |
| ■ In a restaurant<br>■ Impersonal *se*<br>■ Quantifying: *poco/un poco de, suficiente(s), bastante, mucho, demasiado, ninguno (ningún)/ nada*<br>■ Weights and measures | ■ Foods and drinks<br>■ Cooking and restaurants<br>■ Measures and containers | **Oral communication**<br>■ Verbal courtesy (I)<br><br>**Reading**<br>■ Word formation and affixes<br><br>**Writing**<br>■ Writing topic sentences and paragraphs<br>■ Connectors for organizing information |
| ■ Comparatives<br>■ The superlative<br>■ Comparisons of equality<br>■ Relative pronouns<br>■ Expressing and contrasting opinions<br>■ The weather | ■ Cities and services<br>■ Weather and environment<br>■ Problems in the city | **Oral communication**<br>■ Collaboration in conversation (I)<br><br>**Reading**<br>■ Word order in Spanish<br><br>**Writing**<br>■ Adding details to a paragraph<br>■ Connecting information using relative pronouns |
| ■ The Preterit tense<br>■ Uses of the Preterit<br>■ Talking about dates<br>■ Sequencing past events | ■ Biographies<br>■ Historical and socio-political events | **Oral communication**<br>■ Using approximation and circumlocution<br><br>**Reading**<br>■ Following a chronology<br><br>**Writing**<br>■ Writing a narrative (I): past actions and events<br>■ Use of time markers in narratives (I) |

|  | TASK | OBJECTIVES |
|---|---|---|
| <br><br>**11 Gente e historias (II)** *182* | Write a narration related to a specific episode or period of our country's history. | **Communicative**<br>■ Talking about past and circumstances surrounding them<br>■ Relating biographical data: events, and circumstances surrounding them<br><br>**Cultural**<br>■ Nicaragua<br>■ Hispanics in the United States |
| **12 Gente sana** *200* | Create a campaign for the prevention of accidents or health problems | **Communicative**<br>■ Talking about health<br>■ Giving advice and recommendations<br><br>**Cultural**<br>■ Costa Rica<br>■ Hispanics in the United States |

| GRAMMATICAL/ FUNCTIONAL GOALS | VOCABULARY GOALS | STRATEGIES |
| --- | --- | --- |
| ■ The Imperfect tense<br>■ Uses of the Imperfect<br>■ Contrasting Preterit vs. Imperfect<br>■ Relating past events: cause and consequence | ■ Historical and socio-political concepts and events | **Oral communication**<br>■ Collaboration in conversation (II)<br><br>**Reading**<br>■ Summarizing a text<br><br>**Writing**<br>■ Writing a narrative (II): including circumstances that surround events<br>■ Use of time markers in narratives (II) |
| ■ Commands forms<br>■ Recommendations, advice, and warnings<br>■ Impersonal *tú*<br>■ Talking about health<br>■ Adverbs ending in *-mente* | ■ Accidents, symptoms, and illnesses | **Oral communication**<br>■ Verbal courtesy (II)<br><br>**Reading**<br>■ Considering the type of text<br><br>**Writing**<br>■ The good foreign language writer<br>■ Reviewing your text for cohesion |

## Gente 3rd edition – Communicate with a Purpose!

*Gente* is a task- and content-based basic Spanish learning program. With *Gente*, students learn Spanish in the classroom through interaction and collaborative work. They develop an ability to express themselves in real contexts and solve communicative problems. Students also reflect on how the Spanish language works and on their own language learning process; use of the language and discovery are the keys to learning. To a degree unmatched by other textbook programs available in North America, *Gente* promotes integration of the four skills and development of cultural awareness by providing a rich context in which students learn by doing, and the teacher acts as the facilitator of this learning process.

## New to This Edition

✦ **Fewer chapters allow for easier implementation of the *Gente* program**

In response to our reviewers' suggestion to streamline the number of chapters, the third edition now has 20 chapters. This new format allows for easier implementation and easier lesson planning in the traditional semester- and quarter-systems.

✦ **Expanded cultural content provides students with cultural insights to the entire Spanish-speaking world including Hispanics in the United States.**

**NEW** Hispanic/Latinos in the U.S. sections promote awareness of the Spanish-speaking communities in the United States. These new activities foster comparisons and cross-cultural knowledge. Culture permeates all sections of the chapter, from *Acercamientos* to *Comparaciones*. Relevant and authentic cultural input (both visual and verbal) has been revised to reinforce language-culture connections. The carefully selected readings and writing tasks, maps, cultural boxes, and extensive photographic material encourage students to make connections with Spanish-speaking countries and their cultures.

✦ **The culminating task now includes reflection as one of the steps to move students from language usage to language analysis**

At the end of each task, the **NEW** linguistic focus stage serves to clarify and review key structures, meanings, and functions, so that students have the opportunity to reflect upon the contents of the chapter and their

overall language learning. Students go from language usage to language analysis.

✦ **The grammar reference section, *Consultorio gramatical*, is now in English for easier student comprehension**

The *Consultorio gramatical*, a functional and discourse-oriented grammar reference, and the interaction-based examples, have now been translated into English, in order to facilitate processing and understanding of the linguistic and metalinguistic aspects of the language.

✦ **Streamlined sections make work in each chapter more efficient and meaningful**
  • *Nuestra gente* section has been reduced from six to three pages
  • In the **vocabulary** section, the vocabulary lists have been extensively reviewed and reduced to facilitate learning of new words and phrases.

✦ **NEW MySpanishLab saves time and improves results!**

Over 100,000 students have used MyLanguageLabs to improve their results in basic language courses. **MySpanishLab**, part of our MyLanguageLabs suite of online products, combines a learning management system with online instructional and practice materials for students. Students complete meaningful practice with built-in, point-of-need support to help them understand the important concepts that they will practice communicatively in class.

✦ **Annotated Instructor's Edition now brings the instructor annotations to the margins providing point-of-need support for instructors.**

**NEW** updated and useful Teacher's Notes appear on the page where the corresponding item is. The Annotated Instructor's Edition contains an abundance of marginal annotations that suggest warm-up and expansion activities, as well as provide teaching tips, and additional cultural information.

## Learning by Doing: the Task-Based Approach

In second language pedagogy, a **task** is generally defined as a collaborative project with a goal and an observable product. Learners use resources (linguistic and non-linguistic) in order to attain the goal, and the observable product generally takes the form of an oral

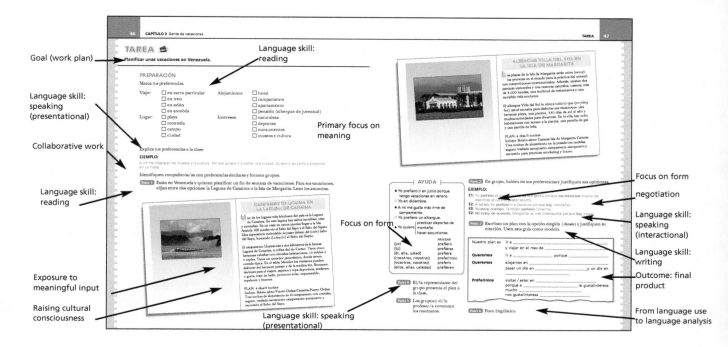

or written text. Normally, tasks require collaborative and interactive work with meaning negotiation and exchange. Tasks engage learners in problem-solving and decision-making activities through interaction (i.e., planning, selecting, and organizing).

When given a linguistic focus, tasks encourage learners to think about, and analyze L2 forms (not simply manipulate forms and apply rules); they allow learners to go from language usage to language analysis, thus promoting attention to, and noticing of grammar forms.

The benefits of a task-based approach to language learning are numerous. Current research in second-language acquisition indicates that frequent exposure to and use of the target language through interaction and meaning negotiation are necessary conditions to learn a foreign language. This research encourages us to go from a product approach to language learning—"learning the L2 to use it"—to a process approach—"using the L2 to learn it." This research also acknowledges the important role that grammar instruction plays in the rate of development toward the ultimate level of attainment in the foreign language. To maintain a better balance between exposure and use, we must provide ample opportunities for interaction in the classroom and involve students in activities where they can process form and meaning. Task-based instruction is an excellent way to promote these productive language-learning conditions.

With task-based language learning students become active users of the language who participate in the learning process. Students who have experience with task-based learning report that they gain confidence in speaking and interacting soon after beginning a task-based course; they can cope with natural spontaneous speech quite easily and tackle tough reading texts in an appropriate way. Most importantly, they become more independent learners.

## Features of the program

### Consistent learning sequence

In the third edition of **Gente**, the instructional sequence—which progresses from contextualized input, to guided output, to free output, to the global/integrative task—is consistent throughout all of the chapters. The classroom textbook has been designed around a single overarching goal: to provide resources for language use in a dynamic communicatively and culturally oriented language classroom. **Gente** is a learner-centered manual, built entirely around a series of activities and pedagogical tasks that require student collaboration, interaction, and meaning negotiation. Its unique structure of 20 chapters, each of them with a final task, serves to motivate students by giving them a sense of accomplishment.

## Chapter Structure

| LAYOUT | SECTION | DESCRIPTION |
|---|---|---|
| 2-page spread | *Acercamientos* | provides an initial approach to the thematic, cultural, and linguistic contents of the chapter through activities geared to activate learners' previous knowledge. |
| 2-page spread | *Vocabulario en contexto* | introduces contextualized active vocabulary and comprehension and production activities so students can learn vocabulary in context. |
| 2-page spread | *Gramática en contexto* | focuses on content-based grammar instruction by presenting the target structures in context. Activities in the section encourage attention to form, form-meaning-usage connections, and effective use of the grammar forms. The in-text grammar yellow boxes serve as quick in-class reference while students work on the sections' activities. |
| 2-page spread | *Interacciones* | targets learners' development of oral discourse and interactional strategies by engaging students in collaborative, meaning-focused, pair- and group-work activities. |
| 2-page spread | *Tarea* | is the central element of each chapter in which students use the contents of the chapter to carry out a collaborative task. The final linguistic focus of each task gives students an opportunity to reflect upon the contents of the chapter and their overall language learning. |
| 4-page spread | *Nuestra gente* | targets the development of reading and writing skills, as well as cross-cultural awareness. |
| | *Gente que lee* *Gente que escribe* | emphasizes the development of discourse-based, strategic reading (*Gente que lee*) and strategic writing (*Gente que escribe*) through content-based, process-oriented reading and writing tasks. The reading activities encourage both comprehension and interpretation of texts. |
| | *Comparaciones* | encourages students to explore the Spanish-speaking cultures, including the U.S. Activities foster development of cultural consciousness, cross-cultural awareness and critical thinking. |
| 1-page | *Vocabulario* | contains the active vocabulary—that is, the words that students need to understand and use in order to successfully complete each chapter's learning sequence. |
| 3-pages | *Consultorio gramatical* | presents explicit grammar instruction from a functional, usage-based perspective. It serves as a useful resource for independent study, and promotes deeper understanding of the Spanish grammar forms, meanings, and uses. |

## Approach to grammar instruction

*Gente's* approach to grammar involves more than the study of grammar forms. For this reason each activity encourages the establishment of connections between *forms* and *meanings*, as well as the *use* of those forms in context, with varied levels of emphasis on the three aspects. This gives students a true understanding of the Spanish language. *Gente* fosters language awareness and discovery, by promoting attention to and noticing of grammar and other sociolinguistic aspects of the language.

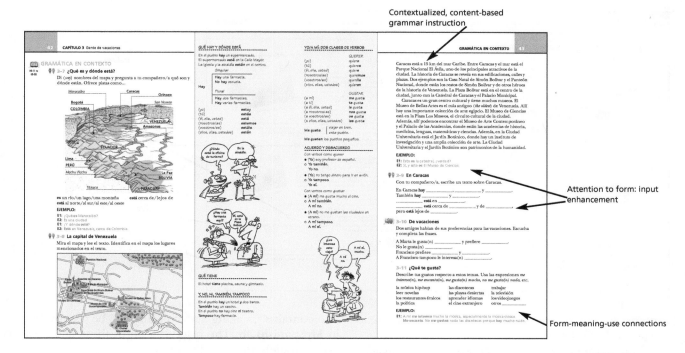

Contextualized, content-based grammar instruction

Attention to form: input enhancement

Form-meaning-use connections

In addition, there are other points of grammar support in the *Gente* program that intend to maximize independent learning opportunities. The pages in *Consultorio gramatical* offer explicit instruction on the target grammar points of the chapter. The grammar tutorials in **MySpanishLab** offer a variety of grammar tutorials in English and Spanish organized by chapter and/or by topic.

## Emphasis on interaction and collaborative learning

For *Gente*, interaction is more than an opportunity to practice the language; it is the way that language is learned. To this end, it incorporates extensive opportunities for students to engage in meaningful interaction and collaborative activities that foster social and affective factors crucial in language learning. The *Interacciones* and *Tarea* sections encourage cooperative learning in pairs and groups to further promote classroom-negotiated interaction. Students learn strategies for effective interaction, such as how to focus on specific information, how to interact in given contexts, or how to ask for clarification. *Gente* also emphasizes the development of discourse abilities, so students practice integrating structures in extended discourse throughout their language-learning process.

In addition, all listening tasks expose the students to naturally spoken Spanish in conversations, and include practice in top-down and bottom-up listening skills.

## Raising cultural consciousness and cross-cultural awareness

*Gente* recognizes the intrinsic role that culture plays in foreign language development and the need for students to develop a critical understanding of the cultures of Spanish-speaking countries. The program intends to raise students' cultural awareness by incorporating a content-based approach to all learning tasks and activities. Every chapter is content-based and culturally oriented, because it revolves around a specific Spanish-speaking country. The *Nuestra gente* section encourages students to reflect on and make comparisons within the Hispanic world, as well as within their own context, in order to develop an increased cross-cultural awareness.

## Development of culture-based, strategic reading and writing

The *Gente que lee* section helps students develop reading skills through an exploration of the Spanish-speaking cultures. Readings are based upon a variety of authentic sources that cover a wide range of topics, countries, and genres. *Gente que lee* provides extensive strategic reading instruction designed to build a core set of reading skills. Focused pre- and post-reading activities develop a range of reading comprehension skills, such as predicting content, understanding the main idea, and identifying topic

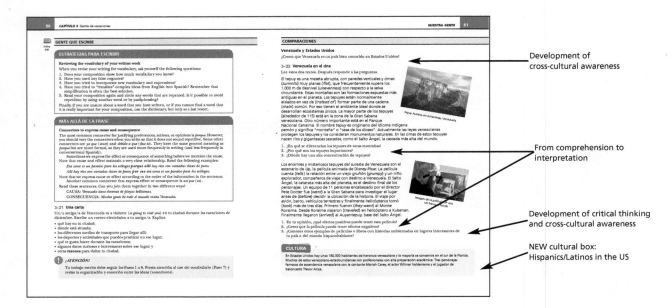

Development of
cross-cultural awareness

From comprehension to
interpretation

Development of critical thinking
and cross-cultural awareness

NEW cultural box:
Hispanics/Latinos in the US

sentences. As a result, students begin to read purposefully and effectively.

The parallel section *Gente que escribe* assigns real-life writing tasks that promote an interactive, discourse-based approach to writing and encourage students to be aware of their audience and its culture. Students learn to write as a process of creating, sharing, and revising ideas and sentences. Each writing task requires brainstorming, drafting, revising, proofreading, and editing. A wide range of writing topics inspires students' self-expression.

## Program Components

### The Complete Program

*Gente* is a complete teaching and learning program that includes a variety of resources for students and instructors, including an innovative offering of online resources.

### For the student

### Student Text

The *Gente* **Student Text** is available both in a complete, paper-bound version, and an à la carte looseleaf edition.

### Student Activities Manual

The **Student Activities Manual**, thoroughly revised for this edition, includes a vast number of vocabulary, grammar, reading and skills practice activities, many of which are audio-based, for each chapter of the text. It

also contains speaking activities that will be recordable in **MySpanishLab**. The organization of these activities now parallels that of the student text. The Student Activities Manual is available both in print and online through **MySpanishLab**.

### Student Activities Manual Answer Key

The **Answer Key** includes answers to all activities in the Student Activities Manual.

### Text Audio CDs

The recordings on this CD set correspond to the listening comprehension activities in the textbook. These recordings are also available within **MySpanishLab** and the Companion Website.

### Student Activities Manual Audio CDs

A second set of audio CDs contains recordings for the listening comprehension activities in the Student Activities Manual. These recordings are also available within **MySpanishLab** and the Companion Website.

### Video on DVD

*Gente en acción* is a series of twenty videos. Each unit shows a group of five native speakers from various Spanish speaking countries carrying out a real life task. In addition, each unit reflects the vocabulary, grammar and functional uses of the language featured in the textbook. The video is available for student purchase on DVD, and it is also available within **MySpanishLab**, with and without captions. In addition, the video is available to instructors on DVD.

## For the instructor

### Annotated Instructor's Edition

The **Annotated Instructor's Edition** contains an abundance of marginal annotations designed especially for novice instructors, instructors who are new to the *Gente* program, and instructors who have limited time for class preparation. A new format allows ample space for annotations alongside full-size pages of the student text. Marginal annotations suggest warm-up and expansion exercises and activities and provide teaching tips and additional cultural information. Answers to discrete point activities are printed in blue type for the instructor's convenience.

### Instructor's Resource Manual

The **Instructor's Resource Manual** now contains complete lesson plans, integrated syllabi for regular and hybrid courses, as well as helpful suggestions for foreign and new instructors. It also provides videoscripts for all episodes of the *Gente en acción* video, audioscripts for listening activities in the Student Activities Manual, and a complete guide to all *Gente* supplements. The Instructor's Resource Manual is available to instructors online at the *Gente* Instructor Resource Center.

### Testing Program

The **Testing Program**, now fully online, has been thoroughly revised and expanded for this edition. The testing content is closely coordinated with the vocabulary, grammar, culture, and skills material presented in the student text. For each chapter of the text, a bank of testing activities is provided in modular form; instructors can select and combine modules to create customized tests tailored to the needs of their classes. Complete, ready-to-use tests are also provided for each chapter. The tests and testing modules are available to instructors online at the Instructor Resource Center and in **MySpanishLab**.

### Testing Audio CD

This CD contains the recordings to accompany the listening comprehension activities in the Gente Testing Program. These recordings are also available within **MySpanishLab**.

### Instructor Resource Center

Several of the instructor supplements listed above—the Instructor's Resource Manual, the Testing Program—are available for download at the access-protected *Gente* Instructor Resource Center. An access code will be provided at no charge to instructors once their faculty status has been verified.

## Online resources

### MYSPANISHLAB

**MySpanishLab** is a widely adopted, nationally hosted online learning system designed specifically for students in college-level language courses. It brings together—in one convenient, easily navigable site—a wide array of language-learning tools and resources, including an interactive version of the *Gente* Student Activities Manual, an interactive version of the *Gente* student text, and all materials from the *Gente* audio and video programs. Readiness checks, practice tests, and tutorials personalize instruction to meet the unique needs of individual students. Instructors can use the system to make assignments, set grading parameters, provide feedback on student work, add new content, access instructor resources, and hold online office hours. Instructor access is provided at no charge. Students can purchase access codes online or at their local bookstore. For more information, including case studies that illustrate how **MySpanishLab** saves time and improves results, visit http://www.mylanguagelabs.com.

### Companion Website

The open-access Companion Website contains all of the audio found on the Text and Student Activities Manual audio CDs. All contents of the Companion Website are also included in **MySpanishLab**.

## Acknowledgments

I am indebted to many members of the Spanish teaching community for their time, candor, and insightful suggestions as they reviewed the drafts of the third edition of *Gente*. Their critiques and recommendations helped me to sharpen the pedagogical focus and improve the overall quality of the program. I gratefully acknowledge the contributions of the following reviewers:

Carole Cloutier, *University of Massachusetts, Amherst*
Gerardo I. Cruz-Tanahara, *Cardinal Stritch University*
Gustavo Fares, *Lawrence University*
Marlene Gottlieb, *Manhattan College*
Jason Jolley, *Missouri State University*
Pedro Koo,  *Missouri State University*
Ana López-Sánchez, *Haverford College*
D. Brian Mann, *North Georgia College & State University*
Frances Matos-Schultz, *University of Minnesota*

Liliana Paredes, *Duke University*
Luisa Piemontese, *Southern Connecticut State University*
Amy Rossomondo, *University of Kansas*
Guadalupe Ruiz-Fajardo, *Columbia University*
Barry Velleman, *Marquette University*
Marianne J. Verlinden, *College of Charleston*
Joseph R. Weyers, *College of Charleston*

I am also grateful for the guidance of Marco Aponte, developmental editor, for all of his work, suggestions, attention to detail, and dedication to the text. His support and spirit helped me to achieve the final product. I would also like to thank the contributors who assisted me in the preparation of the third edition: my colleague and friend Margarita Moreno for the Student Activities Manual, Margaret Snyder for the Feedback for the Student Activities Manual and MySpanishLab, and Frances Matos-Schultz for the Syllabi and Lesson Plans found in the Instructor's Resource Manual. I am very grateful to other colleagues and friends at Pearson Education/Prentice Hall: Meriel Martínez, Media Editor, for helping us produce such great audio programs and Companion Website; Melissa Marolla Brown, Development Editor for Assessment, for the diligent coordination among the text, Student Activities Manual, and Testing Program. I am very grateful to the MySpanishLab Team, Bob Hemmer, Samantha Alducin, and Mary Reynolds for the creation of the *Gente* MySpanishLab course. I would like to give a special thanks to Samantha Alducin for her work on developing a great video. Thanks also to Samantha Pritchard, Editorial Assistant, for attending to many administrative details.

I am very grateful to the marketing team, Kris Ellis-Levy, Denise Miller, and Bill Bliss, for their creativity and efforts in coordinating all marketing and promotion for this edition. Thanks, too, to the production team, Mary Rottino and Janice Stangel, who guided *Gente* through the many stages of production; to our partners at Macmillan Publishing Services, especially Nincis Asencio, for their careful and professional editing and production services. Special thanks to the art team Leslie Osher, Miguel Ortiz, Pat Smythe, and Wanda España for the gorgeous interior and cover designs. I would like to express my most sincere thanks to Phil Miller, Publisher, and Julia Caballero, Executive Editor, for their guidance and support through every aspect of this new edition. Last, but not least, I thank my husband, John, my daughter, Noelle, and my son, Nico, for their infinite patience, encouragement, and unconditional love. I dedicate this work to them.

María José de la Fuente
George Washington University

# GENTE

## Volume 2

## 7–1 ¿Qué necesitas?

Éstas son cosas que la gente necesita habitualmente en los viajes. ¿Qué son? Identifica cada una de ellas. ¿Qué cosas necesitas cuando viajas? ¿Llevas algo especial?

**EJEMPLO:**

**E1:** Yo siempre llevo una cámara de video.

## TAREA

Organizar un viaje a la República Dominicana.

## NUESTRA GENTE

La República Dominicana
Hispanos/latinos en Estados Unidos

guía turística

mochila

maletas

tarjeta de crédito

pasaporte

SANTO DOMINGO
ZONA COLONIAL

plano de la ciudad

## ACERCAMIENTOS

### 7–2 Cuando viajo...

¿Qué haces normalmente antes, durante y después de un viaje? Ordena las actividades siguientes.

comprar los boletos            revelar las fotos            mirar un mapa
tomar fotos                    deshacer la maleta           comprar regalos
hacer la maleta                alquilar un carro            cambiar dinero
escribir postales              buscar alojamiento           obtener un pasaporte
poner fotos en la computadora
otros _____

ANTES            DURANTE            DESPUÉS

 Ahora intercambia tu información con un/a compañero/a.

**EJEMPLO:**
**E1:** Yo primero compro los boletos y después hago las maletas.
**E2:** ¡Yo no, yo primero hago las maletas!

### 7–3 Pasándolo bien (*having fun*)

Mira la guía sobre la República Dominicana. ¿Qué son estos lugares? ¿Dónde están? ¿Qué puedes hacer en ellos?

1. Los Haitises        2. Las Terrenas        3. Los Altos del Chavón        4. La zona colonial

## Pasándolo bien en la República Dominicana

### Zona Colonial

Es uno de los lugares favoritos de los jóvenes, por sus cafés y sus tiendas al aire libre. Aquí hay muchos edificios históricos, como la catedral.

### Las Terrenas

En la costa norte de la isla, se encuentra la playa más larga y bonita de todo el país. Aquí se puede tomar el sol o bucear en las tranquilas aguas.

### Los Haitises

Es un parque nacional formado por un grupo de islas cubiertas de selva tropical. Aquí se pueden apreciar diferentes especies de plantas, pájaros y animales exóticos.

### Altos del Chavón (La Romana)
Es un lugar muy bonito situado en una montaña. Aquí se puede estudiar en la escuela de arte, visitar el museo arqueológico, o escuchar conciertos y festivales de jazz en el gran anfiteatro.

VOCABULARIO EN CONTEXTO

07-01 to
07-07

### 7–4 **Un curso de español en Santo Domingo**

Rick Jordan es un joven estadounidense inscrito (*registered*) en un curso de español en Santo Domingo. Lee la información del folleto (*brochure*) y responde a las preguntas:

1. ¿Dónde está exactamente el Centro de Español Pedro Henríquez Ureña?

2. ¿Cuánto tiempo dura (*lasts*) el curso?

3. ¿Qué viajes se pueden hacer durante el curso?

4. ¿Dónde pueden alojarse los estudiantes?

 ### 7–5 **Por teléfono**

Escucha las conversaciones de Rick Jordan y elige la información correcta.

#### Audio 1

En esta conversación, Rick quiere

a. inscribirse en un curso
b. confirmar la hora de un curso
c. reservar una habitación de hotel

#### Audio 2

En esta conversación, Rick quiere

a. reservar un vuelo a Santo Domingo
b. confirmar un vuelo a Miami
c. cancelar un vuelo a Santo Domingo

#### Audio 3

En esta conversación, Rick quiere

a. reservar un vuelo a una isla del Caribe
b. cambiar su reservación de hotel
c. reservar una habitación de hotel

#### Audio 4

Rick deja este mensaje

a. antes de ir de viaje
b. durante su viaje
c. después de regresar de su viaje

---

**CENTRO DE ESPAÑOL PEDRO HENRÍQUEZ UREÑA**
Calle Las Mercedes 22,
SANTO DOMINGO

## CURSO INTENSIVO DE ESPAÑOL

¿DÓNDE? En una de las más antiguas y hermosas ciudades coloniales del Nuevo Mundo: Santo Domingo, fundada en 1496. Su maravilloso centro colonial es patrimonio mundial de la UNESCO. Santo Domingo es también una próspera ciudad de más de dos millones de habitantes con infinitas posibilidades de ocio. El Centro de Español Pedro Henríquez Ureña está en la zona colonial, en pleno centro de la ciudad.

DURACIÓN: seis semanas
Este curso se ofrece en todos los niveles, desde principiante hasta avanzado. Las clases tienen un máximo de ocho estudiantes.
HORARIO DE CLASES: Las lecciones se ofrecen en la mañana de lunes a viernes, de 8:30 a 1:30.

| | |
|---|---|
| 08:30–10:30 | gramática |
| 11:00–12:30 | conversación |
| 1:00–1:30 | cultura |

Por las tardes, usted tiene tiempo para practicar su español. Para los estudiantes interesados, la escuela ofrece un servicio de intercambio lingüístico con hablantes nativos.

ACTIVIDADES CULTURALES:
– visitas guiadas por la ciudad
– curso de parapente o montañismo
– excursiones a Punta Cana, Saona y las cavernas de San Pedro de Macorí
ALOJAMIENTO: con familias o en hotel (la escuela se ocupa de las reservaciones).
PRECIO DE LA MATRÍCULA: $850 (alojamiento y cursos optativos no incluidos).
FORMA DE PAGO: transferencia bancaria, giro postal o tarjeta de crédito.

---

 ### 7–6 **¿Qué necesita Rick?**

Escucha otra vez las conversaciones y completa estas frases con información más específica.

#### Audio 1

1. El curso comienza el día _____ de _____ a las ocho y media de la mañana.

2. La _____ de la familia dominicana es calle Pedro Bellini, 34. Está muy _____ de la escuela y al lado de la _____.

3. Pero hay un problema: el _____ no está libre hasta el día 3. Por eso el Centro Pedro Henríquez Ureña le va a enviar una lista de _____.

**Audio 2**

4. Hay un _____ Miami-Santo Domingo a las 12:35 y otro a las 5:15 de la tarde.

**Audio 3**

5. Rick quiere _____ una habitación para las noches del 1 y 2 de mayo. Quiere una habitación _____ con _____.

**Audio 4**

6. Rick _____ el día 2 de junio.

**7–7  Una vuelta por la República Dominicana**

Vamos a hacer un juego. Observen el mapa: tiene las etapas de un viaje por la República Dominicana. Cada fase del viaje está marcada con un color diferente.

**DISTANCIAS ENTRE CIUDADES**
Puerto Plata–Barahona: 355 km
Barahona–Santo Domingo: 200 km
Santo Domingo–Juan Dolio: 60 km
Juan Dolio–La Romana: 50 km
La Romana–Punta Cana: 105 km
Punta Cana–Samaná: 205 km
Samaná–Río San Juan: 150 km
Río San Juan–Puerto Plata: 165 km

Ustedes tienen que completar este viaje usando ocho medios de transporte diferentes. Deben hacer el viaje en el menor número de días posible.

**REGLAS DEL JUEGO**

■ Los participantes tienen que utilizar todos los medios de transporte como mínimo una vez y visitar todas las ciudades.

■ Sólo pueden usar un medio de transporte en cada etapa (entre dos ciudades) y tienen que pasar la noche en la ciudad a la que llegan.

■ Gana el equipo que necesita menos días para dar la vuelta al país.

■ Sólo pueden recorrer cada día las distancias máximas con cada medio de transporte que están indicadas en la tabla.

| DISTANCIAS | kilómetros máximos por día |
|---|---|
| A PIE | 25 km |
| EN BICICLETA | 60 km |
| EN MOTOCICLETA | 200 km |
| EN TREN | 300 km |
| EN CARRO | 400 km |
| EN AUTOBÚS | 500 km |
| A CABALLO | 50 km |
| EN AVIÓN | 1,000 km |

**EJEMPLO:**

**E1:** De Juan Dolio a La Romana vamos a pie, porque es más corto.
**E2:** Sí, pero toma dos días. Podemos ir a caballo en un día.

Ahora expliquen a la clase **qué van a hacer** para completar la ruta. Finalmente, decidan qué grupo tiene el viaje más corto.

## GRAMÁTICA EN CONTEXTO

07-08 to
07-28

 **7–8  Los parques nacionales de la República Dominicana**

Lee el texto de forma individual. Fíjate en las expresiones marcadas en negrita para hablar de la Ubicación.

**Parque Nacional Isla Cabritos**
El parque nacional Isla Cabritos está en una pequeña isla situada en Lago Enriquillo, **al oeste del** país, **cerca de** la sierra de Bahoruco y muy **lejos de** Santo Domingo. Tiene una extensión aproximada de 24 km$^2$. Existen especies que son endémicas de la isla, como las iguanas y también una población significativa del cocodrilo americano.

**Parque Nacional de Los Haitises**
El parque nacional de Los Haitises se encuentra situado **al norte de** la República Dominicana, muy **cerca de** la Bahía de Samaná, **a 300 km de** la capital. Tiene un bosque tropical y es uno de los espacios con mayor biodiversidad del país y del Caribe. La riqueza en fauna queda reflejada por la presencia del manatí, un mamífero marítimo en peligro de extinción.

**Parque Nacional del Este**
Este parque **está en** el extremo sureste del país, **cerca de** Punta Cana. Su extensión total es de 310 km$^2$. Al sur del parque está la isla Saona. **Desde** el parque **hasta** la isla hay muy poca distancia. Hay 112 especies de aves dentro de los límites del parque. Además, en él se pueden encontrar manatíes y delfines.

Ahora identifiquen en el mapa el lugar donde están los tres parques nacionales. Hagan preguntas a su compañero/a para identificar los parques correctamente.

**EJEMPLO:**

**E1:** ¿**Dónde está** el parque Isla Cabritos?
**E2:** Aquí, **al oeste**, **cerca de** Bahoruco.

 **7–9  Posada Caribe**

Estás trabajando como recepcionista de una pequeña posada en Punta Cana, una zona turística dominicana. La posada sólo tiene nueve habitaciones. Algunos clientes quieren hacer reservaciones, cambiarlas (*change them*) o confirmarlas. Escucha y anota los cambios en el libro de reservaciones.

---

**REFERENCIAS ESPACIALES**

**DISTANCIAS**
● ¿Cuántos kilómetros hay
**de** | Santo | **a**
**desde** | Domingo | **hasta** | Punta Cana?
o 205 kilómetros.

**estar a... de...**
Punta Cana **está a** 205 km **de** Santo Domingo.

**estar al norte / al sur / al este / al oeste de...**
Punta Cana **está al este de** Santo Domingo.

**estar cerca / lejos de...**
Punta Cana **está lejos de** Santo Domingo.

**PUNTO DE PARTIDA Y DESTINO**
De ... a...
desde... hasta...
De Santo Domingo a Punta Cana vamos en moto.

**DIRECCIÓN**
hacia...
Va **hacia** Santiago.

**LÍMITE**
hasta...
Voy **hasta** Santo Domingo en carro.

**RUTA**
pasar por...
¿**Pasas por** La Romana para ir a Santo Domingo?

**DÍAS Y MESES**

¿Qué día
¿Cuándo     llegas / te vas / ...?

el (día) veintitrés
el veintitrés **de** mayo
el viernes (próximo)

la semana
el mes          que viene
el año

enero, febrero, marzo, abril, mayo, junio, julio, agosto, septiembre, octubre, noviembre, diciembre

## LA HORA

● ¿**A qué hora** abren/cierran/empiezan/...?

○ **A las**
{
ocho.
ocho y cinco.
ocho **y cuarto.**
ocho **y veinte.**
ocho **y media.**
ocho **y veinticinco.**
**Un cuarto para** las diez.
Cinco **para las** nueve.[2]
}

a las diez **de la mañana** = 10 a.m.
a las diez **de la noche** = 10 p.m.

a la una **de la tarde** = 1 p.m.
a la una y media **de la tarde** = 1.30 p.m.

Está abierto **de** ocho **a** tres.
Está cerrado **de** tres **a** cinco.

● ¿**Qué hora** es?
  ¿**Tiene hora,** por favor?
○ **Las cinco y diez.**

Perdone, ¿tiene hora?

Sí, las cinco y diez.

Gracias.

## IR + A + INFINITIVO

El día 1... / A las 4... / El martes...

| voy | | |
| vas | | salir |
| va | **a** | llegar |
| vamos | | venir |
| vais | | ir |
| van | | ... |

## ESTAR A PUNTO DE + INFINITIVO
## ACABAR DE

● ¿Está abierto el restaurante?
○ Sí, pero **están a punto de** cerrar.

● ¿Está abierta la piscina?
○ Sí, **acaban de** abrirla.

[2]En España se dice:
nueve **menos** cuarto
nueve **menos** cinco

| habitación número | viernes **11** | sábado **12** | domingo **13** |
|---|---|---|---|
| 1 | GONZÁLEZ | GONZÁLEZ | – |
| 2 | MARQUINA | MARQUINA | MARQUINA |
| 3 | VENTURA | – | – |
| 4 | – | MAYORAL | MAYORAL |
| 5 | SÁNCHEZ PINA | SÁNCHEZ PINA | SÁNCHEZ PINA |
| 6 | – | – | IGLESIAS |
| 7 | LEÓN | SANTOS | COLOMER |
| 8 | – | – | – |
| 9 | BENITO | BENITO | – |

### 7–10  ¿Qué van a hacer?

Según la información de los turistas de la Posada Caribe (en 7–9) ¿qué **va a hacer** cada uno de ellos?

1. El señor Marquina _____

2. El señor Pérez _____

3. La señora Benito _____

4. El señor Galán _____

### 7–11  El horario

Es martes y son las 7:55 de la noche. Tienes que ir al supermercado, a la farmacia y al dentista. Pregunta a tu compañero si están abiertos o cerrados estos lugares. Pregunta sobre sus horarios.

**EJEMPLO:**

**E1:** ¿Sabes si **está abierta** la clínica dental?
**E2:** No, los martes abren **de 9 de la mañana a 12 del mediodía.** Por las tardes **está cerrada.**
**E1:** ¿Y la farmacia?
**E2:** Sí, **está abierta** pero **están a punto de** cerrar.

RIZOS Peluquería
9 a.m.–8 p.m.
(sábados 10 a.m.–2 p.m.)

Restaurante EL ARENQUE
12:00 p.m.–4 p.m.

AYUNTAMIENTO
8 a.m.–3 p.m.

Farmacia IBÁÑEZ
9:30 a.m.–8 p.m.

Dr. Sánchez Trueba
CLÍNICA DENTAL PENÍNSULA
9 a.m. 12 p.m. Lu, mi, vi 6 p.m. 8 p.m.

Supermercado PENÍNSULA
8:30 a.m.–8:30 p.m.

Gimnasio en forma
fitness
aeróbic
artes marciales
8 a.m.–11 p.m.

Ahora son las tres y diez de la tarde y tienes que ir al ayuntamiento, al supermercado y al restaurante.

**EJEMPLO:**

**E1:** ¿**Está abierto** el ayuntamiento?
**E2:** No, **acaban de cerrar.** Cierran a las **3 de la tarde.**

INTERACCIONES

07-29 to
07-32

---

### ESTRATEGIAS PARA LA COMUNICACIÓN ORAL

**Beyond *sí* and *no*: emphasizing affirmative or negative replies**

There are questions that require a *yes/no* reply. The person who asks this type of question is asking for confirmation or rejection of his/her request or idea. However, answering with a simple **sí** or **no** may be considered impolite or uncooperative. One way to show more cooperation is to add more information to the **sí/no** reply. Another possibility is to use different types of affirmative or negative replies.

Observe the following examples:

- ¿Hiciste las maletas (*luggage*)?          • ¿Hiciste las maletas?
  ○ Sí.                                       ○ Por supuesto. (*Of course.*)

The second reply is more emphatic, and its effect on the recipient is very different. Here are other ways to answer the question affirmatively:

■ Claro. (*Of course; Sure.*)               ■ Por supuesto que sí. (*Of course.*)
■ Claro que sí. (*Of course.*)              ■ Sí, cómo no. (*Yes, of course.*)
■ Desde luego. (*Of course.*)

There are also various ways to reject the following request:

- ¿Puedes llevar mis maletas?
  ○ No.
    ■ Ni hablar. (*No way.*)                 ■ Lo siento, pero no. (*Sorry, but the answer is no.*)
    ■ Claro que no. (*Of course not.*)        ■ Desde luego que no. (*Of course not.*)
    ■ Por supuesto que no.
      (*Of course not; absolutely not.*)

---

**7-12 En mi ausencia…**

Vas a viajar a la República Dominicana por seis semanas para estudiar en la escuela Pedro Henríquez Ureña. Antes de salir, necesitas pedirle muchos favores a tu amigo/a. Escribe una lista de seis favores.

**EJEMPLO:**

limpiar el apartamento, recoger el correo…

 Ahora pídele a tu amigo/a estos favores. El/ella va a responder de forma afirmativa o negativa. Después intercambien sus papeles (*roles*).

**EJEMPLO:**

**E1:** ¿Puedes limpiar mi apartamento mientras (*while*) estoy fuera?
**E2:** No. ¡Ni hablar!

**7-13 Tu próximo viaje**

Seguro que van a viajar en los próximos días o meses; quizá (*maybe*) al final de sus estudios. Sus viajes pueden ser de vacaciones, de trabajo, para visitar a un familiar… Prepara una lista de preguntas para tu compañero/a. Ésta es la lista de temas:

| | | |
|---|---|---|
| lugar donde viaja | acompañantes | alojamiento |
| itinerario | actividades planeadas | transporte |
| razón o razones del viaje | fechas y duración del viaje | |

**EJEMPLO:**

¿Cuándo **vas a viajar**? ¿Qué mes? ¿Qué días?

Ahora conversa con tu compañero/a para saber más de su próximo viaje.

**7–14 Situaciones:** *un viaje en septiembre*

Two friends go to a travel agency to get information on trips to the Dominican Republic in September. The travel agent gives them information and makes recomendations.

Éstas son las ofertas de viajes de la agencia.

**ESTUDIANTE A**

You are a travel agent. Two customers are interested in visiting the Dominican Republic. Think about some questions you may ask them to find out their preferences.

1. ¿_____?
2. ¿_____?
3. ¿_____?

| DESTINO | VIAJE | DURACIÓN | SALIDA | TRANSPORTE | PRECIO | ALOJAMIENTO |
|---------|-------|----------|--------|------------|--------|-------------|
| **PUNTA CANA** | 🏊 🌲 📷 | 6 días | 12 y 19 de septiembre | avión y barco | $2.500 | hoteles *** |
| **PLAYA DORADA** | 🏊 🤿 🚶 | 17 días | a diario | avión y carro | $2.775 | hoteles **** y tiendas |
| **SANTO DOMINGO** | 🏛 📷 🌲 | 15 días | 2 y 6 de septiembre | avión y autobús | $780 | hoteles ** |

📷 **Fotografía**   🏛 **Cultura**   🏊 **Mar y playa**   🤿 **Buceo**   🌲 **Naturaleza**   🚶 **Caminatas**

**ESTUDIANTE B**

You are in a travel agency. You are interested in visiting the Dominican Republic in September. Choose one of these situations and talk with the travel agent.

**ESTUDIANTE C**

You are in a travel agency. You are interested in visiting the Dominican Republic in September. Choose one of these situations and talk with the travel agent.

**1. MARÍA LÓPEZ RUEDA**

Mi novio/a y yo comenzamos las vacaciones el 4 de septiembre y tenemos 18 días. Este año queremos salir de Estados Unidos y viajar al Caribe. Nos interesa mucho la República Dominicana, especialmente su historia y su cultura. También nos encanta hacer excursiones y el contacto con la naturaleza. No queremos gastar mucho dinero.

**2. JUAN RODRÍGUEZ PALACIOS**

Somos dos amigos y queremos viajar unas dos semanas. Empezamos las vacaciones el día 9 de septiembre. Nos gustaría ir a una buena playa y estar en un buen hotel. Ah, y queremos hacer actividades acuáticas: buceo, vela…

**EJEMPLO:**

**E1:** Mire, yo le recomiendo un viaje a Punta Cana porque _____.

**E2:** Pero ¿tienen hoteles de cuatro estrellas?

**E1:** Por supuesto que sí. Pero son más caros, claro.

# TAREA  Gente en acción

## Organizar un viaje a la República Dominicana.

### PREPARACIÓN

 Ustedes van a hacer una pasantía (*internship*) en una compañía en la República Dominicana. Tienen que ir a Santo Domingo para un taller (*worskhop*) preliminar y a Puerto Plata para una reunión. Organicen su viaje, seleccionen los vuelos y busquen hotel.

**Paso 1** Ésta es su agenda de trabajo. Revísenla bien antes de comenzar.

- El día 13 están en Miami.
- El día 14 tienen un taller en Santo Domingo a las 9:30 de la mañana en el centro de la ciudad.
- Tienen una reunión de trabajo en Puerto Plata el día 17 a las 9 de la mañana.
- Tienen que regresar a Miami el día 18 antes de las 6 de la tarde.
- En Santo Domingo quieren alojarse en un hotel céntrico pero sólo pueden pagar $125 por noche.
- En Puerto Plata van a alojarse en casa de la familia de un amigo.

**Paso 2** El vuelo

Éste es el fax que recibieron de su agencia de viajes. Examinen todas las opciones y decidan qué reservación de vuelo de ida y vuelta (*round-trip flight*) van a hacer.

|  | LUNES | MARTES | MIÉRCOLES | JUEVES | VIERNES | SÁBADO | DOMINGO |
|---|---|---|---|---|---|---|---|
|  |  | 1 | 2 | 3 | 4 | 5 | 6 |
|  | 7 | 8 | 9 | 10 | 11 | 12 | 13 |
|  | 14 | 15 | 16 | 17 | 18 | 19 | 20 |
|  | 21 | 22 | 23 | 24 | 25 | 26 |  |
|  | 28 | 29 | 30 |  |  |  |  |

**FAX** **DE/FROM** Carolina Mayoral

**PARA/TO:** estudiantes de español de esta clase

**VIAJES DE LA FUENTE, S.A.**
CENTRAL DE EMPRESAS
TEL. 433 3533 - FAX 433 0102

**Número de páginas/number of pages:** 1

---

### AYUDA

el (vuelo) **de las** 7:33 de la noche
el (vuelo) de Copa

Con el vuelo de las 7:33 vamos a llegar
...**a tiempo.**
...**demasiado tarde / temprano**
...**antes de / después de las** doce
...**de día / de noche**

Quiero reservar...
...un boleto para Santo Domingo,
en el vuelo de las...
...una habitación para el día...

| **MIAMI / SANTO DOMINGO** | | **salida** | **llegada** |
|---|---|---|---|
| AA423 | MIA/SDQ | 7:33 p.m. | 9:46 p.m. |
| AA783 | MIA/SDQ | 4:20 p.m. | 6:36 p.m. |
| COPA301 | MIA/PTY/SDQ | 8:20 a.m. | 2:05 p.m. |

| **SANTO DOMINGO / PUERTO PLATA** | | | |
|---|---|---|---|
| VIVA106 | SDQ/PPL | 7:45 a.m. | 8:35 a.m. (ju, vi) |
| VIVA447 | SDQ/PPL | 4:00 p.m. | 4:50 p.m. (mi, sa, do) |

—— NO HAY VUELOS DIRECTOS PUERTO PLATA / MIAMI ——

| **PUERTO PLATA / SANTO DOMINGO / MIAMI** | | | |
|---|---|---|---|
| VIVA3473 | PPL/SDQ | 1:40 p.m. | 2:40 p.m. |
| AA4743 | SDQ/MIA | 6:40 p.m. | 8:45 p.m. |

| **PUERTO PLATA / SANTO DOMINGO / MIAMI** | | | |
|---|---|---|---|
| VIVA6654 | PPL/SDQ | 9:05 p.m. | 10:05 p.m. |
| AA4743 | SDQ/MIA | 12:50 p.m. | 3:30 p.m. |

Códigos:
Líneas aéreas   AA = American Airlines   VIVA = Viva Airlines   COPA = Copa Airlines
Ciudades   SDQ = Santo Domingo   PTY = Panama City   PPL = Puerto Plata

**Paso 3** El hotel
También tienen que hacer una reservación de hotel en Santo Domingo. Éstos son los hoteles que les propone la agencia. ¿Cuál van a reservar?

H
* * *
HOTEL UNIVERSIDAD
* * *
♦ A una cuadra de la Universidad Católica
♦ A 10 minutos del centro de la ciudad
♦ 40 habitaciones con aire acondicionado
♦ Tranquilo y bien comunicado
♦ Sauna y gimnasio

HOTEL SAN PLÁCIDO
HP
* * * *
**EN EL CENTRO DE SANTO DOMINGO**
Un "cuatro estrellas" muy especial…
• Aire acondicionado • Música • Teléfono
• Caja fuerte • Antena parabólica • Jacuzzi

Hotel EMBAJADOR
* * * * *
• Situación estratégica: primera línea de playa
• Piscina, sauna, sala de ejercicio
• Estacionamiento propio

Vamos a reservar un cuarto en el hotel _____ porque _____.

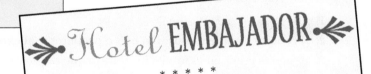 **Paso 4** Escuchen estas llamadas de teléfono. ¿Tienen que cambiar sus planes de hotel? ¿Por qué?

**Paso 5** El plan de viaje
Escriban detalladamente su plan del viaje, incluyendo cómo y cuándo van a viajar y dónde van a alojarse. Justifiquen sus decisiones.

**Paso 6** El representante de cada grupo presenta su plan de viaje a su profesor/a y a la clase. Los grupos y el/la profesor/a comentan los planes y deciden quién tiene el mejor plan.

**Paso 7** Foco lingüístico.

**NUESTRA GENTE**

07-33 to
07-34

### GENTE QUE LEE

---

**ESTRATEGIAS PARA LEER**

**Skimming and scanning texts**

Skimming and scanning are different styles of reading and information processing.

**Skimming** is used to quickly identify the main ideas of a text. It enables you to predict what will be in the text before you read it in detail. It is usually done at a much higher speed than normal reading. Some people read the first paragraph, a summary, or other organizers as they move down the page or the screen. You might read the title, subtitles, subheadings, and look at the illustrations. Consider reading the first sentence of each paragraph. Skimming works well for finding dates, names, and places. It might also be used to quickly go over graphs, tables, and charts.

In contrast, **scanning** consists of reading in order to find specific pieces of information. You might want to scan to find data that confirms predictions you have made, or maybe to find answers to particular questions, for example, to look for the price of an airline ticket, the time of arrival of a train, or the address of a hotel. When you scan, you are not interested in the main idea of the passage, but, rather, in a particular bit of information.

---

*ANTES DE LEER*

### 7–15  Viajar al extranjero

1. ¿Te gusta viajar? ¿Por qué?

2. ¿Prefieres viajar en tu propio país o prefieres ir al extranjero? ¿Por qué?

3. ¿Quieres tener en el futuro un trabajo que requiera viajar mucho?

4. ¿Cuál es el lugar más lejos de tu casa que conoces?

5. Para viajar a la República Dominicana necesitas varios documentos. ¿Cuáles crees que necesitas?

_____ un pasaporte                      _____ un certificado de salud

_____ una visa                          _____ un permiso de trabajo

_____ una tarjeta de turismo            _____ una carta oficial explicando el motivo del viaje

_____ una licencia de conducir          _____ un certificado de nacimiento

### 7–16  Activando estrategias

1. Lee el título del texto. ¿Qué tipo de información vas a leer?

2. Lee por encima (*skim*) el texto de lectura. Fíjate en los detalles (susbtítulos, estructura). ¿Qué tipo de texto es? ¿Qué información específica nos va a ofrecer?

*DESPUÉS DE LEER*

### 7–17  ¿Comprendes?

1. ¿Qué necesita un ciudadano mexicano para entrar en el país?

2. ¿Cuánto tiempo se demora (*takes*) obtener una visa de turismo?

3. Marca los que son correctos. Los ciudadanos de _____ necesitan visa de visitante.

☐ Guatemala   ☐ Panamá   ☐ Colombia

☐ Perú        ☐ Ecuador   ☐ México

☐ Venezuela   ☐ Canadá    ☐ Brasil

4. Si eres de Honduras, ¿qué necesitas?

5. ¿Cuánto cuesta la visa de entrada múltiple? ¿Cuánto tiempo es válida una visa de este tipo?

*A LEER*

## INFORMACIÓN PARA VIAJAR A LA REPÚBLICA DOMINICANA

Los siguientes países requieren una visa de visitante para estar en tránsito:

Costa Rica, Guatemala, Nicaragua, Bolivia, Ecuador, Guyana, Panamá, Colombia, El Salvador, Honduras.

Los ciudadanos de los siguientes países *no* requieren visa de visitante para estar en tránsito o entrar en la República Dominicana pero deben comprar una tarjeta de turismo a la llegada:

Antigua y Barbuda, Chile, México, San Vicente y las Granadinas, Argentina, Dominica, Paraguay, Trinidad y Tobago, Bahamas, Estados Unidos, Perú, Uruguay, Barbados, Granada, San Kitts y Nevis, Venezuela, Brasil, Haití, Santa Lucía, Canadá, Jamaica, Surinam.

Todas las personas deben estar en posesión de un pasaporte válido para entrar en la República Dominicana, excepto los ciudadanos de Canadá y de Estados Unidos que tengan documento de identidad apropiado, como una licencia de conducir o un certificado de nacimiento.

### Documentación requerida para visa de visitante

| | |
|---|---|
| Un pasaporte válido | cuatro fotos |
| Fotocopia del pasaporte | Boleto de avión de ida |
| Formulario de solicitud | y vuelta |
| | Certificado de salud |

### Método para depositar la solicitud

La **solicitud** se debe hacer en persona en el consulado o en el departamento de servicios consulares de la embajada.

### Tiempo de procesamiento

De dos a cuatro días para las tarjetas de turismo; de seis a ocho semanas para las visas de visitante y de negocios que tienen que ser aprobadas por las autoridades en la República Dominicana.

### Tipos de visas

Usted puede obtener visa de visitante, visas sencillas y múltiples, y visas de negocios. Las visas de visitante sencillas son válidas por 60 días. Las visas de múltiple entrada y de negocios son válidas hasta por un año. Las tarjetas de turismo son tramitadas para visitantes en la República Dominicana con propósitos de turismo para **estadías** de hasta 90 días. Costo de la solicitud: US $17.

### Para más información

Comuníquese con la Embajada o con el Departamento de Servicios Consulares de la Embajada.

---

### 7-18  Activando estrategias

1. ¿Qué significa la palabra "estadía"? ¿Cómo lo sabes? ¿Es nombre, verbo o adjetivo?
2. Busca la palabra "solicitud" en el diccionario. ¿Es nombre o adjetivo? ¿Es masculina o femenina? ¿Cuántos significados aparecen en el diccionario? ¿Cuál es el más apropiado?
3. Busca en el texto (*scan*) y averigua si los ciudadanos de tu país necesitan visa y pasaporte. ¿Qué documentos necesitas para entrar en el país?

### 7-19  Expansión

Compara estos requisitos con los que tiene tu país para permitir la entrada a ciudadanos de otros países. ¿Es tu país más estricto, igual de estricto, o menos estricto? ¿Puedes viajar a algún lugar sin pasaporte?

## GENTE QUE ESCRIBE

### ESTRATEGIAS PARA ESCRIBIR

**Using a bilingual dictionary when writing**

The writing process may involve using a bilingual dictionary to look up Spanish equivalents of English words and expressions. To use the dictionary correctly, you need to familiarize yourself with it. Look at the entries to learn the meaning of the abbreviations used. Each dictionary is different. Let's work with the following example:

You are writing about the problems that a U.S. citizen **faces** when travelling to Cuba. You really want to use this same idea (to face a problem), so you look up the word **face**.

> **face**   **I**.n (ANAT) *cara, rostro;* (of clock) *esfera;* (side) *cara;* (surface) *superficie* f.
> **II**. vt *mirar a:* (fig) *enfrentarse a;* ~ **down** (person, card) *boca abajo;* **to lose ~** *desprestigiarse;* **to save** ~ *salvar las apariencias;* **to make a** ~ *hacer muecas;* **in the ~ of** (difficulties, etc) *en vista de;* ~ **to** ~ *cara a cara.*

What do these abbreviations (ANAT, n, vt, f, fig) mean? Are you looking for a noun or a verb? Are you looking just for a verb, or an expression? If you followed this process, you will come up with ***enfrentarse a***, a reflexive verb that takes a direct object (vt). Likewise, you would use ***esfera*** to write about the face of your clock, or ***cara*** when referring to people.

### MÁS ALLÁ DE LA FRASE

**Using spatial references when writing descriptions**

In spatial descriptions, all the locational expressions are often placed at the beginning of sentences (e.g., *To the south, you can find a beautiful river*). This is done to emphasize the importance of location and position. You may need to write spatial descriptions when giving directions to visitors (to your campus or your city), after a trip, to describe where you went, etc. It is not necessary to place all spatial references at the beginning of sentences, but you need to be consistent so that you don't confuse your reader.

Read these sentences:

1. Al norte está Playa Dorada, Santo Domingo al sur, al este Punta Cana y Barahona al oeste.
2. Al norte está Playa Dorada, al sur Santo Domingo, al este Punta Cana y al oeste Barahona.

The second sentence is easier to understand because the writer used space as an organizing principle.

### 7–20 Un artículo descriptivo

Escribe un artículo sobre un estado o región de tu país para la sección de viajes de un periódico. Describe el mapa del estado y una ruta especialmente interesante. Incluye:

1. referencias espaciales (al norte, al sur…; a… kilómetros de…; de… a…; etc.)
2. registro informal (tú)
3. información sobre la existencia (¿qué hay?) y localización (¿dónde está/n?) de monumentos, parques, museos, etc.
4. otra información relevante (transportes, alojamientos…)

Considera el propósito de este artículo sus lectores (¿quiénes son?) y el registro (informal).

## COMPARACIONES

### 7-21 Viaje a la tierra del béisbol

¿Adónde tienes que viajar en América Latina si te gusta el béisbol? Lee este texto para saber más.

**San Pedro de Macorís**
La ciudad de San Pedro de Macorís, fundada en el siglo XIX por inmigrantes cubanos, está al este de Santo Domingo, a una hora en carro. La ciudad tiene 125.000 habitantes, una universidad y una bonita catedral. San Pedro es cuna de muchos beisbolistas de fama mundial, como Sammy Sosa de los Texas Rangers. Sosa es el primer latinoamericano y el quinto hombre en alcanzar los 600 jonrones en las Grandes Ligas de Estados Unidos. La influencia de las raíces cubanas de San Pedro se observa no sólo en el béisbol sino también en la industria del azúcar.

**La ciudad del béisbol**
Entre San Pedro de Macorís y Santo Domingo, a unos kilómetros al oriente del aeropuerto internacional, está la Ciudad del Béisbol. Es un gigantesco complejo de academias de béisbol, campos de juego y jaulas de bateo, dedicado a la producción de jugadores profesionales del béisbol dominicano para exportar al mercado laboral de Estados Unidos. Más del 10% de los jugadores de las Grandes Ligas vienen de la isla, incluyendo varias de sus principales estrellas, como Alex Rodríguez, Vladimir Guerrero, David Ortiz, Pedro Martínez o Manny Ramírez. Seis equipos de las Grandes Ligas de béisbol de Estados Unidos tienen residencia en la Ciudad del Béisbol.

1. ¿Qué información te parece más interesante? ¿Por qué?
2. ¿Conoces otros deportistas dominicanos de origen o de herencia dominicana en Estados Unidos?

### 7-22 Un Premio Pulitzer dominicano

¿Conoces algunos escritores latinos que triunfan en Estados Unidos? Aquí tienes uno.

Junot Díaz es un escritor dominicano nacionalizado estadounidense que escribe en inglés. Sus libros describen la dura realidad de los emigrantes hispanoamericanos en Estados Unidos. Sus libros más famosos son la colección de cuentos *Drown* (1997) y su novela *The Brief Wondrous Life of Oscar Wao* (2007). En sus libros Díaz expresa la alienación de las personas que se sienten ajenas a dos culturas, la hispánica y la estadounidense, pero también su admiración por el ser humano que sobrevive y supera los problemas de ese contacto cultural. Díaz es el segundo latino en Estados Unidos en ganar el premio Pulitzer, después del escritor cubano-estadounidense Óscar Hijuelos.

1. ¿Cuál es la temática de los libros de Junot Díaz? ¿Crees que les interesa a las personas de Estados Unidos que no son de ascendencia hispana? ¿Por qué?
2. ¿Por qué crees que Junot escribe en inglés?

### CULTURA

Los dominicanos forman uno de los grupos más numerosos de latinos en Estados Unidos. Hay aproximadamente 1.200.000 personas de nacimiento o ascendencia dominicana en Estados Unidos. La mayor parte de esta población está en las ciudades del este del país, especialmente en Nueva York. A diferencia de los latinos de ascendencia cubana o mexicana, los dominicano-estadounidenses no están tan activamente involucrados en la política de Estados Unidos. Sin embargo, destacan en numerosas áreas. Algunos dominicanos que triunfan en Estados Unidos son Óscar de la Renta, diseñador, Juan Luis Guerra, cantante, y Thomas E. Pérez, hijo de padres dominicanos, quien es Secretario Auxiliar de Justicia para la División de Derechos Civiles desde 2009.

## 🔊 VOCABULARIO

### Los viajes *(Trips)*

| | |
|---|---|
| el aeropuerto | *airport* |
| el boleto | *ticket* |
| el boleto de ida | *one-way ticket* |
| el boleto de ida y vuelta | *round-trip ticket* |
| la cámara de fotos | *camera* |
| la cancelación | *cancellation* |
| el destino | *destination* |
| la dirección | *address* |
| el equipaje | *luggage* |
| la excursión | *field trip* |
| el/la extranjero/a | *foreigner* |
| el folleto | *prospect, brochure* |
| el/la guía | *guide* |
| la habitación | *room* |
| el hotel | *hotel* |
| el itinerario | *itinerary* |
| la llegada | *arrival* |
| la maleta | *suitcase* |
| la mochila | *backpack* |
| la moneda | *currency* |
| el pasaporte | *passport* |
| la pensión | *a lodging house* |
| el permiso de conducir | *driver's license* |
| la recepción | *reception desk* |
| el/la recepcionista | *receptionist* |
| el requisito | *requirement* |
| el retraso | *delay* |
| la salida | *departure* |
| la tarjeta de crédito | *credit card* |
| la tienda de campaña | *tent* |
| el viaje | *trip* |
| la visa, el visado | *visa* |
| el/la visitante | *visitor* |
| el vuelo | *flight* |

### Actividades relacionadas con el viaje *(Travel-related activities)*

| | |
|---|---|
| cancelar una reservación | *to cancel a reservation* |
| comprar los billetes | *to buy the tickets* |
| deshacer la(s) maleta(s) | *to unpack* |
| facturar la(s) maleta(s) | *to check luggage* |
| tomar fotos | *to take pictures* |
| hacer la(s) maleta(s) | *to pack* |
| hacer cola/fila | *to wait in line* |
| hacer una reservación | *to make a reservation* |
| ir de camping, acampar | *to go camping* |

| | |
|---|---|
| irse del hotel | *to check out* |
| llegar a tiempo | *to arrive on time* |
| llegar tarde | *to arrive late, to be late* |
| llegar con retraso | *to be delayed* |
| montarse en el tren, avión… | *to get on the train, plane . . .* |
| inscribirse en el hotel | *to check in* |
| salir del avión, tren, autobús… | *to get off the plane, train, bus . . .* |
| solicitar una visa | *to apply for a visa* |

### Medios de transporte *(Means of transportation)*

| | |
|---|---|
| el autobús (bus, omnibus) | *bus* |
| el avión | *plane* |
| el barco | *boat, ship* |
| la bicicleta | *bicycle* |
| el caballo | *horse* |
| el carro (coche, auto) | *car* |
| el taxi | *cab* |
| el tren | *train* |

### Adjetivos *(Adjectives)*

| | |
|---|---|
| aburrido/a | *boring* |
| cerrado/a | *closed* |
| divertido/a | *fun* |
| gratis | *free* |
| lento/a | *slow* |
| lleno/a | *booked* |
| ocupado/a | *busy* |
| rápido/a | *fast* |
| vacío/a | *empty* |

### Verbos *(Verbs)*

| | |
|---|---|
| aterrizar | *to land* |
| descubrir | *to discover* |
| despedirse de | *to say goodbye* |
| despegar | *to take off* |
| empezar (ie) | *to start* |
| esperar | *to wait* |
| irse | *to leave* |
| llegar | *to arrive* |
| ocuparse (de) | *to take care of* |
| recoger | *to pick up* |
| regresar | *to return* |
| reunirse (con) | *to meet* |
| volar | *to fly* |
| volver | *to return* |

# CONSULTORIO GRAMATICAL

## 1 Spatial References

| | | |
|---|---|---|
| POINT OF DEPARTURE AND DESTINATION | de... a... | **De** Santo Domingo **a** Punta Cana vamos en moto. |
| | desde... hasta... | **Desde** Santo Domingo **hasta** Punta Cana vamos en moto. |
| | from . . . to . . . | We travel by motorcycle **from** Santo Domingo **to** Punta Cana. |
| DIRECTION | hacia... | Va **hacia** Santo Domingo. |
| | toward... | S/he/it is going **toward** Santo Domingo. |
| LIMIT | hasta... | Voy **hasta** Santo Domingo en carro. |
| | to . . . | I'm going **to** Santo Domingo by car. |
| DISTANCE | estar a... de... | Punta Cana **está a** 450 km **de** Santo Domingo. |
| | to be . . . from . . . | Punta Cana **is** 450 km **from** Santo Domingo. |
| | estar cerca / lejos de... | **¿Está lejos de** Punta Cana? |
| | to be near / far from . . . | **Is it far from** Punta Cana? |
| | | Mi pueblo **está muy cerca de** aquí. |
| | | My town **is very near** here. |
| ROUTE | pasar por... | **¿Pasas por** La Romana para ir a Santo Domingo? |
| | to go by . . . | Do you go **by** La Romana on your way to Santo Domingo? |
| SPEED | a... kilómetros por hora | Va **a** 100 **kilómetros por hora** (100 km/h). |
| | at . . . kilometers per hour | It moves **at** 100 **kilometers per hour.** |

## 2 Time References

### Indicating dates and months

In the past
**ayer**
(yesterday)
**anteayer / antes de ayer**
(the day before yesterday)
**el** lunes; **el** lunes **pasado**
(**on** Monday; **last** Monday)
**el pasado** 16 de julio
(**last** July 16)

In the future
**mañana**
(tomorrow)
**pasado mañana**
(the day after tomorrow)
**el próximo** lunes = **el** lunes **que viene**
(**next** Monday)
**el próximo** 16 de julio
(**next** July 16)

Note that when you give a date in American English, the month goes first, followed by the day. In Spanish it's the other way around, as in British English, so 10/4 is always **10 de abril** and not **4 de octubre**.

The article is not used when stating the date:

Hoy **es** lunes 4 **de** septiembre **de** 2006.
Today **is** Monday, September 4, 2006.

Mañana **es** 5 **de** septiembre.
Tomorrow **is** September 5.

The article is used when asking or talking about dates of events:

● **¿Cuándo / Qué día** es tu cumpleaños?　　—**When** is your birthday?
○ **El** dos **de** marzo.　　　　　　　　　　—**The** second **of** March.

Nos vamos de vacaciones **el** 24 de agosto.
We'll go on vacation on August 24.

Months in Spanish are not capitalized, e.g.: **enero.**

**El** lunes tenemos que viajar a Santo Domingo.
On Monday we have to visit Santo Domingo.

### Indicating periods of time

| In the past | In the future |
|---|---|
| **la semana pasada** | **la semana que viene / la próxima semana** |
| (last week) | (next week) |
| **el mes pasado** | **el mes que viene / el próximo mes** |
| (last month) | (next month) |
| **el verano pasado** | **el verano que viene / el próximo verano** |
| (last summer) | (next summer) |
| **el año pasado** | **el año que viene / el próximo año** |
| (last year) | (next year) |

**La semana que viene** viajamos a Santo Domingo.
*Next week we are travelling to Santo domingo.*

- ● **¿Cuándo** van de vacaciones? —*When are they/you going on vacation?*
- ○ El **próximo mes.** —*Next month.*

### Indicating parts of the day

| | |
|---|---|
| **por/en la mañana** | **de día** |
| (in the morning) | (during the day) |
| **al mediodía** | **de noche** |
| (at noon) | (at night) |
| **por/en la tarde** | **esta noche** |
| (in the afternoon) | (tonight) |
| **por/en la noche** | **esta mañana** |
| (in the evening) | (this morning) |
| **anoche** (= ayer por la noche) | **esta tarde** |
| (last night) | (this afternoon) |
| **antenoche** (= anteayer por la noche) | |
| (the night before last night) | |

- ● Me gusta trabajar **de noche / por la noche.** ¿Y a ti? —*I like to work at night. And you?*
- ○ Yo prefiero trabajar **por la mañana.** —*I prefer to work in the morning.*

## 3  The Time

To tell time, the article **las** (except for **la una**) is used.

- ● ¿Qué hora es? —*What time is it?*
- ○ **Las** cinco / **La** una. —*Five / one*

| | | |
|---|---|---|
| las dos | **(en punto)** | **(de la madrugada)** |
| | | (in the early morning) |
| las cuatro | y cinco | **(de la mañana)** |
| | | (in the morning) |
| las doce | **y cuarto** | **(del mediodía)** |
| | | (in the early afternoon) |
| las tres | **y media** | **(de la tarde)** |
| | | (in the afternoon) |
| veinte | **para las** diez | **(de la noche)** |
| | | (in the evening) |
| **un cuarto para** | las cinco | **(de la mañana)** |
| | | (in the morning) |

IN SPAIN

| | | | |
|---|---|---|---|
| las diez **menos** veinte | **(de la noche)** | las cinco **menos cuarto** | **(de la mañana)** |
| twenty **to** ten | (in the evening) | quarter **to** five | (in the morning) |

To indicate the time when something takes place, the structure **a + las** (**la**) is used.

- ● **¿A qué hora** abre el club? —**At what time** does the club open?
- ○ **A la** una de la madrugada. —**At** one o'clock in the morning.

To talk about work schedules, store hours, etc. the prepositions **de... a** or **desde... hasta** are used.

- ● ¿Qué horario tiene la biblioteca? —What are the library's working hours?
- ○ **De** nueve **a** cinco. —**From** nine **to** five.

- ● ¿Cuántas horas trabajas? —How many hours do you work?
- ○ **Desde las** ocho y media **hasta las** seis. —**From** eight-thirty **until** six.

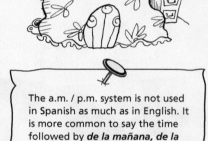

## 4  Talking about the Future

The use of a marker indicating a future time period + the present indicative is one way of expressing future actions. This structure presents a future action as part of a plan that has already been decided upon.

| | |
|---|---|
| Mañana | **voy** a San Pedro. |
| | (**I'm going to** San Pedro.) |
| El mes que viene | **regreso** a la República Dominicana. |
| | (**I am going back** to the Dominican Republic.) |
| El 15 de julio | **vamos** al teatro. |
| | (**we are going to** the theater.) |
| Esta tarde | **nos reunimos** con Marco. |
| | (**we are meeting** with Marco.) |

Another way to express future actions is to use **IR a** + infinitive (with or without an explicit indication of time). This form expresses plans or intentions that refer to future actions.

| (yo) | **voy** | |
|---|---|---|
| (tú) | **vas** | |
| (él, ella, usted) | **va** | **a** + INFINITIVE |
| (nosotros/as) | **vamos** | |
| (vosotros/as) | **vais** | |
| (ellos, ellas, ustedes) | **van** | |

(El próximo año) **vamos a hacer** un viaje por el norte de la isla.
(Next year) **we're going to make** a trip in the north of the island.

¿El señor López? Creo que **va a ir** a Santo Domingo mañana.
Mr. López? I think **he's going to** Santo Domingo tomorrow.

>
>
> The a.m. / p.m. system is not used in Spanish as much as in English. It is more common to say the time followed by *de la mañana, de la tarde, de la noche.*

> Note that unlike English, in Spanish we cannot use the present progressive to express a future arrangement (I'm eating lunch with Margarita tomorrow.); instead, we use the present indicative with a temporal marker: *Mañana como con Margarita.*

Future actions can also be expressed with the future indicative (with or without explicit indication of a future time). The future indicative is a very consistent tense.

| | INFINITIVE + ENDINGS | |
|---|---|---|
| (yo) | | **-é** |
| (tú) | viaj**ar** | **-ás** |
| (él, ella, usted) | com**er** | **-á** |
| (nosotros/as) | dorm**ir** | **-emos** |
| (vosotros/as) | | **-éis** |
| (ellos, ellas, ustedes) | | **-án** |

## 5  *Estar a punto de..., acabar de...*

To be more precise about the exact moment in which something takes place or has taken place, the structures **ESTAR a punto de** + infinitive (to express the immediate future) and **ACABAR de** + infinitive (to express a very recent past) are used.

El concierto **está a punto de** empezar.           El concierto **acaba de** empezar.
The concert is about to start.                              The concert just started.

- ● ¿Está abierta la farmacia? —Is the pharmacy open?
- ○ No, **acaban de cerrar.** —No, they just closed.

# 8 GENTE que come BIEN

## 8–1 Platos (*dishes*) internacionales

¿Qué tipo de cocina te gusta más? ¿De qué país o países? ¿Por qué? Mira estas fotos. ¿Qué plato prefieres?

Carbonada (Argentina)

Tacos, burritos y enchiladas (México)

Arroz con frijoles negros
(Cuba y Puerto Rico)

Pollo con arroz y frijoles (Cuba)

Paella (España)

Frutas tropicales (Costa Rica, El Salvador...)

## TAREA

Escribir una receta de cocina.

## NUESTRA GENTE

Cuba
Hispanos/latinos en Estados Unidos

## CULTURA

La gastronomía de Cuba es una fusión de cocina española, africana y caribeña. Entre los ingredientes más usados están el arroz, el plátano, las legumbres y la carne de cerdo. El plato nacional es el ajiaco criollo, un conjunto de viandas, vegetales y carnes de diversos tipos. Otros platos cubanos típicos son los tostones o chatinos (trozos de plátano verde aplastados y fritos), el congrí (guiso de arroz con frijoles colorados) y la carne de cerdo asada o frita.

ESTADOS UNIDOS — LAS BAHAMAS

La Habana, Pinar del Río, Cienfuegos, Santa Clara, Trinidad, **CUBA**, Camagüey, Holguín, Santiago de Cuba

*Mar Caribe*

**JAMAICA**

## ACERCAMIENTOS

### 8–2 ¡A comer!

Mira las fotos de la página 128. ¿Qué ingredientes usan estos platos? Usa la lista y pide ayuda a tu profesor o a tus compañeros/as.

**EJEMPLO:**

**E1:** ¿Qué es esto?
**E2:** Fresas.
**E1:** ¿Cómo se dice *meat* en español?
**E2:** Carne.

¿Cuáles te gustan? Márcalos con estos signos.

+ = Me gusta/n.
− = No me gusta/n.
? = No lo sé.

| | | |
|---|---|---|
| ☐ frijoles | ☐ tomates | ☐ pollo |
| ☐ bananas | ☐ judías verdes | ☐ cebolla |
| ☐ maíz | ☐ zanahoria | ☐ naranja |
| ☐ papas (patatas) | ☐ carne | ☐ mango |
| ☐ arroz | ☐ pimiento | ☐ melón |
| ☐ sandía | ☐ tortillas | ☐ pescado |
| ☐ uvas | ☐ aguacate | ☐ marisco |
| ☐ guisantes | ☐ calabaza | ☐ verdura |
| ☐ mejillones | ☐ ajo | ☐ fruta |
| ☐ gambas | ☐ melocotón | |

### 8–3 ¿Y a ti qué te gusta?

Comenta tus gustos con dos compañeros/as.

**EJEMPLO:**

**E1:** A mí me gustan mucho las habichuelas. ¿Y a ti?
**E2:** A mí no, no me gustan nada. Me gusta la fruta, pero la verdura, no.
**E3:** A mí sí, mucho.

Un/a representante del grupo va a explicar al resto de la clase qué gustos comparten.

**EJEMPLO:**

A todos nos gustan mucho las naranjas, la piña y el pollo; pero a nadie le gusta el ajo.

¿Cuáles son los dos productos que más le gustan a la clase? ¿Y los que menos le gustan?

| Más | 1. | 2. |
|---|---|---|
| Menos | 1. | 2. |

VOCABULARIO EN CONTEXTO

08-01 to
08-09

 **8-4 Tienda Blasco**

En el mercado (*grocery store*) Blasco, Celia, la dependienta, está hablando con la señora Millán.
Escucha y marca qué compra la señora Millán.

2 **kilos** de naranjas
2 naranjas
1/2 docena de huevos
1 **docena** de huevos
1 **paquete** de café Cubita
1 paquete de azúcar
200 **gramos** de queso fresco

200 gramos de jamón
2 **botellas** de leche
2 **bolsas** de leche
1 botella de ron Legendario
1 botella de ron Varadero
6 **latas** de refresco de cola
10 latas de refresco de cola

Mira las palabras en negrita. ¿Qué otras cosas puedes comprar en este formato?

 **8-5 La pirámide de alimentos
(*food*)**

Miren las recomendaciones para comer bien. Usen los dibujos para adivinar el significado de las palabras que no conocen. Después respondan a estas preguntas:

1. ¿Qué hay que comer cada día?
2. ¿Qué debemos comer sólo de vez en cuando?
3. ¿De qué alimentos hay que comer dos o más tazas diarias?
4. ¿Qué debemos beber diariamente?
5. ¿Hay que comer mucha carne cada día?

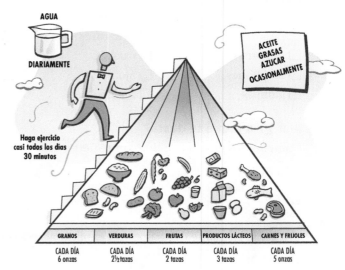

**8-6 ¿Cómo comes?**

Vamos a averiguar cómo es la dieta de nuestros compañeros para luego darles algunos consejos. Haz una entrevista a tu compañero/a con estas preguntas. Añade dos preguntas más.

| | SÍ | NO |
|---|---|---|
| ¿Comes mucho pescado? | | |
| ¿Comes mucha verdura? | | |
| ¿Comes mucha carne? | | |
| ¿Bebes vino? | | |
| ¿Cocinas con aceite de oliva? | | |
| ¿Bebes leche? | | |
| ¿Comes muchos huevos? | | |
| ¿Comes legumbres? | | |
| | | |
| | | |

Según sus respuestas y las recomendaciones de la pirámide, tu compañero/a come…

muy bien          bien          no muy bien          mal          muy mal

¿Tiene que cambiar algún hábito? Informa a la clase.

**EJEMPLO:**

Josh se alimenta bien. Bebe mucha agua y come mucha verdura, pero tiene que comer menos grasas y dulces.

 **8-7 En el restaurante cubano**

Noelle, una estudiante estadounidense, va a comer a un restaurante cubano. No conoce la cocina cubana y la mesera le describe cada plato.

Lee el menú y después escucha.

1. Noelle pide, primero, _____
2. Noelle pide, después, _____
3. Noelle pide, de postre, _____

Ahora escucha otra vez. ¿Puedes hacer una lista de algunos ingredientes de estos platos?

**8-8 En un restaurante cubano**

Imagina que vas a ese restaurante cubano. Piensa qué vas a pedir.

**EJEMPLO:**

Yo, primero, sopa de pollo.

Ahora unos/unas estudiantes hacen de (*play the role of*) meseros y toman nota de lo que quieren sus compañeros/as. ¿Cuáles son los platos más populares en la clase?

**RESTAURANTE HABANERA**

MENÚ DEL DÍA

frijoles negros
arroz con maíz a la criolla
sopa de pollo

costillas de cerdo con piña
camarones borrachitos

pudín de piña
arroz con leche de coco

 **8-9 Programa de adelgazamiento (*weight loss*)**

El hotel balneario Gente Sana ofrece un programa de adelgazamiento. Los clientes pueden adelgazar seis kilos en seis días, pero de una forma sana. ¿Puedes elaborar el menú con tu compañero/a? Compartan luego su propuesta con la clase.

| * * * HOTEL BALNEARIO GENTE SANA * * * | | |
|---|---|---|
| | **VIERNES** | **SÁBADO** | **DOMINGO** |
| **Desayuno** | | | |
| **Almuerzo**<br>Primer plato:<br>Segundo plato:<br>Postre: | | | |
| **Cena**<br>Primer plato:<br>Segundo plato:<br>Postre: | | | |

📖 GRAMÁTICA EN CONTEXTO

08-10 to
08-25

### 8–10 Platos típicos y fiestas típicas

Lee estas definiciones de platos y bebidas típicos cubanos. ¿Sabes cómo se llama cada uno?

buñuelos

sopón

carne de cerdo con papaya

mojito

**1**

Es una sopa típica de Holguín. **Se hace** con carne de cerdo, de pollo, jamón, plátano verde, boniato, yuca, calabaza, arroz y agua. **Se acompaña** con rodajas de limón.

**2**

Es una bebida muy típica. **Se prepara** con ron blanco, hierbabuena, azúcar y jugo de limón.

**3**

Es un plato que **se elabora** con carne de cerdo. Lleva cebolla, sal y pimienta. **Se pone** además azúcar y jugo de piña, papaya verde y pimientos rojos.

**4**

Es un postre muy popular. **Se come** especialmente en fin de año. **Se cocina** con yuca, malanga y boniato. Lleva anís y canela, además de huevos, harina, azúcar y vino. **Se hacen** roscas y se fríen en aceite. Luego **se sumergen** las roscas en un almíbar y se dejan enfriar.

Fíjate en las palabras marcadas en negrita. Ahora completa este texto con formas similares. Usa estos verbos: *comer, beber, servir*.

Las fiestas navideñas en Cuba tienen por lo general un carácter familiar. El 24 de diciembre (Nochebuena y víspera de Navidad) la familia se reúne para celebrar la fecha. Por supuesto, en estas fechas en Cuba se _____ muy bien. _____ cerdo asado, congrí (arroz con frijoles negros) y postres caseros. Además _____ vinos, cerveza fría y licores. Para postre _____ nueces, avellanas o dátiles y, como herencia de España, _____ turrón. El 31 de diciembre es un día para la familia, y en el menú _____ otra vez cerdo; además ese día _____ las 12 uvas a medianoche para despedir el año.

Describe ahora un plato típico de tu país o región y cuándo se come. Sigue los modelos anteriores. Luego, explícaselo a tus compañeros/as.

👥 8–11 ¿Qué frutas y verduras se comen en Cuba?

Lean el texto sobre los hábitos alimentarios de los cubanos.

Las frutas y las verduras son excelentes fuentes de vitaminas y nutrientes. El Instituto de Farmacia y Alimentos de la Universidad de La Habana hizo una investigación con el objetivo de evaluar el consumo de fruta y verdura. Respecto a la fruta, según los datos obtenidos, los cubanos comen **mucha**; en cuanto a la verdura, consumen **suficiente**. Las frutas que más se consumen son el mango, la naranja, la piña, el plátano, el aguacate y el tomate. En cambio, se comen **pocas** uvas porque es un producto de cantidad limitada en la isla. Las frutas y verduras menos populares son la acelga, el apio, la berenjena, la coliflor, la espinaca y la remolacha. El 18% de los cubanos consume **bastante** fruta (a diario) y el 60% la come tres ó cuatro veces por semana. La verdura se come menos: el 39% de los cubanos afirma que come **bastante**, el 48% dice que come **poca** y el 13% afirma que no come **nada de** verdura en una semana.

---

**LA FORMA IMPERSONAL**

*Con complemento directo*

SINGULAR     En Cuba **se come** una **carne** muy buena.

PLURAL     En Cuba **se fabrican** excelentes **cigarros** habanos.

*Sin complemento directo*

Aquí **se vive** muy bien.
En Cuba **se trabaja** mucho.

**EN EL RESTAURANTE**

● ¿Qué van a comer/pedir?
○ Yo,...
   Primero / después...
   De / para postre,

● ¿Para beber?
○ Vino tinto / blanco / rosado.
   Agua con gas/sin gas.
   Cerveza.
   Jugo de naranja

¿Es carne o pescado?
¿Es fuerte / picante / graso?
¿Qué lleva?
¿Lleva salsa?

## CUANTIFICADORES

### ANTES DEL NOMBRE

*SINGULAR*
**demasiado** arroz/**demasiada** leche
**mucho** arroz/**mucha** leche
**suficiente/bastante** arroz/leche
**poco** arroz/**poca** leche
**un poco de** arroz (= una pequeña cantidad)

*PLURAL*
**demasiados** huevos/**demasiadas** peras
**muchos** huevos/**muchas** peras
**suficientes/bastantes** huevos/peras
**pocos** huevos/**pocas** peras

### ANTES DE UN VERBO
Come **poco / mucho.**
Fuma **bastante.**
Trabaja **demasiado.**

## CUANTIFICADORES NEGATIVOS

*Nombres no contables*
No hay azúcar.
**No** hay **nada de** azúcar.

*Nombres contables*

*SINGULAR*
No tengo **ningún** No tengo **ninguno.**
plátano.
No tengo **ninguna** No tengo **ninguna.**
botella.

*PLURAL*
No tengo plátanos.    No tengo.

## PESOS Y MEDIDAS

**100 gramos de**
**200 gramos de**

**un cuarto de** kilo/litro de
**medio** kilo/litro de
**tres cuartos de** kilo/litro de
**un** kilo/litro de

**un paquete de** arroz/sal/azúcar/harina
**una botella de** vino/agua mineral/aceite
**una lata de** atún/aceitunas/tomate
**una caja de** galletas/leche...

---

Ahora conversen sobre estos hábitos para ver si son iguales en su país y en sus casos particulares.

**EJEMPLO:**

**E1:** En Cuba se come **mucha** fruta y verdura, pero aquí se come **poca** fruta.
**E2:** Yo no como verdura, pero como **bastante** fruta.

 **8-13** **Comida de excursión a Pinar del Río**

La familia Zalacaín va a pasar siete días de campamento en Pinar del Río, una ciudad al oeste de Cuba donde se encuentran dos de las cuatro reservas mundiales de la biosfera declaradas por la UNESCO.

Son cinco personas, tres adultos y dos niños. Tienen que llevar toda la comida porque van a acampar en una zona donde no hay tiendas. Miren la lista. ¿Olvidan algo importante? Eliminen o añadan (*add*) cosas a la lista.

| | |
|---|---|
| 1 docena de huevos | 7 kilogramos de carne |
| 15 litros de leche | 50 gramos de queso |
| 1/2 litro de aceite | 2 plátanos |
| 2 kilogramos de papas | 12 kilogramos de manzanas |
| 3 kilogramos de espaguetis | 100 gramos de azúcar |
| 1 lata de tomate | 11 botellas de vino |
| 2 yogures | |

**EJEMPLO:**

**E1:** Llevan **pocos** huevos, ¿verdad?
**E2:** Sí, es verdad. Y llevan **poco** azúcar, ¿no?
**E1:** Sí, no tienen **bastante** azúcar.

**8-13** **Tu plato favorito**

Piensa en tu plato favorito y en cómo se prepara. Haz una lista de ingredientes y cantidades aproximadas. Después explica a tu compañero/a el procedimiento para prepararlo.

**EJEMPLO:**

**E1:** **Se necesita** un tomate, un poco de cebolla, carne picada (ground), una rebanada de queso, un poco de ketchup y mostaza.
**E2:** ¿Y cómo **se prepara?**
**E1:** **Se pone** en el pan la carne y **se coloca** encima la cebolla, el tomate y el queso.

INTERACCIONES

08-26 to
08-28

**Verbal courtesy (I)**

Verbal courtesy is a universal concept; however, ways of expressing courtesy vary from culture to culture. You already know that when interacting in formal contexts, it is generally more appropriate to use *usted*.

Read this dialogue between a waiter and a customer at a restaurant. Identify all the ways in which verbal courtesy is used.

- *Buenas tardes. **Disculpe**, ¿tienen mesas libres?*
- *Sí, **pase, pase**. **Siéntese** aquí, por favor. ¿Qué va a pedir?*
- *¿Me trae primero una ensalada?*
- *Cómo no. ¿Y después?*
- ***Tráigame** por favor un bistec con papas fritas.*
  *[…]*
- ***Oiga**, por favor.*
- *Sí, **dígame**.*
- *¿Me puede traer una botella de agua sin gas?*
- *Ahora mismo.*

Note how the use of *usted* is reflected in the verb conjugations. Also, note how the use of command forms (*tráigame, pase, siéntese*) can be considered courteous in certain cases, such as when used to attract someone's attention (*oiga, disculpe*) or to respond (*sí, dígame*). When used alongside expressions such as *por favor*, these command forms can also become courteous.

 **8–14 Situaciones: *En el restaurante***

Three students visiting Cuba want to try authentic homemade Cuban food, so they go to a *paladar*. They are looking at the menu and have some questions for the owner about the various dishes and drinks. Then they order their food.

*Menú del día*

Frijoles negros
Sopón de Holguín

Carne de cerdo con papaya

Buñuelos o flan

Vino o agua
Café

**ESTUDIANTE A**

You are the owner of this *paladar*. Ask these two visitors questions to find out what they would like to eat. Answer their questions about the dishes. You can also make recommendations. Remember to use verbal courtesy and the *usted* forms.

**ESTUDIANTE B**

You and your friend are in a Cuban *paladar*. You are lactose intolerant and want to know the ingredients in the dishes. Remember to use verbal courtesy and the *usted* forms.

**ESTUDIANTE C**

You and your friend are in a Cuban *paladar*. You don't drink coffee or wine, but you love sweets and desserts. Remember to use verbal courtesy and the *usted* forms.

**8-15 ¿Qué comes?**

¿Consumes alguno de estos productos? Completa la siguiente tabla.

| DEMASIADO | BASTANTE | POCO/UN POCO DE | NADA DE | PRODUCTO |
|---|---|---|---|---|
| | | | | café / té |
| | | | | pescado |
| | | | | fruta |
| | | | | verduras |
| | | | | agua |

Ahora intercambia la información con tu compañero/a. Pregúntale a tu compañero/a qué productos consume y en qué cantidad. Luego tu compañero/a te va a preguntar a ti.

**EJEMPLO:**

**E1:** ¿Bebes **mucho** café?
**E2:** No, muy **poco**. Pero tomo **mucho** té. ¿Y tú?
**E1:** No, yo no bebo **nada de** té. Bebo **mucho** café. **Demasiado**.

 **8-16 ¿A qué restaurante vamos?**

Están visitando La Habana en viaje de estudios y quieren ir a comer. Lean la información sobre tres lugares y decidan dónde van y por qué. Justifiquen su decisión con datos del texto. Luego expliquen a la clase su decisión.

### Paladar *La Cocina de Lilliam*

Éste es uno de los restaurantes más acogedores de la capital. La cocinera y dueña del paladar es Lilliam Domínguez. La residencia está decorada con hermosas antigüedades. Los más distinguidos personajes han comido en este restaurante, entre ellos el presidente estadounidense Carter. Aquí se puede comer la famosa "ropa vieja", un plato tradicional cubano preparado con carne de cordero.

*Precio promedio*: $9,00

### Restaurante *La Mina*

Está ubicado en la esquina de la Plaza de Armas. En este restaurante se puede disfrutar de una gran variedad de menús cubanos, como los tamales, arroz congrí (frijoles negros con arroz blanco) y cerdo asado. También se sirven excelentes cócteles como el mojito y el daiquirí, postres hechos en casa, y el delicioso café "Cubita".

*Precio promedio*: $17,00

### Restaurante *La Bodeguita del Medio*

A un lado de la Plaza de la Catedral, en el casco histórico de la ciudad, está este prestigioso restaurante. La Bodeguita es famosa por ser lugar de encuentro de importantes intelectuales y artistas desde su apertura en 1940, como el famoso escritor estadounidense Ernest Hemingway. La presencia de estas personalidades se ve en cada detalle, fotografías y objetos traídos de todas partes. Es la cuna del famoso cóctel "mojito".

*Precio promedio*: $25,00

**EJEMPLO:**

**E1:** Yo quiero ir al paladar porque es más barato. Además, tienen comida tradicional. Dice que se puede comer "ropa vieja".
**E2:** No sé... La Mina parece interesante. Y hay comida tradicional también.

# TAREA  Gente en acción

**Escribir una receta de cocina.**

## PREPARACIÓN

Antes de escribir su receta, vamos a examinar con detalle un plato típico cubano, sus ingredientes y preparación. Se trata del *ajiaco cubano*, el plato nacional de Cuba.

El ajiaco es una sopa propia del campo, pero se come en todos los hogares cubanos. Se compone de diversos ingredientes: vegetales como la yuca o mandioca, la malanga, el ñame o el boniato y diferentes carnes, todo mezclado. También se pueden agregar plátanos verdes y maíz. Éste es un plato tradicional de las poblaciones indígenas de la isla.

Ahora vamos a repasar los ingredientes para preparar el ajiaco.

### AYUDA

Se pone/n en { una sartén. / una cazuela. / una bandeja.

**Se** pon**e** un huevo.
**Se** pon**en** tres huevos.

| | |
|---|---|
| se echa/n | se añade/n |
| se fríe/n | se asa/n |
| se hierve/n | se pela/n |
| se corta/n | se saca/n |
| se mezcla/n | |

**primero…**
**después…**
**luego…**
**al final…**

## AJIACO CUBANO

**DIFICULTAD:** media
**TIEMPO:** 120 minutos
**INGREDIENTES** (para seis personas):

| | |
|---|---|
| tasajo (cecina) : | 150 g |
| carne de cerdo: | 145 g |
| tocino: | 80 g |
| plátano pintón: | 200 g |
| malanga: | 200 g |
| maíz tierno: | 200 g |
| calabaza: | 200 g |
| boniato: | 200 g |
| salsa criolla: | 75 g |
| sal: | 40 g |
| aceite vegetal: | 60 ml |
| agua (aprox.): | 2,3 l |

Escuchen a Ramón, un cocinero cubano, explicar cómo se prepara el ajiaco. Luego, ordenen los pasos de la receta.

☐ Se corta el tocino.
☐ Se pone el maíz en el caldo.
☐ Se ponen las viandas.
☐ Se fríe el tocino en aceite.
☐ Se corta el tasajo en cinco pedazos.

☐ Se mezcla la carne de cerdo con la salsa criolla.
☐ Se cocina el tasajo durante 30 minutos.
☐ Se añade la carne de cerdo al tasajo.
☐ Se cocina todo 10 minutos más.

Lean ahora la transcripción para comprobar que el orden es correcto.

> Bueno, para hacer ajiaco uno tiene primero que remojar el tasajo durante 12 horas. Luego el tasajo se pone a cocinar en agua, durante 30 minutos más o menos. Después se le añade la carne de cerdo y se deja cocinar hasta que esté blando. A continuación se sacan las carnes, se limpia el tasajo y se corta en cinco pedazos. Después de hacer esto, se cuela el caldo, se vierte en la cazuela que usamos antes, se pone al fuego y se incorpora en primer lugar el maíz. Bueno, entonces se deja cocinar el maíz unos 45 minutos y luego se ponen las viandas cortadas en pedazos por orden de dureza, es decir, las más duras primero, las más blandas después. Se cocinan hasta que estén blandas. Después, se corta el tocino en cubos pequeños, se fríe en aceite un poquitico y se mezcla con la salsa criolla. Todo esto se añade al ajiaco. Finalmente, se cocina todo 10 minutos más, ¡y ya está!

**Paso 1** Formen grupos de tres o cuatro personas. Decidan entre todos qué plato van a presentar para una colección de recetas de la clase. Puede ser una receta de su país o de un país hispanohablante.

**Paso 2** Completen ahora esta ficha. Incluyan una lista detallada de los ingredientes y las cantidades necesarias.

**Paso 3** Escriban la receta. Pueden usar la receta del ajiaco como modelo.

**Paso 4** Cada grupo explica a la clase el plato que propone y cómo se prepara. La clase puede elegir las mejores recetas.

**Paso 5** Foco lingüístico.

DIFICULTAD: _____

TIEMPO: _____

INGREDIENTES: _____
_____
_____
_____
_____
_____
_____
_____
_____

# NUESTRA GENTE

## GENTE QUE LEE

### ESTRATEGIAS PARA LEER

**Word formation and affixes**

As you already know, words can take on markers of gender or number (*camarero/a/os/as*). Words can also take other endings that change their category. For example, if you add *-ar* to the noun *cocina*, you get the verb *cocinar*.

   **Affixes** are placed either before words (as prefixes) or after them (as suffixes). For example, the word *cierto* (certain) can take the prefix *in-* and form a new word: *incierto* (uncertain). The word *pescado* can become *pescadería* by adding the affix *-ería* to the first part of the word.

   **Compound words** are single words that are formed by combining two or more other words. For example, the word *paraguas* (umbrella) is formed by two words: *parar* (to stop) and *aguas* (waters). Can you guess what the word *abrelatas* means?

   Now take a look at these words: *la verdura* (*verde* + *-ura*), *la naranjada* (*naranja* + *-ada*), *azucarar* (*azúcar* + *-ar*), *abrebotellas* (*abre* + *botellas*), *frutero* (*fruta* + *-ero*). *Can you guess what they mean?*

### ANTES DE LEER

#### 8–17 En La Habana

Mira las fotos y pregunta a tu profesor/a sobre estos lugares. Después piensa cuáles te gustaría visitar. Puedes ponerlos en orden de más interesante (1) a menos interesante (6).

1. Catedral de La Habana
2. El capitolio, La Habana
3. Memorial de José Martí
4. Universidad de La Habana
5. Los castillos de La Habana
6. Museo de la Revolución
7. Casa de África

¿En qué lugar has colocado el museo?

#### 8–18 Visitando museos

¿Conoces algún museo sobre comidas o bebidas? ¿Por qué crees que se hacen estos museos? ¿Crees que las comidas y bebidas son elementos que reflejan la cultura de un país? ¿Tienes algunos ejemplos?

#### 8–19 Activando estrategias

Mira durante unos segundos la foto, el texto, su título y subtítulos. ¿De qué crees que trata?

*A LEER*

# EL RON Y EL TABACO DE CUBA: DOS MUSEOS EN LA HABANA

### El Museo del Ron

La Fundación Habana Club está situada en el corazón de La Habana Vieja, en un palacio del siglo XVIII. Esta institución **difunde** el conocimiento sobre el ron y su vínculo natural con la cultura cubana. Entre otras atracciones, la Fundación ofrece un museo viviente que reproduce el proceso tradicional de fabricación del ron. El recorrido por este museo termina con una **degustación**. Además hay una galería de arte, una tienda y un bar-restaurante. En la tienda se puede **adquirir** todo tipo de ron Habana Club, además de música tradicional, libros sobre la historia del ron y sobre los bares más famosos de la ciudad considerada centro de la **coctelería** mundial. Dentro del edificio hay un bar, heredero del primer Bar Habana Club del año 1934. Este bar **recrea** el ambiente típico de las mejores bodegas de los años 30. Además es lugar de encuentro de artistas cubanos como pintores y músicos. Aquí se preparan los famosos cócteles cubanos al ritmo del tradicional *son*. En el restaurante se encuentra una buena oportunidad para degustar el sabor de la comida cubana, ya que además de comida internacional se sirven excelentes platos criollos.

### El Museo del Tabaco

El Museo del Tabaco es la única institución en Cuba destinada a conservar y mostrar colecciones vinculadas a la cultura del tabaco. Fundado en 1993, está ubicado en un edificio del siglo XVIII en el centro histórico de La Habana. En el museo se puede hacer un recorrido por los aspectos históricos y culturales del tabaco cubano y el proceso de cultivo de la hoja y de fabricación de los famosos puros habanos. También se muestra una colección de utensilios del fumador de los siglos XIX y XX confeccionados con diferentes tipos de metales **preciosos** y otros materiales. Esto demuestra la notable influencia de la industria del habano en artes como la orfebrería, la artesanía, la pintura, la litografía y la cerámica. Es muy interesante también la colección de fotos sobre las grandes personalidades mundiales consumidoras de los famosos puros.

Finalmente, en el mismo museo está La Casa del Habano, una tienda donde se vende todo tipo de habanos y útiles del fumador (encendedores, **cortapuros**, tabaqueras, **ceniceros**...).

---

*DESPUÉS DE LEER*

### 8–20 ¿Comprendes?

1. ¿Cuántas partes tiene la Fundación Habana Club?
2. ¿Cuáles de estos productos se puede obtener en la tienda del Museo del Ron?
   a. música           b. libros           c. arte
3. ¿Cuál de estos datos sobre el Museo del Tabaco es falso?
   a. Tiene una tienda de tabaco.     b. Expone arte y fotografía.     c. Se funda en el siglo XVIII.

### 8–21 Activando estrategias

1. ¿Qué significan las palabras "degustación", "coctelería" y "cortapuros"? ¿Puedes dividirlas en partes? Si la palabra *ceniza* significa *ash*, ¿qué significa "cenicero"?
2. ¿Qué significan las palabras "recrear", "adquirir" y "preciosos"? ¿Cómo lo sabes?
3. Busca en el diccionario la palabra "difunde". ¿Es nombre, verbo o adjetivo? ¿Qué necesitas buscar? ¿Qué significado es más apropiado en este contexto?

### 8–22 Expansión

¿Existe algún museo en tu país de este tipo? ¿Cómo es? Si no existe, piensa en un museo hipotético para el pueblo o ciudad donde vives. Justifica tu idea.

## GENTE QUE ESCRIBE

08-31 to
08-35

### ESTRATEGIAS PARA ESCRIBIR

**Writing topic sentences and paragraphs**

A good topic sentence (a) is normally at the beginning of a paragraph, (b) states the main idea of the paragraph, (c) focuses exclusively on one topic of interest, and (d) attracts the attention of the reader.

　　Here is a list of possible topic sentences for an opening paragraph about Santiago de Cuba. Which ones do you think are appropriate? Why?

> En Santiago está la primera catedral de Cuba.
> El clima de Santiago se caracteriza por tener dos estaciones.
> Santiago de Cuba es una ciudad al este de la isla.
> Santiago es una ciudad que atrae a muchos turistas.

The remaining sentences in the paragraph should contain details that develop the main idea stated in the topic sentence. When editing your paragraphs, be sure to get rid of any ideas that don't help develop the topic of the paragraph.

### MÁS ALLÁ DE LA FRASE

**Connectors for organizing information**

We have already discussed the importance of organizing and sequencing ideas when writing. Let's review and expand some of these discourse markers:

- First idea: *primero…*(first)*, en primer lugar…*(in the first place)*, para empezar…*(to start)*.
- Intermediate ideas: *segundo / tercero…*(second, third)*, a continuación…*(next)*, después…*(next, after that)*, luego…*(next)*, en segundo / tercer lugar…*(second / third)*.
- Final idea: *finalmente…*(last)*, al final…*(at the end)*, por último…*(finally, last)*, para terminar* (to conclude)*.

### 8–23 Crítica de un restaurante o comedor

Escribe una crítica de un restaurante que conoces bien para el periódico en español. La crítica debe tener tres partes: el tipo de cocina, el ambiente y un plato especialmente recomendado.

Piensa en los lectores de esta crítica y decide el registro que vas a usar (formal o informal). Después escribe **frases temáticas** para el párrafo de apertura, las tres partes de la crítica y un párrafo final. Presta atención a las frases temáticas:

- ¿Están al principio del párrafo?
- ¿Dan la idea central del párrafo?
- ¿Se centran en un solo tema de interés?
- ¿Atraen la atención del lector?

 *¡ATENCIÓN!*

Tu trabajo escrito debe seguir (*follow*) los Pasos 1 a 8 y tener contenidos bien organizados y relevantes. Usa conectores para organizar la información y sigue una secuencia lógica.

## COMPARACIONES

### 8–24 El café en Latinoamérica

¿Cuáles de estos países latinoamericanos producen más café? Ordénalos de mayor a menor.

☐ El Salvador     ☐ Guatemala     ☐ México

☐ Colombia     ☐ Cuba     ☐ Costa Rica

### 8–25 Café y cultura cubana

¿Sabías que el café de Cuba es de una calidad excelente? Lee este texto para saber más. Luego responde a las preguntas.

El café forma parte importante de la cultura cubana. Para los cubanos, es parte inseparable de la identidad y cotidianeidad de su gente. El primer cafetal de Cuba data de 1748, pero es después de 1791 cuando se produce en Cuba una avalancha de haciendas cafetaleras con la llegada de colonos franceses de Haití, debido a la revolución en ese país.

Cuba posee la mayor cantidad de ruinas de haciendas cafetaleras con valor arqueológico en todo el mundo, muchas de ellas en buen estado de conservación. Son los primeros cafetales franco-haitianos de Santiago de Cuba y están ubicados al sureste de esa provincia. Además, son patrimonio de la humanidad (UNESCO) desde el año 2000 por su valor histórico. Hay cerca de un centenar, la mayoría ubicados en la provincia de Santiago de Cuba, aunque también hay muchos en Guantánamo. Estos lugares forman un extenso cinturón cafetalero en la región sudeste de Cuba.

Por regla general, los cafetales cubanos están en las serranías de la isla entre 500 y 800 metros sobre el nivel del mar. Esto es debido a que el cafeto, la planta del café, crece muy bien en este microclima. Hoy en día el café cubano no sobresale por grandes volúmenes de exportación, sino por su excelente calidad, sobre todo en la especie *arábica*, que lo ubica entre los preferidos del mundo. Entre las marcas más famosas están Cubita, Hola y la famosa Crystal Mountain.

Roel Caboverde Liacer
*Recolectores de café*

1. El café forma parte integral de la cultura de Cuba desde sus orígenes. Habla con la clase sobre el papel que tiene el consumo de café en tu propia cultura.
2. Piensa en las diferencias entre el café cubano y el café que se bebe en tu país. ¿Cuáles son?
3. Los patrimonios de la humanidad son lugares históricos y culturales de incalculable valor para la humanidad y pertenecen a todo el mundo. ¿Por qué crees que los cafetales de Cuba están en este grupo? ¿Puedes mencionar algunos lugares en tu país que son patrimonio de la humanidad?

## CULTURA

En la actualidad hay en Estados Unidos más de 1,6 millones de cubano-estadounidenses, quienes forman el tercer grupo hispano más grande del país. En Miami y otras áreas de Florida reside el grupo más numeroso, seguido de Nueva Jersey y el oeste de Nueva York. Los cubanos tienen una larga historia de inmigración a Estados Unidos como consecuencia de cambios políticos en la isla y más tarde de factores económicos. La comunidad de origen cubano de Estados Unidos tiene mucha influencia en el mundo de los negocios y la política. Cuatro miembros del Congreso de Estados Unidos y dos del Senado son de ascendencia cubana.

Además de destacarse en la política y los negocios, hay cubano-estadounidenses que sobresalen en el deporte (como Gilbert Arenas, jugador de baloncesto para los Washington Wizards, o Robert Andino, jugador de béisbol con los Orioles de Baltimore), el cine (Rosario Dawson o Eva Mendes), la literatura (el Premio Pulitzer Oscar Hijuelos), o la moda (los diseñadores Narciso Rodríguez e Isabel Toledo).

Oscar Hijuelos

 VOCABULARIO

### Alimentos *(Food)*

| | |
|---|---|
| el aceite | *oil* |
| el aguacate | *avocado* |
| el ajo | *garlic* |
| el apio | *celery* |
| el arroz | *rice* |
| el azúcar | *sugar* |
| la calabaza | *pumpkin* |
| el camarón | *shrimp* |
| la cebolla | *onion* |
| el cerdo | *pork* |
| el champiñón | *mushroom* |
| la fresa | *strawberry* |
| los frijoles | *beans* |
| las habichuelas | *green beans* |
| el huevo | *egg* |
| el jamón | *ham* |
| la lechuga | *lettuce* |
| el limón | *lemon* |
| el maíz | *corn* |
| la mantequilla | *butter* |
| el marisco | *seafood* |
| la naranja | *orange* |
| el pan | *bread* |
| el pavo | *turkey* |
| la papa / patata | *potato* |
| el pepino | *cucumber* |
| la pera | *pear* |
| la pimienta | *pepper (spice)* |
| el pimiento | *pepper (vegetable)* |
| la piña | *pineapple* |
| el plátano | *banana* |
| el pollo | *chicken* |
| el queso | *cheese* |
| la sandía | *watermelon* |
| el tomate | *tomato* |
| la uva | *grape* |
| la zanahoria | *carrot* |

### Bebidas *(Drinks)*

| | |
|---|---|
| el agua | *water* |
| el café | *coffee* |
| el jugo | *juice* |
| la leche | *milk* |
| el refresco | *soft drink, soda pop* |
| el ron | *rum* |
| el té | *tea* |
| el vino | *wine* |

### Las medidas y los envases
*(Measures and containers)*

| | |
|---|---|
| la botella | *bottle* |
| la caja | *box* |
| la cantidad | *quantity* |
| la docena | *dozen* |
| el gramo | *gram* |
| el kilo | *kilogram* |
| la lata | *can* |
| el litro | *liter* |
| el paquete | *pack, package* |
| el peso | *weight* |
| la taza | *cup* |

### La cocina y el restaurante
*(Cooking and restaurant)*

| | |
|---|---|
| el aperitivo | *appetizer* |
| la cazuela | *casserole, pot* |
| el cocido; el guiso | *stew* |
| el/la cocinero/a | *chef, cook* |
| la copa | *wine glass* |
| la cuenta | *check, bill* |
| la ensalada | *salad* |
| el/la mesero/a | *waiter/waitress* |
| la parrilla | *grill* |
| el postre | *dessert* |
| la propina | *tip* |
| la sartén | *frying pan* |
| la sopa | *soup* |

### Adjetivos relacionados con la cocina
*(Adjectives related to cooking)*

| | |
|---|---|
| asado/a | *roasted* |
| blando/a | *soft* |
| caliente | *warm, hot* |
| crudo/a | *raw* |
| delicioso/a | *delicious* |
| duro/a | *hard* |
| fresco/a | *fresh* |
| frito/a | *fried* |
| fuerte | *strong* |
| picante | *hot, spicy* |
| rico/a | *tasty, delicious* |
| salado/a | *salty* |
| soso/a | *tasteless* |
| tierno/a | *tender* |

### Verbos *(Verbs)*

| | |
|---|---|
| añadir | *to add* |
| asar | *to roast* |
| batir | *to beat* |
| calentar (ie) | *to heat* |
| cocinar | *to cook* |
| cortar | *to cut* |
| freír (i) | *to fry* |
| hervir (ie) | *to boil* |
| merendar (ie) | *to have a snack* |
| mezclar | *to mix* |
| pedir | *to order (in a restaurant)* |
| pelar | *to peel* |

# CONSULTORIO GRAMATICAL

## 1 In a Restaurant

### To inquire about the menu

**¿Qué lleva la sopa?**
*What is in the soup?*

**¿Lleva mucha sal?**
*Does it have a lot of salt?*

**¿Es fuerte / picante?**
*Is it strong / spicy?*

**¿Qué hay / tienen de postre?**
*What is for dessert?*

**¿Tienen pastel de chocolate?**
*Do you have chocolate cake?*

When asking someone for something, the main difference between English and Spanish is that in English the verb or the action is projected towards the person who asks: **May/Can I have some more bread, please?** In Spanish the verb or the action is projected towards the person being asked: **¿Puede traerme un poco más de pan?**

### To order

- **Yo** (voy a tomar) los macarrones y el bistec.    —*I'll have the maccarroni and a steak.*
  **Primero / después / para postre,...**    *To start / then / for dessert . . .*
  **Para beber**, agua sin gas.    *I will have non-sparkling water, please*
- **Para mí,** un café por favor.    —*I will have a coffee, please.*

### To ask the waiter to bring something

- **¿Me puede traer...**    *Can I have . . .*
  **la cuenta?**
  **un** cuchillo / **una** botella de agua...?

  **otro** vaso de vino / café?    *(WITH NOUNS THAT CAN BE COUNTED)*
  **otra** cerveza / ensalada?

  **un poco de** pan / salsa / agua / vino?    *(WITH NOUNS THAT CANNOT BE COUNTED)*

Note that **un otro** or **una otra** is not correct in Spanish.

*¿Me puede traer un poco de sal?*

*Otro café, por favor.*

*¿Me trae otra ensalada, por favor?*

## 2 Impersonal Se

When the object in a sentence is a singular noun, the verb is also singular.

Aquí **se come un pescado** muy rico.
*They eat very good fish here.*

En estas tierras **se cultiva arroz.**
*They grow rice in this land.*

When the object is a plural noun, the verb is also plural.

En Cuba **se fabrican** excelentes **cigarros** habanos.
*In Cuba **they make** excellent **cigars.***

When the object is not a noun, the verb is always singular.

En Cuba **se cena** tarde.
*In Cuba **they have dinner late.***

El ajiaco **se prepara** con carne.
**They cook** *ajiaco with meat.*

There is no one-to-one equivalent in English for **se**. Instead, in English the impersonality or lack of subject in a sentence is expressed by using a symbolic subject such as **people**, as in: **People in Cuba have dinner late. / They have dinner late in Cuba.** Rather than a literal translation, a Spanish speaker would employ the impersonal **se** form to convey the same idea.

## 3 Quantifying

When these words are used as adjectives before nouns, they change form to agree in gender and number.

| SINGULAR | | PLURAL | | |
|---|---|---|---|---|
| MASCULINE | FEMININE | MASCULINE | FEMININE | |
| poco | poca | pocos | pocas | (few, little, very little) |

| | | | | |
|---|---|---|---|---|
| much**o** | much**a** | much**os** | much**as** | *(many, much, very much, a lot)* |
| demasiad**o** | demasiad**a** | demasiad**os** | demasiad**as** | *(too many, too much)* |
| | suficient**e** | | suficient**es** | *(enough)* |
| | bastant**e** | | bastant**e** | *(enough, quite a lot)* |

Bebe demasiad**o** alcohol.      Toma much**os** helados.

Come poc**a** fibra.       Come demasiad**as** hamburguesas.

No hace suficient**e** ejercicio.     Tiene bastant**es** amigos.

When modifying verbs, these words don't change form, since in these cases
they function as adverbs. Their form is always the masculine singular.

Come **poco**.       Lee **mucho**.

*S/he eats very **little**.*     *S/he reads **a lot**.*

Fuma **bastante**.      Trabaja **demasiado**.

*S/he smokes **quite a lot**.*     *S/he works **too much**.*

Come demasiadas golosinas y
demasiados bocadillos.

### Cuantificadores negativos

*To indicate the complete absence of something, we make the sentence negative. The negative quantifying of something
depends on what we are quantifying.*

1.  When the noun is something that cannot be counted, we always use
     the singular form:

**No** hay azúcar.      **No** pongo sal en la ensalada.

*There is **no** sugar.*     *I **don't** put salt in the salad.*

**No** tengo harina.

*I **don't** have **any** flour.*

*To emphasize complete absence, sometimes we use **nada** (**de**).*

En la nevera **no** hay **nada de** leche.     **No** pongo **nada de** sal en la ensalada.

*There is **no** milk in the refrigerator.*    *I **don't** put **any** salt in the salad.*

Esta receta **no** lleva **nada de** aceite.

*That recipe **doesn't** include **any** oil.*

*If the noun has been mentioned previously, we use the word **nada**.*

● ¿Pones sal en la ensalada?     —Do you put salt in the salad?

○ No, no pongo **nada**.      —No, I don't put **any**.

2.  When the noun is something that can be counted:

SINGULAR:  **No** tengo **ningún** plátano.    **No** hay **ninguna** manzana.

         *I **don't** have **any** bananas.*    *There **aren't any** apples.*

*If the noun has been mentioned previously, it may be expressed in subsequent references by the pronouns ninguno/ninguna
without repeating the original noun:*

● ¿Tienes muchos plátanos?      —Do you have a lot of bananas?

¿Hay manzanas?       —Are there any apples?

SINGULAR  ○ No, **no** tengo **ninguno**.    —No, I **don't** have **any**.

        No, **no** hay **ninguna**.     —No, there **isn't any**.

PLURAL   ○ **No** tengo plátanos.      —I **don't** have **any** bananas.

        **No** tengo.      —I **don't** have **any**.

To ask about the existence or presence
of something in English, we use the
word **any**:

*Are there **any** strawberries?*
*Is there **any** milk?*

In the same context, in Spanish we don't
need a particle corresponding to **any**:

*¿**Hay** fresas?*
*¿**Hay** leche?*

To give a negative answer in Spanish,
the verb takes a negative form:

*No hay manzanas.*
*No hay leche.*

This is in contrast to English:

*There are no strawberries.*
*There is no milk.*

**¡ATENCIÓN!**

*Several kinds of nouns that can be counted, however, don't follow this rule. In these cases, we use singular nouns, without articles or adjectives.*

Nouns designating facilities, services, or appliances, which tend to be the only one of their kind in a given location: **piscina, teléfono, aire acondicionado, aeropuerto, garaje, jardín...**

No hay piscina en el hotel.     No tengo teléfono en casa.
*There is no pool in the hotel.*    *I don't have a phone at home.*

Nouns designating personal objects, garments, facial hair, or jewelry, which tend to be the only one of their kind used or worn by an individual at any given time: **computadora, carro, chaqueta, barba, bigote, anillo...**

● ¿Tienes coche?    —Do you have a car?
o No, no tengo coche.    —No, I don't have a car.

Nouns designating personal relationships: **madre, novio, jefe...**

María tiene novio.
*María has a boyfriend.*

## Weights and Measures

| | |
|---|---|
| **un kilo de** carne | 1 kg |
| **un litro de** leche | 1 l |
| **un cuarto de kilo de** carne | 1/4 kg |
| **un cuarto de litro de** leche | 1/4 l |
| **medio kilo de** carne | 1/2 kg |
| **medio litro de** leche | 1/2 l |
| **tres cuartos de kilo de** carne | 3/4 kg |
| **tres cuartos de litro de** leche | 3/4 l |
| 100 **gramos de** jamón | 100 g |
| 250 **gramos de** queso | 250 g |
| **una docena de** huevos | (= 12) |
| **media docena de** huevos | (= 6) |

Use the metric system in Spanish-speaking countries.

1 pound ≈ **0.45 kilos**
1 gallon ≈ **4 liters**

# 9 GENTE de CIUDAD

## 9–1 Ciudades peruanas ✓

Mira las fotos de estas tres ciudades. Descríbelas con detalle. ¿Qué ves en ellas? ¿En qué se parecen y en qué se diferencian?

## TAREA

Identificar y evaluar los problemas de una ciudad universitaria y proponer soluciones.

## NUESTRA GENTE

Perú
Hispanos/latinos en Estados Unidos

Arequipa

Lima

Cuzco

## CULTURA

Perú es el cuarto país más poblado de Sudamérica. El 76% de la población vive en ciudades y el 24% en el campo. Las mayores ciudades se encuentran en la costa, como Piura, Chiclayo, Trujillo o Lima, su capital. En la sierra se destacan las ciudades de Arequipa, Cajamarca, Ayacucho y Cuzco. Finalmente, en la selva la más importante es Iquitos.

# ACERCAMIENTOS

 **9–2 ¿Qué ciudad es?**

¿A qué ciudades creen que corresponden estas informaciones? Hay algunas que pueden referirse a varias ciudades. Traten de averiguarlo con la ayuda de las fotos, el mapa y su profesor/a.

| | a | b | c | d | e | f | g | h | i | j | k | l | m | n | ñ | o | p |
|---|---|---|---|---|---|---|---|---|---|---|---|---|---|---|---|---|---|
| Cuzco | | | | | | | | | | | | | | | | | |
| Iquitos | | | | | | | | | | | | | | | | | |
| Lima | | | | | | | | | | | | | | | | | |
| Arequipa | | | | | | | | | | | | | | | | | |

a. Tiene más de ocho millones de habitantes y es una de las 28 ciudades más pobladas del mundo.

b. Es la segunda ciudad más importante del Perú.

c. Está situada en la sierra al sur del Perú.

d. Es la capital de Perú y la ciudad más grande del país.

e. Es la capital del antiguo imperio inca y patrimonio de la humanidad.

f. Está ubicada a orillas del río Amazonas y es la ciudad más importante de la amazonía peruana.

g. Está a orillas del océano Pacífico y tiene playas por toda su costa.

h. Es una ciudad moderna y cosmopolita con mucho entretenimiento y vida cultural.

i. Su clima es tropical, cálido, húmedo y lluvioso, con una temperatura promedio anual de unos 28°C. La temporada de lluvias es de diciembre a marzo y la seca de mayo a septiembre.

j. En el idioma quechua, su nombre significa "ombligo" o centro del mundo.

k. Sus principales industrias son la madera, el ecoturismo y el comercio fluvial.

l. Tiene un puerto marítimo muy importante: El Callao.

m. Su clima es templado, seco y soleado todo el año, con una temperatura diurna de entre 15°C y 18°C, y una temperatura nocturna de hasta 0°C.

n. Sólo se puede llegar a esta ciudad por vía aérea o fluvial.

ñ. Está rodeada de tres volcanes: Misti, Chachani y Pichu Pichu.

o. Hay muchas iglesias y monumentos de estilo colonial.

p. Su clima es templado, nublado y extremadamente húmedo. La temperatura varía entre 13°C y 22°C en el invierno y entre 24°C y 32°C en el verano.

**EJEMPLO:**

**E1:** Me parece que la A es Lima porque es la capital de Perú.

**E2:** Y la B es Cuzco.

**E1:** ¿Cuzco? No, yo creo que es Arequipa.

 **9–3 Otras ciudades**

¿Saben en qué países están estas ciudades? Gana el grupo con más respuestas correctas.

Guadalajara _____    Guayaquil _____    Mendoza _____    Medellín _____

Sucre _____    Maracaibo _____    Valparaíso _____    Sevilla _____

**VOCABULARIO EN CONTEXTO**

09-01 to
09-09

### 9–4 Calidad de vida

El ayuntamiento (*city council*) de la ciudad donde estás estudiando te da este cuestionario para conocer la opinión de los estudiantes sobre la calidad de vida de ese lugar.

Contesta individualmente al cuestionario. Luego lee tus respuestas y dale una "calificación" global a la ciudad o pueblo (máximo 10, mínimo 0).

AYUNTAMIENTO DE...
Área de Urbanismo

*Encuesta sobre la calidad de vida*

| | SÍ | NO |
|---|---|---|
| **TAMAÑO** | | |
| ¿Cree usted que es una ciudad demasiado grande? | ☐ | ☐ |
| ¿Piensa que es demasiado pequeña? | ☐ | ☐ |
| ¿Cree que tiene el tamaño apropiado? | ☐ | ☐ |
| **TRANSPORTES Y COMUNICACIÓN** | | |
| ¿Está bien comunicada? | | |
| ¿Hay mucho tráfico? ¿Hay embotellamientos? | ☐ | ☐ |
| ¿Funciona bien el transporte público? | ☐ | ☐ |
| ¿Se puede caminar? ¿Hay aceras? | ☐ | ☐ |
| **CULTURA Y OCIO** | | |
| ¿Hay suficientes instalaciones deportivas? | ☐ | ☐ |
| ¿Tiene monumentos o museos interesantes? | ☐ | ☐ |
| ¿Hay suficiente vida cultural (conciertos, teatros, cines, conferencias...)? | ☐ | ☐ |
| ¿Hay ambiente nocturno (discotecas, restaurantes...)? | ☐ | ☐ |
| ¿Son bonitos los alrededores? | ☐ | ☐ |
| **ECOLOGÍA** | | |
| ¿Hay mucha contaminación? | | |
| ¿Tiene suficientes zonas verdes (jardines, parques...)? | ☐ | ☐ |
| ¿Se recicla en esta ciudad? | ☐ | ☐ |

**CLIMA**

| | sí | no |
|---|---|---|
| ¿Nieva mucho? | ☐ | ☐ |
| ¿Hace demasiado frío/calor? | ☐ | ☐ |
| ¿Llueve demasiado? | ☐ | ☐ |

**COMERCIO**

| | sí | no |
|---|---|---|
| ¿Es caro/a? | ☐ | ☐ |
| ¿Hay suficientes tiendas? | ☐ | ☐ |

**LA GENTE**

| | sí | no |
|---|---|---|
| ¿La gente es amable? | ☐ | ☐ |
| ¿La gente participa? | ☐ | ☐ |
| ¿La gente es solidaria? | ☐ | ☐ |

**PROBLEMAS SOCIALES**

| | sí | no |
|---|---|---|
| ¿Existen problemas de drogas? | ☐ | ☐ |
| ¿Hay mucha delincuencia? | ☐ | ☐ |
| ¿Hay violencia? | ☐ | ☐ |

Para mí, lo mejor es...
Lo peor es...
Yo pienso que falta/n...

**9–5 Mi opinión**

Informa a tus compañeros/as de tu decisión. Coméntales los aspectos positivos o negativos que consideras más importantes. Compara tus opiniones con las de tus compañeros/as de grupo.

**EJEMPLO:**

**E1:** Mi calificación es cuatro. A mí me parece que no hay suficientes instalaciones deportivas. Además, hay demasiado tráfico.

**E2:** Pues yo creo que es un siete porque hay mucha vida cultural y entretenimiento, y eso es muy importante.

**9–6 Prioridades**

Imagina que, por razones de trabajo, tienes que vivir dos años en una ciudad del Perú. ¿Qué es para ti lo más importante que tiene que tener una ciudad? Repasa los aspectos (ecología, clima, cultura y ocio, etc.) del cuestionario de la actividad 9–4 y establece tus prioridades.

Para mí, lo más importante es _____ y también _____.
Lo menos importante es _____ y _____.

**9–7 Dos ciudades peruanas para vivir**

Lee los textos. Después, haz una lista de los pros y contras de cada ciudad y luego decide qué ciudad prefieres. Explícales a tus compañeros/as de clase las razones de tu elección.

**Iquitos**

La ciudad de Iquitos, con unos 250.000 habitantes, está a orillas del Amazonas. A pesar de ser la ciudad más grande de la amazonía peruana, sólo se puede acceder a ella por vía aérea o fluvial. En Iquitos sobreviven algunas muestras arquitectónicas de interés, como la Casa Eiffel, o los lujosos hoteles y casonas de estilo *art nouveau*, decorados con objetos traídos directamente de Europa. Su Biblioteca Amazónica es una de las más importantes de América. En los alrededores de la ciudad existen algunas etnias nativas que mantienen rasgos culturales originales.

Iquitos tiene además una vida nocturna de gran vitalidad en el boulevard del Malecón Maldonado, en el que hay pubs y restaurantes muy concurridos.

**Lima**

La ciudad de Lima es una metrópoli de ocho millones de habitantes situada a orillas del río Rímac, frente al océano Pacífico. Es una ciudad moderna en constante crecimiento, pero que mantiene la riqueza de su casco antiguo, declarado por la UNESCO patrimonio cultural de la humanidad. Lima es el primer centro industrial y financiero del Perú. Es una ciudad donde se pueden ver muestras del período de la cultura prehispánica (como por ejemplo el santuario de Pachacamac) y del período colonial (como la Catedral, la plaza de Armas o el Convento de Santo Domingo). Además de su maravilloso casco antiguo con impresionantes conventos e iglesias, y de sus museos y plazas, también está la Lima moderna, con sus grandes edificios, centros comerciales, modernos hoteles, restaurantes, discotecas, bares y una animadísima vida nocturna. Por supuesto, como toda gran ciudad, Lima sufre de problemas como la contaminación, el tráfico y la inseguridad.

| | LIMA | IQUITOS |
|---|---|---|
| **pros** | 1. | 1. |
| | 2. | 2. |
| | 3. | 3. |
| **contras** | 1. | 1. |
| | 2. | 2. |
| | 3. | 3. |

## GRAMÁTICA EN CONTEXTO

09-10 to
09-32

### 9–8 Mi ciudad

Compara tu ciudad natal con la ciudad donde estudias. Contrasta tu información con la de tu compañero/a.

**EJEMPLO:**

**E1:** Mi ciudad tiene **más** discotecas y restaurantes y es **más** bonita **que** ésta. Es divertid**ísima**.

**E2:** En mi ciudad no hay **tantos** museos **como** en ésta y además es **más** aburrida. Es aburrid**ísima**.

### 9–9 Atención a la gramática

Lee este texto sobre Cuzco. Fíjate en los pronombres relativos en negrita y clasifícalos en tres grupos. Identifica a qué o quién se refieren.

### CUZCO

De día o de noche, Cuzco es una ciudad **que** tiene miles de encantos y atractivos, y **en la que** se puede disfrutar de tantas actividades y diversiones como en una gran ciudad. Es un lugar **donde** se funden la influencia española con el pasado andino, **en el que** todavía hoy se celebra el Inti Raymi o Fiesta del Sol durante el solsticio de invierno el 24 de junio de cada año. Es una ciudad **que** vive principalmente de la agricultura y el turismo. También tiene varias universidades a las que asisten miles de estudiantes cada año. Cuzco es una ciudad **a la que** viajan casi todas las personas **que** visitan Perú y tiene un aeropuerto **al que** se necesita ir para volar a las ruinas de Machu Picchu. En fin, es un lugar **del que** nunca puedes olvidarte.

| | PRONOMBRES | SE REFIERE A... |
|---|---|---|
| Grupo 1 | que | *ciudad* |
| Grupo 2 | | |
| Grupo 3 | | |

### 9–10 ¿Qué tipo de ciudad te gusta?

Completa estas frases:

A mí me gustan las ciudades **que** _____

A mí me gustan las ciudades **en las que** _____

A mí me gustan las ciudades **donde** _____

A mí me gustan las ciudades **a las que** _____

A mí me gustan las ciudades **de las que** _____

A mí me gustan las ciudades con/sin _____

 Ahora comparte la información con tu compañero/a.

---

## COMPARACIÓN

Lima: 8.000.000 de habitantes
Arequipa: 1.000.000 de habitantes

Lima tiene **más** habitantes **que** Arequipa.
Arequipa tiene **menos** habitantes **que** Lima.

Lima es **más** grande **que** Arequipa.
Arequipa es **más** pequeña **que** Lima.

más bueno/a ⟶ **mejor**
más malo/a ⟶ **peor**

## SUPERLATIVO

Lima es **la** ciudad **más** grande **de** Perú.

## COMPARACIONES DE IGUALDAD

CON UN NOMBRE

Lima tiene { **tanto** encanto / **tanta** contaminación / **tantos** monumentos / **tantas** iglesias } **como** Cuzco.

CON UN ADJETIVO

Cuzco no es **tan** grande **como** Lima.

Luis y Héctor tienen { **la misma** edad. / **el mismo** color de pelo. / **los mismos** problemas. / **las mismas** ideas. }

Son iguales.

Sí, ése es tan guapo como ése.

## PRONOMBRES RELATIVOS

Lima es una ciudad...

| | |
|---|---|
| **en la que / donde** | se vive muy bien. |
| **que** | tiene muchos museos. |
| **a la que** | vamos todos los veranos. |

Son unas ciudades...

| | |
|---|---|
| **en las que / donde** | se puede ver arte. |
| **que** | tienen muchos museos. |
| **a las que** | vamos todos los veranos. |

A mí me parece que...
(Yo) pienso / creo que...

Yo (no) estoy de acuerdo {
con Juan.
contigo.
con eso.
}

Sí, tienes razón.

Sí, claro, pero...
Eso es verdad, pero... } + OPINIÓN
Bueno, pero...

ME GUSTARÍA

Me gustaría {
ir a Lima.
visitar Lima.
}

**Le gustaría** vivir cerca del mar.

### 9–11 Ciudades del mundo

Piensa en una ciudad mundialmente famosa y escribe cuatro frases para describirla. El resto de la clase va a adivinar qué ciudad es.

**EJEMPLO:**

Es una ciudad **donde** hay muchos rascacielos.
Es una ciudad **a la que** van muchos turistas.

### 9–12 ¿París, Londres o Lima?

Elige ciudades para completar las frases.

| París | Tokio | Berlín | Moscú |
|---|---|---|---|
| Rabat | Calcuta | Lima | La Habana |
| Barcelona | Acapulco | Monte Carlo | Ámsterdam |
| Dublín | Hong Kong | Managua | Las Vegas |
| Helsinki | Ginebra | Viena | Jerusalén |

- A mí **me gustaría** pasar unos días en _____ porque _____
- A mí **me gustaría** ir de vez en cuando a _____ porque _____
- Yo quiero visitar _____ porque _____
- A mí **me gustaría** trabajar una temporada en _____ porque _____
- A mí **me gustaría** vivir en _____ porque _____
- No **me gustaría** nada tener que ir a _____ porque _____

Ahora compara tus deseos (*wishes*) con los de tu compañero/a.

### 9–13 ¿Campo o ciudad?

Escucha las opiniones de estos dos amigos sobre el campo y la ciudad. ¿Qué prefieren y por qué?

| | ¿QUÉ PREFIERE? | ¿POR QUÉ? |
|---|---|---|
| Gonzalo | | _____ *tiene menos/más* _____ *que* _____ |
| | | _____ *hay menos/más* _____ *que* _____ |
| | | *Hace menos/más* _____ *que* _____ |
| Gabriela | | _____ *tiene menos/más* _____ *que* _____ |
| | | _____ *hay menos/más* _____ *que* _____ |
| | | *Hace menos/más* _____ *que* _____ |

### 9–14 ¿Y tú?

Piensa en más ventajas y desventajas de vivir en el campo o en la ciudad y después comparte tus opiniones con tu compañero/a. ¿Están de acuerdo?

**EJEMPLO:**

**E1:** **A mí me parece que** en el campo necesitas el carro para todo.
**E2:** **No estoy de acuerdo** porque en la ciudad también lo necesitas.
**E1:** **Tienes razón,** pero en el campo es **más** difícil vivir sin carro **que** en la ciudad.

## INTERACCIONES

09-33 to
09-36

### ESTRATEGIAS PARA LA COMUNICACIÓN ORAL

**Collaboration in conversation (I)**

Communicating in conversation is very different from communicating in writing. When having a conversation, speakers need to make sure they are understood, and that they understand. In real-life conversations there is ambiguity, sentences are shorter and often incomplete, there are many pauses and repetitions... and there is no time for planning. Speakers usually help each other out. This is even more the case when you are speaking a foreign language you are just acquiring.

At certain points in the conversation you need to ascertain whether others are following what you are saying and whether or not they are agreeing with you. These are some of the most common ways that Spanish speakers request this confirmation:

| | |
|---|---|
| *¿(Me) entiendes? / ¿(Me) comprendes?* | Do you understand? |
| *¿Sabes?* | You know? |
| *¿Entiendes/sabes lo que quiero decir?* | Do you understand / know what I mean? |
| *¿OK? ¿Ya? ¿Mmmm?* | |

Likewise, you can show that you understand by using expressions such as:

| | |
|---|---|
| *(Sí), claro* | (Yes), of course |
| *(Sí), entiendo / comprendo* | (Yes), I understand |
| *Ya (veo)* | I see |

These rhetorical questions are important for maintaining the natural flow of conversation, and therefore you should try to incorporate them into your regular interactions.

| | |
|---|---|
| *¿Verdad?* | Right? |
| *¿No? ¿No te parece? ¿No crees?* | Right? Don't you think? |

 Escucha otra vez el diálogo de 9–13. Fíjate en estas expresiones que usan Gonzalo y Gabriela. ¿Puedes cambiar las palabras en negrita por otras que expresen lo mismo?

En el campo se está más fresco, **¿no?**
**Ya**, pero es aburrido, no hay nada, **¿comprendes?**
**Sí, claro**, pero tiene otras ventajas, **¿sabes?** La tranquilidad, el aire puro... A mí me encanta la naturaleza. Hay personas a las que no les gusta el ruido, **¿entiendes?**
**Sí, pero** viviendo en el campo no tienen acceso a la vida cultural. Pierden algo, **¿no crees?**

### 9–15 ¿Frío o calor?

Uno de ustedes va a defender las ventajas de vivir en una ciudad como Fargo (ND) donde hace mucho frío. El otro va a defender las ventajas de vivir en una ciudad donde hace mucho calor como Brownsville (TX). Luego compartan sus opiniones con su compañero/a. ¿Están de acuerdo o no?

**EJEMPLO:**

**E1:** **Yo prefiero el calor. Pienso que** en una ciudad como Fargo el invierno debe ser my aburrido, **¿no?**
**E2:** **No estoy de acuerdo.** Hay nieve y los deportes de invierno son divertidos, **¿no crees?**

**9–16  ¿El Barrio Chino o Barranco?**

Están en Lima visitando la ciudad. Hoy tienen que decidir qué área de la ciudad desean visitar. Después de leer la información, decidan adónde van. No olviden que deben hacer comparaciones y llegar a un acuerdo.

### El Barrio Chino

La colonia china en el Perú es la tercera en importancia fuera de la República Popular China, con una población de más de 300.000 habitantes. El Barrio Chino está ubicado en pleno casco antiguo de Lima, a muy pocas cuadras del Congreso y del Palacio Presidencial. En esta parte de la ciudad, bohemios, compositores e intelectuales visitan sus conocidos salones de té, pastelerías y restaurantes (chifas) de comida china cantonesa acriollada que hoy forman parte importante de la gastronomía peruana. En esta zona de la capital peruana destacan el Arco Chino, la iglesia de las Trinitarias o el Molino de Santa Clara, entre otros monumentos interesantes.

### Barranco

Actualmente, Barranco es el principal barrio bohemio y nocturno de Lima. Aquí se ven casonas de estilo colonial y floridos parques, calles y avenidas, además de acogedores sitios frente al mar. Su clima es seco, a diferencia de otros distritos de la ciudad que son húmedos. En esta parte de la ciudad hay numerosos restaurantes donde se puede degustar la variada gastronomía peruana a cualquier hora. Los espectáculos musicales y culturales abundan en sus calles y en acogedores rincones a orillas del mar. Se debe visitar el viejo Puente de los Suspiros, rincón predilecto de los enamorados, y su malecón.

**EJEMPLO:**

**E1:** A mí me parece que el Barrio Chino es **más interesante que** Barranco porque es más exótico, **¿no?**

**E2:** ¿Más interesante que Barranco? Yo creo que no... creo que Barranco tiene más cosas que ver... **¿no creen?**

**E3:** Bueno, los dos tienen muchas cosas, pero el Barrio Chino es **el** tercero **más importante del** mundo...

 **9–17  Situaciones: ¿Nueva York o Los Ángeles?**

A Peruvian student wants to visit the United States in February. S/he needs to decide between New York and Los Angeles, and calls a friend in the United States to ask for his/her opinion.

### ESTUDIANTE A

You will be visiting the United States for the first time. You love big cities but can't decide between New York and Los Angeles. Call a friend in the United States to ask for his/her opinion. You want to compare different aspects in order to make the best decision. Also, keep in mind that

- you don't like to drive and prefer public transportation.
- you don't like cold weather.
- you love nightlife.
- you enjoy museums.

### ESTUDIANTE B

A friend from Lima is coming to the United States for the first time. S/he loves big cities, but can't decide between New York and Los Angeles. Help her/him by comparing different aspects of both cities.

# TAREA  Gente en acción

**Identificar y evaluar los problemas de una ciudad universitaria y proponer soluciones.**

## PREPARACIÓN

Una ciudad universitaria o campus universitario se parece bastante a una ciudad real, con sus calles, tiendas, lugares de ocio, viviendas o dormitorios universitarios... Lean esta información sobre una ciudad universitaria que tiene 45.000 estudiantes. Van a tener que tomar decisiones importantes sobre el futuro del campus.

**CAMPUS UNIVERSITARIO VILLANUBLA**

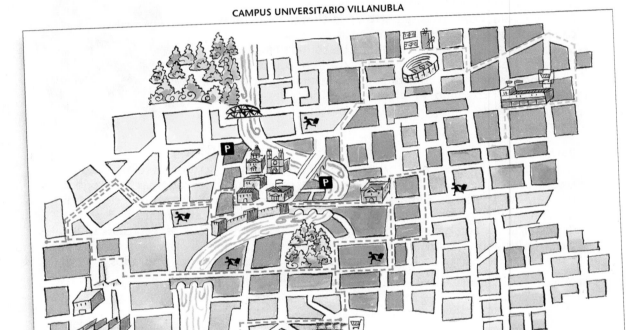

P Estacionamiento — Facultad — Supermercado

### TRANSPORTES Y COMUNICACIÓN

- Pocas líneas de transporte público llegan al campus.
- No hay transporte para ir de una parte a otra del campus.
- Hay graves problemas de estacionamiento, ya que sólo existen dos estacionamientos con capacidad para 600 carros. El decanato dice que no va a construir más estacionamientos.

### COMERCIO

- Hay pocas tiendas y sólo dos supermercados en el campus

(uno de ellos está muy lejos).
- Todo es carísimo.
- Una cadena de hamburgueserías quiere construir dos restaurantes, pero no hay otras alternativas.
- La comida de las cafeterías es muy mala.

### CULTURA Y OCIO

- Solamente hay un cine y un teatro. El teatro tiene graves problemas económicos y el edificio está en muy mal estado.

- La biblioteca es muy pequeña.
- Hay dos bares.
- Instalaciones deportivas: Hay un estadio de fútbol, una piscina al aire libre y un complejo deportivo (baloncesto, tenis y gimnasio). No hay piscina cubierta ni canchas de tenis.

### VIVIENDA

- Las residencias estudiantiles son muy pequeñas y las habitaciones también.
- No hay casas para los estudiantes.

### SALUD

- Hay un ambulatorio estudiantil pero no hay hospital. Hay pocos médicos.

### SERVICIOS PARA FAMILIAS

- No hay guardería para estudiantes con hijos.

### SEGURIDAD

- La delincuencia ha aumentado un 22% con respecto al año anterior.
- No hay policía en el campus.

Escucha ahora la encuesta de radio hecha a algunos estudiantes. Escribe cuáles son los problemas que ellos señalan.

1. _____
2. _____
3. _____
4. _____
5. _____
6. _____

**Paso 1** Identifiquen ahora los problemas de su propio campus o escuela. Decidan cuáles son los cuatro problemas más urgentes y ordénenlos según su importancia, de mayor a menor.

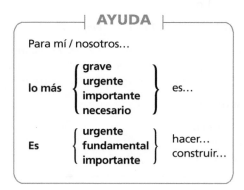

**Paso 2** Piensen en las soluciones posibles para cada uno de estos problemas. Ustedes tienen 1.000 millones. ¿Cómo van a gastarlos?

Problema                                              Solución

1. _____    _____
2. _____    _____
3. _____    _____
4. _____    _____

**Paso 3** Ahora escriban un informe con toda la información.

**EJEMPLO:**

Lo más importante es la falta de estacionamientos. Es fundamental construir más. Por eso vamos a invertir 200 millones para construir tres nuevos estacionamientos.

**Paso 4** Informe para la clase.
Su representante va a defender las decisiones de su grupo ante las autoridades del campus.

**Paso 5** La clase, con la ayuda de su profesor/a, compara los planes de los diferentes grupos.

**EJEMPLO:**

El grupo 2 piensa que el estacionamiento es más importante que la comida, pero nosotros creemos que no es tan importante.

**Paso 6** Foco lingüístico.

**NUESTRA GENTE**

09-37 to
09-38

## GENTE QUE LEE

---

### ESTRATEGIAS PARA LEER

**Word order in Spanish**

In Spanish, the order of the words that make up a sentence is quite flexible. This means that

1. the subject of a sentence can appear before or after the verb. Look at these examples:

   ***Juan** me llama todos los días.*          *Todos los días me llama **Juan**.*

2. the direct object can appear before or after the verb. Look at these examples:

   *Juan compra **los boletos para Perú.***      ***Los boletos para Perú** los compra Juan.*

The most important elements are moved to the front of the sentence for emphasis. Thus, in the case of 1.2, the speaker or writer wants to emphasize the fact that it is everyday that Juan calls him/her. In the case of 2.2, the emphasis is on the tickets and not on who purchases them.

   Identify the subject and object in the following sentences:

1. La lengua quechua la habla el 24% de la población peruana.
2. En Perú está la antigua ciudadela inca de Machu Picchu.
3. A la costa peruana puedes viajar de diciembre a abril (verano).

---

### *ANTES DE LEER*

#### 9–18 **Grandes ciudades**

Contesta a las siguientes preguntas y después intercambia la información con tu compañero/a.

1. ¿Eres de una gran ciudad, de una ciudad pequeña o de un pueblo? ¿Cuál de estos tres lugares prefieres? ¿Por qué? Compara unos con otros.
2. ¿Qué tiene de atractivo tu ciudad? ¿Cuáles son los lugares más interesantes, las zonas más conocidas? ¿Hay buenas comunicaciones con otras ciudades o países?

#### 9–19 **Activando estrategias**

1. Lee por encima el texto, su título y el mapa. ¿De qué crees que trata?
2. Observa su estructura y lee las frases temáticas de cada párrafo. ¿Qué información vas a leer?

### *DESPUÉS DE LEER*

#### 9–20 **¿Comprendes?**

1. ¿Por qué Lima es una ciudad superpoblada?
2. Según el mapa, ¿qué está más lejos del casco antiguo: San Isidro, Barranco o Miraflores?
3. ¿Dónde puedo ir para ver cerámica precolombina? ¿Y para ver construcciones precolombinas?
4. ¿Y si quiero salir por la noche a divertirme?

*A LEER*

## LIMA, CIUDAD DE LOS REYES

Lima es una ciudad de más de ocho millones de habitantes (un tercio de la población total del Perú) y está en proceso de megalopolización. Es la quinta ciudad más poblada de América Latina y una de las 30 áreas metropolitanas más grandes del mundo. Esta **superpoblación** es producto de la migración rural de las últimas décadas. En esta ciudad se aplica como en ninguna otra ciudad del país el concepto de **comodidad**, ya que facilita la vida de sus habitantes manteniendo muchos de los restaurantes, farmacias, supermercados, **gasolineras** (en Perú llamadas *grifos*), bancos, centros comerciales y tiendas abiertos al público 24 horas al día.

Lima ofrece impresionantes construcciones coloniales, museos que recrean el milenario pasado peruano en arqueología, historia y arte, y yacimientos arqueológicos **preincaicos**. El casco antiguo, declarado patrimonio de la humanidad en 1988, **alberga** monumentos de valor incalculable. La plaza de Armas es el punto de partida para conocer Lima y la Catedral está a un costado de la plaza. El Palacio de Gobierno es la vivienda del presidente. <u>Muy cerca está la Plaza de San Martín</u>, dedicada al famoso libertador y considerada una de las más lindas de Lima. Para conocer mejor la cultura peruana, lo mejor es visitar alguno de los numerosos museos de Lima, como el Museo Arqueológico Rafael Larco Herrera, que expone la mayor colección de cerámica precolombina, o el Museo del Oro. Es posible también encontrar un legado arqueológico en diferentes construcciones y templos prehispánicos como

Pachacamac, centro de peregrinación prehispánico, o el centro ceremonial de Huallamarca.

Lima cuenta además con una amplia variedad de restaurantes donde se puede probar la cocina peruana, reconocida en todo el mundo. En 2006 Lima fue (*was*) declarada capital gastronómica de América Latina en la Cumbre Internacional de Gastronomía. En la cocina peruana se encuentra el aporte de las culturas preincaicas, de la cocina española, de los esclavos africanos, de los chefs franceses de la época de la revolución, y de chinos-cantoneses, japoneses e italianos (llegados entre los siglos XIX y XX).

San Isidro, Barranco y Miraflores son los distritos de mayor **atractivo** turístico. San Isidro es un área residencial con buenos restaurantes, centros comerciales y un bonito parque. El distrito de Barranco alberga a artistas y escritores, y por las noches ofrece espectáculos de todo tipo. Finalmente, los mejores hoteles, restaurantes, centros comerciales y discotecas están en el distrito de Miraflores. <u>En Miraflores está también el Parque Kennedy</u>, punto de reunión de artistas y bohemios.

### 9–21 Activando estrategias

1. ¿Qué significa la palabra "superpoblación"? ¿Es: nombre o adjetivo? ¿Puedes dividirla en partes?
2. Si "gasolina" significa *gas*, ¿qué significa la palabra "gasolinera"?
3. ¿Qué significa la palabra "comodidad"? ¿De qué palabra viene? ¿Es nombre o adjetivo?
4. Divide la palabra *preincaico* en tres partes. ¿Es nombre o adjetivo? ¿Qué significa?
5. Busca la palabra *atractivo* en el diccionario. Elige su significado según el contexto.
6. Según su contexto, ¿qué significa la palabra *alberga*? ¿Es nombre o verbo?
7. Lee las dos frases subrayadas e identifica el sujeto y el complemento en cada una.

### 9–22 Expansión

¿Cuáles son las otras cuatro ciudades más grandes de América Latina? ¿Y de tu país? ¿En qué se parecen estas megalópolis y en qué se diferencian?

## GENTE QUE ESCRIBE

### ESTRATEGIAS PARA ESCRIBIR

**Adding details to a paragraph**

Every sentence in a paragraph should contribute details that develop the idea stated in the topic sentence. Make a list in Spanish of related ideas that develop the topic. Then, organize them in a logical sequence. Write the paragraph and try to make it flow smoothly by using discourse markers. Eliminate anything you don't consider important. Lastly, rewrite your paragraph.

Look at the following topic sentence:

> *Cuzco es un ejemplo de ciudad inca precolombina.*

Which of the following sentences gives unrelated information?

- *Es una ciudad construida con piedra tallada o adobe.*
- *En Perú hay muchas ciudades precolombinas.*
- *Cuzco tiene una gran plaza en el centro.*
- *Las calles de Cuzco son estrechas y rectas.*

Look at the final paragraph, which includes two connectors: *y* and *que* (relative pronoun):

> *Cuzco es un ejemplo de ciudad inca precolombina. Es una ciudad construida con piedra tallada o adobe **que** tiene una gran plaza en el centro **y** calles estrechas y rectas.*

### MÁS ALLÁ DE LA FRASE

**Connecting information using relative pronouns**

Relative pronouns are used to connect two sentences, one dependent on the other. These sentences have two pieces of information: the main idea and the secondary one. Thus, instead of writing two separate sentences such as:

> *Lima es una ciudad muy bonita. Tiene muchos monumentos.*

You may want to integrate both sentences:

> *Lima es una ciudad muy bonita **que** tiene muchos monumentos.*

Don't forget to use prepositions when needed.

> *Lima es una ciudad muy bonita. Voy **a** Lima todos los veranos.* $\longrightarrow$ *Lima es una ciudad muy bonita **a la que** voy todos los veranos.*

## 9–23 Carta al alcalde de tu ciudad

Haz una lista de los tres problemas principales que tiene la ciudad en la que vives (tráfico, contaminación, falta de servicios, etc.) y otra lista de tres soluciones posibles. Después escribe una carta al alcalde (*mayor*) para exponerle los problemas y ofrecer soluciones.

Toma en cuenta cuál es el propósito de esta carta y quién es el lector. Elige el registro adecuado. Después escribe un párrafo inicial donde presentas el tema, seguido de (*followed by*) tres párrafos con sus respectivas frases temáticas. Presta atención al desarrollo de cada párrafo.

 **¡ATENCIÓN!**

Tu trabajo escrito debe seguir los Pasos 1 a 8 y tener contenidos bien organizados y relevantes. Usa conectores para organizar la información.

## COMPARACIONES

### 9–24  ¿Desde cuándo existen las ciudades?

Las primeras ciudades conocidas aparecen en Mesopotamia y Egipto hace 5.000 años. ¿De cuándo crees que datan estas ciudades?

Chichén Itzá (México)       Teotihuacán (México)       Cádiz (España)       Jamestown (Virginia)

Tikal (Guatemala)       Cholula (México)       San Agustín (Florida)       Cuzco (Perú)

### 9–25  Caral

¿Sabes cuál es la ciudad más antigua del mundo? ¿Y de América? Lee este texto y responde a las preguntas.

#### Caral, la primera ciudad de América

El descubrimiento arqueológico de una ciudad de 5.000 años de antigüedad en el norte de Perú es de una magnitud extraordinaria porque permite mostrar que una civilización florecía (*was flourishing*) en el antiguo Perú al mismo tiempo que las civilizaciones de Mesopotamia, China, Egipto e India. La ciudad preincaica de Caral está en el valle de Supe, a 200 kilómetros al norte de Lima. Se trata de la ciudad y la cultura más antiguas del continente americano. El sitio arqueológico de Caral-Supe es una de las primeras "cunas de la civilización" del mundo.

Entre los años 3000 y 1600 a.C., Caral fue (*was*) una ciudad de 65 hectáreas y alrededor de 3.000 habitantes. Sus construcciones de arquitectura monumental y residencial indican la existencia de una economía sólida y de una sociedad con una organización sociopolítica estatal, con una élite gobernante y una población dedicada a la producción agrícola y a la construcción. Con el paso del tiempo, las construcciones en Caral adquieren estructuras cada vez más complejas, lo que indica la evolución de las técnicas de construcción y el conocimiento de las ciencias exactas (aritmética, geometría, astronomía) de las antiguas culturas peruanas.

Caral tiene edificios con plataformas en las que caben dos estadios de fútbol y construcciones de cinco plantas. Algunas de las 32 pirámides encontradas tienen hasta 18 metros de altura. Al pie del Templo Mayor hay grandes plazas circulares, espacios de congregación para los habitantes de la ciudad.

1.  ¿Qué similitudes y qué diferencias hay entre una ciudad antigua como ésta y una ciudad moderna?
2.  ¿Por qué es importante recuperar los restos de estas ciudades? ¿Qué nos muestran las ruinas de una ciudad milenaria sobre las sociedades que las habitan?
3.  ¿Cuáles son otros ejemplos de restos arqueológicos importantes en países hispanohablantes?

## CULTURA

En Estados Unidos la comunidad de origen peruano asciende al millón de personas, siendo aproximadamente la mitad ciudadanos estadounidenses. Es una comunidad relativamente reciente; gran parte llegó (*arrived*) al país después de 1990. Esta comunidad vive en muchos lugares pero particularmente en el norte de Nueva Jersey, Nueva York, el Sur de Florida, y el área metropolitana de Washington, DC. La cocina peruana es muy popular en Estados Unidos, especialmente el ceviche y el pollo asado. La Inca Kola, el refresco de Perú, y el pisco, el licor nacional, se venden en muchas áreas con población latina. Los estadounidenses Carlos Noriega (astronauta) y Benjamin Bratt (actor) son de origen peruano.

Mario Vargas Llosa

El tenor Juan Diego Flórez, considerado uno de los mejores del mundo, y el escritor Mario Vargas Llosa, uno de los más importantes novelistas de América Latina, y Premio Nobel de Literatura en 2010, son dos de los peruanos más famosos en todo el mundo.

## VOCABULARIO

### La ciudad y los servicios (Cities and services)

| | |
|---|---|
| la acera | *sidewalk* |
| el alcalde, la alcaldesa | *mayor* |
| los alrededores | *outskirts* |
| el aparcamiento | *parking lot* |
| el ayuntamiento | *city council* |
| el barrio | *neighborhood* |
| la cafetería | *coffee shop* |
| la carretera | *road* |
| el casco antiguo | *historic district* |
| la ciudad universitaria | *college campus* |
| el edificio | *building* |
| los espectáculos | *shows* |
| el estacionamiento | *parking lot* |
| el estadio | *stadium* |
| la gasolinera | *gas station* |
| la guardería | *daycare, preschool* |
| el habitante | *inhabitant* |
| la iglesia | *church* |
| el jardín | *garden* |
| las obras públicas | *public works* |
| el parque | *park* |
| el peatón | *pedestrian* |
| la plaza | *square* |
| la población | *population* |
| el puerto | *harbor* |
| los rascacielos | *skyscraper* |
| la residencia estudiantil | *dorm* |
| el semáforo | *traffic light* |
| la señal de tráfico/tránsito | *traffic sign* |
| la urbanización | *housing development* |
| la vida nocturna | *nightlife* |
| la zona peatonal | *pedestrian zone* |
| la zona verde | *green zone* |

### Problemas de la ciudad (Problems of the city)

| | |
|---|---|
| la basura | *garbage, trash* |
| la calidad de vida | *quality of life* |
| el caos | *chaos* |
| la delincuencia | *crime* |
| el desempleo | *unemployment* |
| la droga | *drugs* |
| el embotellamiento | *traffic jam* |
| el humo | *smoke* |
| el olor | *smell* |
| la pobreza | *poverty* |
| el ruido | *noise* |
| la violencia | *violence* |

### El clima y el medio ambiente (Weather and environment)

| | |
|---|---|
| el aire | *air* |
| el calor | *heat* |
| el clima | *climate, weather* |
| la contaminación | *pollution* |
| la ecología | *ecology* |
| la lluvia | *rain* |
| el medio ambiente | *environment* |
| la niebla | *fog* |
| la nieve | *snow* |
| la polución | *pollution* |

### Adjetivos (Adjectives)

| | |
|---|---|
| acogedor/a | *welcoming, friendly, warm* |
| ambiental | *environmental* |
| bien/mal situado/a | *well/badly located* |
| cálido/a | *warm* |
| caluroso/a | *hot (weather)* |
| colorido/a | *colorful* |
| grave | *serious* |
| húmedo/a | *humid* |
| limpio/a | *clean* |
| nublado/a | *foggy* |
| peligroso/a | *dangerous* |
| poblado/a | *populated* |
| seco/a | *dry* |
| soleado/a | *sunny* |
| sucio/a | *dirty* |
| superpoblado/a | *overpopulated* |
| templado/a | *cool (weather)* |

### Verbos (Verbs)

| | |
|---|---|
| aburrirse | *to get bored* |
| construir | *to build* |
| contaminar | *to pollute* |
| crecer (zc) | *to grow* |
| criticar | *to criticize, to critique* |
| destinar | *to assign* |
| disponer de algo | *to have something* |
| faltar | *to lack* |
| funcionar | *to function, to work* |
| instalar | *to install* |
| instalarse | *to settle down* |
| llover (ue) | *to rain* |
| manejar | *to drive* |
| ocurrir | *to happen* |
| rebasar | *to exceed* |
| recibir | *to receive* |
| reciclar | *to recycle* |
| rodear | *to surround* |

# CONSULTORIO GRAMATICAL

## 1 Comparatives

We compare things that are different. The comparative forms **más... que...** and **menos... que...** can be used to compare nouns or adjectives.

Lima tiene **más** habitantes **que** Arequipa.
Lima has **more** inhabitants **than** Arequipa.

Arequipa tiene **menos** habitantes **que** Lima.
Arequipa has **less** inhabitants **than** Lima.

Lima es **más** grande **que** Arequipa.
Lima is **bigger than** Arequipa.

Arequipa es **más** pequeña **que** Lima.
Arequipa is **smaller than** Lima.

Some adjectives have special forms.

| | | | |
|---|---|---|---|
| más bueno/a, más bien | = | **mejor** (better) | El campo es **mejor que** la ciudad. |
| más malo/a, más mal | = | **peor** (worse) | La ciudad es **peor que** el campo. |
| más grande / de más edad | = | **mayor** (older) | Ana es **mayor que** mi padre. |
| más pequeño/a / de menos edad | = | **menor** (younger) | Raúl es **menor que** su novia. |

When referring to size you can use one of two forms: **mayor** or **más grande**, and **menor** or **más pequeño**.

Comparatives can also be used to compare actions (verbs).

VERB + **más / menos** + QUE

Raúl trabaja **más que** su novia.
Raúl works more than his girlfriend.

## 2 The Superlative

We use this form when we want to stress the superiority of something or someone against all others.

Lima es **la** ciudad **más** grande de Perú.
Lima is the **biggest** city in Peru.

El Amazonas es **el** río **más** caudaloso de Perú.
The Amazon is the **largest** river in Peru.

When it is clear from the context, we do not need to mention the others.

● ¿Cuál es **la ciudad más grande de** Perú?
○ Lima es **la más grande**.

—Which is the **largest** city in Peru?
—Lima is the **largest**.

## 3 Comparisons of Equality

### Nouns

We use **tanto** + noun + **como...** The adjective **tanto** must agree in gender and number with the noun: **tanto/a/os/as... como**.

Arequipa
- (no) tiene **tanto** turismo **como**
- (no) tiene **tanta** contaminación **como**
- (no) tiene **tantos** restaurantes **como**
- (no) tiene **tantas** zonas verdes **como**
Iquitos.

Arequipa
- doesn't have / has **as much** tourism as
- doesn't have / has **as much** pollution as
- doesn't have / has **as many** restaurants as
- doesn't have / has **as many** green areas as
Iquitos.

### Verbs

With comparisons of equality involving actions (verbs), the form of **tanto** never changes: **tanto... como**.

María (**no**) duerme **tanto como** Laura.
María doesn't sleep / sleeps **as much as** Laura.

### *Adjectives*

When comparing using an adjective, we use **tan... como...** The adverb **tan** never changes.

Lima es **tan** bonita **como** Arequipa.　　Tu país es **tan** bonito **como** mi país.
*Lima is **as** beautiful **as** Arequipa.*　　*Your country is **as** beautiful **as** my country.*

We can also use **igual de... que ...**

Lima es **igual de** bonita **que** Arequipa.
*Lima is **as** beautiful as **Arequipa**.*

Another way to compare two things is to use the adjective **mismo/a/os/as.**

Las dos ciudades tienen {
**el mismo** 　　tamaño.
**la misma** 　　reputación.
**los mismos** 　problemas.
**las mismas** 　instalaciones deportivas.

Son dos regiones muy diferentes.

Claro, no tienen el mismo clima.

Both cities have {
*the same* 　　size.
*the same* 　　reputation.
*the same* 　　problems.
*the same* 　　sports facilities.

## 4 Relative Pronouns

*Relative pronouns introduce clauses that have the same function as an adjective.*

Es una ciudad **que tiene mucha belleza** = Es una ciudad muy bella.

The relative pronoun **que** doesn't require a preposition when it relates to a subject or a direct object (except when the direct object requires the personal **a**).

Es una ciudad **que** tiene mucho encanto.
Es un plato **que** comemos mucho en Perú.

*Relative pronouns require a preposition when they relate to any other part of the sentence that originally had a preposition.*

Es una persona que hace yoga.

Es un lugar　　　　　　**en el que** (*in which*)
Es una ciudad　　　　　**en la que** (*in which*)　　se vive muy bien.
Es un lugar/una ciudad　**donde** (*where*)
(**En** ese lugar / **En** esa ciudad se vive muy bien)

Es un lugar　　　　　　**al que** (*to which*)
Es una ciudad　　　　　**a la que** (*to which*)　　voy mucho.
Es un lugar/una ciudad　**adonde** (*where*)
(**A** ese lugar / **A** esa ciudad voy mucho)

Es un lugar　　　　　　**por el que** (*through which*)
Es una ciudad　　　　　**por la que** (*through which*)
Es un lugar　　　　　　**por donde** (*where*)　　paso cada día.
(**Por** ese lugar paso cada día)

## 5 Expressing and Contrasting Opinions

To give your opinion, you can use:

**Yo pienso/creo que** } + *OPINION*
**A mí me parece que** } la ciudad necesita otra escuela.

Yo no estoy de acuerdo con él.

¡Sí, tiene razón!

Bla, Bla, Bla...

PLAS PLAS

|  | PENSAR |
|---|---|
| (yo) | pienso |
| (tú) | piensas |
| (él, ella, usted) | piensa |
| (nosotros/as) | pensamos |
| (vosotros/as) | pensáis |
| (ellos, ellas, ustedes) | piensan |

*When others give their opinion, you can react by agreeing, disagreeing, and/or adding more arguments to theirs.*

| Yo (no) estoy de acuerdo | con Juan. | I (don't) agree | with Juan. |
|---|---|---|---|
| | contigo. | | with you. |
| | con eso. | | with that. |

In Spanish the preposition **with** in the first and second persons is just one word and has a special form: **conmigo, contigo.**

Dice que quieren ir **contigo.**(= He/She says they want to go **with you.**)

Sí, tienes razón.  }
Sí, claro,  } + OPINION
Eso es verdad, pero  }
Bueno, pero  }

Yes, you are right.  }
Yes, of course,  } + OPINION
That's true, but  }
Right, but  }

In this context **lo más** + **adjective** expresses the highest priority. The neuter article **lo** expresses the Spanish equivalent of the English **the thing** or **the idea.** For example: **The most** important thing now is to talk to her. (= *Lo más importante ahora es hablar con ella.*)

*To establish priorities:*

| | | | INFINITIVE | | | | INFINITIVE |
|---|---|---|---|---|---|---|---|
| Lo más { | grave | es | solucionar el problema de la escuela. | The most { | serious thing | is | to solve the problem of the school. |
| | urgente | | NOUNS | | urgent thing | | NOUNS |
| | importante | es | la escuela nueva. | | important thing | is | the new school. |
| | necesario | son | las escuelas nuevas. | | needed thing | are | the new schools. |

| Es { | importantísimo | | | It is { | very important | |
|---|---|---|---|---|---|---|
| | fundamental | construir una escuela nueva. | | | fundamental | to build a new school. |
| | urgente | | | | urgent | |
| | necesario | | | | necessary | |

## Me gustaría

*To express wishes or desires, it is common to use the conditional form fo the verb gustar:* **gustaría.** *It can only be followed by a verb.*

**Me gustaría** vivir en esta ciudad.
*I would like to live in this city.*

**Me gustaría** solucionar los problemas de la escuela.
*I would like to solve the school's problems.*

## 6 The Weather

| Tiene un clima { | muy bueno / suave / agradable. |
|---|---|
| | tropical / templado / húmedo / seco. |

|  |  |  |
|---|---|---|
| | (no) llueve / llueve. (*it does(not) rain*) | |
| | (no) nieva. (*it does(not) snow*) | |
| | (no) hace frío (*it is (not) cold*) | |
| En  verano | calor (*it is (not) hot*) | |
| invierno | sol (*it is (not) sunny*) | |
| primavera | viento (*it is (not) windy*) | |
| otoño | buen / mal tiempo (*the weather is (not) good / bad*) | |
| | (no) hay  niebla (*fog*) | |
| | tormentas (*storms*) | |
| | huracanes (*hurricanes*) / ... | |

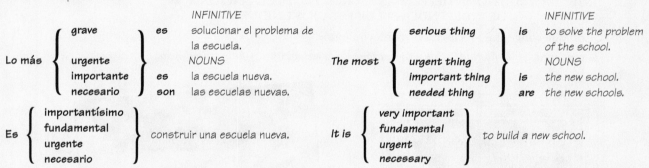

In English one talks about the weather using the "dummy subject" **it**, a pronoun for inanimate subjects. In Spanish the same idea is conveyed without using a subject pronoun at all: *Hace calor / Llueve...* (= **It's hot / It's raining...**)

## 10–1 Acontecimientos (*events*) en la historia de América

Mira las imágenes y asocia cada una con un acontecimiento y una fecha. ¿Por qué son importantes en la historia de América?

| | |
|---|---|
| 1492 | 1. MÉXICO SE INDEPENDIZÓ DE ESPAÑA |
| 1521 | 2. CRISTÓBAL COLÓN LLEGÓ A AMÉRICA |
| 1565 | 3. LOS ESPAÑOLES FUNDARON SAN AGUSTÍN (FLORIDA) |
| 1776 | 4. HERNÁN CORTÉS DERROTÓ EL IMPERIO AZTECA |
| 1821 | 5. THOMAS JEFFERSON ESCRIBIÓ LA DECLARACIÓN DE INDEPENDENCIA DE ESTADOS UNIDOS |

¿Con qué conceptos asocias cada acontecimiento?

*la conquista     la libertad     la colonización     la esclavitud     la independencia*

## ✓ TAREA

Escribir la biografía de un personaje famoso a partir de datos previos.

## NUESTRA GENTE

Chile
Hispanos/latinos en Estados Unidos.

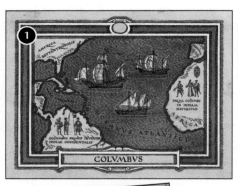

## ACERCAMIENTOS

 **10–2 Acontecimientos en la historia de Chile**

Miren las fechas y asocien cada una con un acontecimiento de la historia de Chile.

| | |
|---|---|
| 1535 | 1. SALVADOR ALLENDE ES ELEGIDO PRESIDENTE DE CHILE. |
| 1550 | 2. CHILE RECUPERA LA DEMOCRACIA DESPUÉS DE LA DICTADURA DE AUGUSTO PINOCHET. |
| 1818 | 3. HAY UN GOLPE DE ESTADO EN CHILE Y COMIENZA LA DICTADURA DE AUGUSTO PINOCHET. |
| 1970 | 4. EL CONQUISTADOR DIEGO DE ALMAGRO LLEGA A CHILE. |
| 11/09/1973 | 5. COMIENZA LA GUERRA DE ARAUCO, ENTRE EL PUEBLO INDÍGENA MAPUCHE Y LOS HISPANO-CRIOLLOS DE CHILE. |
| 11/03/1990 | 6. CHILE SE INDEPENDIZA DE ESPAÑA. |
| 03/2010 | 7. SEBASTIÁN PIÑERA GANA LAS ELECCIONES PRESIDENCIALES. |

**EJEMPLO:**

**E1:** La guerra de Arauco en 1818.
**E2:** ¡Nooo! En 1550.

Comparen sus respuestas con las de otros/as compañeros/as de clase.

### 10–3 Personajes famosos de la historia de América

Piensa en dos personajes de la historia de América. ¿En tu opinión, por qué son importantes? Comparte esta información con la clase.

Ahora mira las fotos y relaciona a estos cuatro personajes con las descripciones.

■ Simón Bolívar (1783–1830)
Nació en Caracas, Venezuela, el 24 de julio de 1783. En 1813 luchó contra el ejército español y fue proclamado "El Libertador" de Venezuela. Además, dirigió las guerras independentistas de Colombia, Perú y Ecuador. También fundó Bolivia. Bolívar es considerado uno de los militares más brillantes de todos los tiempos. Murió en Colombia en 1830.

■ Cristóbal Colón (1451–1506)
Nació en 1451 (hay muchas teorías sobre su lugar de nacimiento) y murió en España en 1506. Fue navegante, almirante y gobernador general de las Indias al servicio de la Corona de Castilla, y es famoso por iniciar la conquista de América en 1492. Hizo cuatro viajes a tierras americanas en 1492, 1495, 1498 y 1502.

■ Bernardo O'Higgins (1778–1842)
Nació en Chile el 20 de agosto de 1778. En 1808 comenzó su vida política y más tarde su actividad revolucionaria. En 1813 se inició la guerra de la independencia y O'Higgins se incorporó al ejército. Consiguió la independencia de Chile en 1818. Murió en Perú en 1842.

■ Abraham Lincoln (1809–1865)
Fue el décimosexto presidente de Estados Unidos desde 1861 hasta 1865 cuando fue asesinado. Durante este período ocurrió la Guerra Civil. Lincoln consiguió la abolición de la esclavitud con su Proclamación de Emancipación en 1863.

##  VOCABULARIO EN CONTEXTO

 **10–4 Cuatro décadas**

Éstas son las descripciones de cuatro décadas de la historia reciente: los sesenta, los setenta, los ochenta y los noventa. Incluyen algunos de los acontecimientos más importantes. Lean las descripciones e identifiquen a qué década se refiere cada una.

**EJEMPLO:**

**E1:** Yo creo que la número dos es de los setenta.
**E2:** No, no puede ser, porque la invasión de Panamá es de los ochenta.

---

**1**

Los _____

La Unión Soviética **invade** Afganistán y **comienza** la Revolución Islámica en Irán. Richard Nixon **dimite** después del escándalo de Watergate. También en esta década **ocurre** el golpe de estado en Chile contra Salvador Allende y el General Augusto Pinochet **toma** el poder para establecer una dictadura militar. En esta década aparecen los primeros microprocesadores, las calculadoras de bolsillo y los videojuegos. Además Estados Unidos **lanza** el primer trasbordador espacial. **Termina** el período de crecimiento y prosperidad económica de las naciones desarrolladas y **comienza** uno de crisis. **Muere** Elvis Presley y los Beatles **se separan**.

---

**2**

Los _____

Se **descubre** el virus del SIDA. También se popularizan las computadoras personales, los videocasetes y los discos compactos. **Ocurre** el accidente nuclear de Chernobyl. La Guerra Fría **se intensifica**. Gorbachev **instaura** la Perestroika en la Unión Soviética. El muro de Berlín **cae** y las dos Alemanias **se unifican**. Israel **invade** Líbano. La guerra Irán-Irak **causa** cientos de miles de muertos. Unas 120.000 personas **salen** de Cuba en el barco Mariel con destino a Estados Unidos. En Chile, Augusto Pinochet **proclama** una nueva Constitución, **pierde** las elecciones y **se restaura** la democracia. Estados Unidos **invade** Panamá. David Chapman **asesina** a John Lennon.

---

**3**

Los _____

Esta década **es** muy turbulenta y **está** llena de revoluciones. La Unión Soviética **pone** al primer hombre (Gagarin) en el espacio y Estados Unidos pone al primer hombre en la Luna. **Se construye** el muro de Berlín. Estados Unidos trata de terminar con el régimen comunista de Fidel Castro en Cuba. En Estados Unidos **tiene lugar** el movimiento de derechos civiles y **asesinan** a Martin Luther King Jr. Un gran terremoto en el sur de Chile **causa** miles de muertos. Hay muchas protestas estudiantiles en Francia, México y Checoslovaquia. Muchos países europeos **experimentan** un gran crecimiento económico. **Nace** el rock and roll y los Beatles **se convierten** en el grupo musical más popular del mundo.

---

**4**

Los _____

En esta década **crece** la globalización y el capitalismo global. **Aumentan** los ataques terroristas en el mundo. **Ocurre** la explosión del Internet y se inventa el DVD. Los científicos **consiguen** clonar a un animal y **empiezan** a usar el ADN para la investigación criminal. La Unión Soviética se desintegra y **termina** la Guerra Fría. En Sudáfrica **se declara** el fin del apartheid. En Chile comienza la Transición a la democracia y en Irlanda **del Norte** el proceso de paz. **Desaparece** la Comunidad Económica Europea y **se crea** la Unión Europea. La música rap y el tecno pop son muy populares.

### 10–5 Historia y política

Fíjate en los verbos en negrita de los textos anteriores. Expresan acciones relacionadas con contextos históricos o sociopolíticos. Algunos se refieren a personas o países y otros se refieren a acontecimientos. ¿Puedes hacer dos listas?

| CAMPO | VERBOS |
|---|---|
| PERSONAS/PAÍSES | Ejemplo: invadir |
| ACONTECIMIENTOS | Ejemplo: ocurrir |

Ahora haz otra lista con sustantivos relacionados con la historia y la política que aparecen en el texto.

| CAMPO | SUSTANTIVOS |
|---|---|
| HISTORIA/POLÍTICA | Ejemplo: revolución |

 ### 10–6 Una biografía: Michelle Bachelet, la primera presidenta de Chile

Lean los datos biográficos de Michelle Bachelet. Asocien los datos con el vocabulario de esta lista.

| | | |
|---|---|---|
| casarse | vivir | tener |
| crecer | enamorarse | separarse |
| la infancia | el nacimiento | la vida |
| estudiar | la juventud | la niñez |
| ser | nacer | estar |

**Datos biográficos**
— Santiago, 29 de septiembre de 1951
— Bases aéreas de Chile (1952–1962)
— Washington, DC (1962–1965)
— Medicina–Universidad de Chile (1972–1975; 1979–1982)
— Exilio en Australia y Alemania (1975–1979)
— Esposo Jorge Dávalos (1977–1984)
— Tres hijos
— Ministra de Salud en 2000 y de Defensa en 2002
— Presidenta de Chile (2006–2010)
— Primera presidenta de la historia de Chile

**EJEMPLO:**

**E1:** Santiago, 29 de septiembre de 1951 se refiere al **nacimiento**, ¿no?
**E2:** Sí, **nació** en 1951.

¿Conocen otros presidentes de América? Compartan esta información con la clase.

## GRAMÁTICA EN CONTEXTO

10-05 to
10-31

### 10–7 **La vida de Marcelo Ríos**

Escucha este fragmento de una entrevista con Marcelo Ríos, tenista chileno ex-campeón del mundo. Luego completa el cuadro con los acontecimientos mencionados.

| 1975 | **Nació** en Santiago |
|------|------------------------|
| 1992 | |
| 1993 | |
| 1994 | |
| 1995 | |
| 1998 | |

### 10–8 **¿Cuándo fue?**

Escucha las respuestas de dos concursantes del programa "¿Cuándo fue?" ¿Cuál de los dos tiene más respuestas correctas? Completa el cuadro.

| | Pregunta 1 | | Pregunta 2 | | Pregunta 3 | |
|--------------|----------|------------|----------|------------|----------|------------|
| | Correcto | Incorrecto | Correcto | Incorrecto | Correcto | Incorrecto |
| Concursante 1 | | | | | | |
| Concursante 2 | | | | | | |

### 10–9 **Años muy importantes**

Piensa en años y acontecimientos específicos especialmente importantes en tu vida y completa el cuadro.

| | Familia/relaciones | Estudios | Trabajo | Viajes | Otros |
|------|--------------------|----------|---------|--------|-------|
| 2004 | | | | | |
| | | | | | |
| | | | | | |
| | | | | | |

 Ahora compartan y comparen sus datos. ¿Hay algún año importante?

**EJEMPLO:**

**E1:** Yo **comencé** mis estudios en la universidad **en 2009**.
**E2:** Yo también, ¿y tú?
**E3:** Yo **en el 2008**.

---

## EL PRETÉRITO

*VERBOS REGULARES*

| TERMIN**AR** | CONOC**ER**, VIV**IR** |
|-------------|------------------------|
| termin**é** | conoc**í** |
| termin**aste** | conoc**iste** |
| termin**ó** | conoc**ió** |
| termin**amos** | conoc**imos** |
| termin**asteis** | conoc**isteis** |
| termin**aron** | conoc**ieron** |

*VERBOS IRREGULARES MÁS FRECUENTES*

| SER/IR | TENER | ESTAR |
|--------|--------|-----------|
| fui | tuve | estuve |
| fuiste | tuviste | estuviste |
| fue | tuvo | estuvo |
| fuimos | tuvimos | estuvimos |
| fuisteis | tuvisteis | estuvisteis |
| fueron | tuvieron | estuvieron |

| HACER | DECIR |
|--------|----------|
| hice | dije |
| hiciste | dijiste |
| hizo | dijo |
| hicimos | dijimos |
| hicisteis | dijisteis |
| hicieron | dijeron |

| SABER | DAR |
|--------|--------|
| supe | di |
| supiste | diste |
| supo | dio |
| supimos | dimos |
| supisteis | disteis |
| supieron | dieron |

## FECHAS

| ¿Cuándo | } | nació? |
|---------|---|--------|
| ¿En qué año/mes | | fue? |
| ¿Qué día | | llegó? |

| Nació | } | en 1987/en el 87. |
|-------|---|-------------------|
| Fue | | en junio. |
| Llegó | | el (día) 6 de junio de 1987. |

Tuve un accidente.

No me digas... ¿cuándo fue?

## USO DEL PRETÉRITO

Presenta la información como acontecimientos. Se usa con marcadores como:

Ayer
Anteayer
Anoche
El otro día
El lunes/martes } **fui** a Santiago de Chile.

El día 6
La semana pasada
El mes pasado
El año pasado }

**¿Y cuándo la conociste?**

**El mes pasado, cuando fui a Chile.**

## SECUENCIA DE ACONTECIMIENTOS

Luego
Después
Entonces
Antes } **viajamos** a Valparaíso.

Fui a la facultad pero **antes** estuve en la biblioteca.

Estuve en la biblioteca y **después** fui a casa.

**Antes de** + *INFINITIVE*
**Antes de** ir a mi casa, estuve en la biblioteca.

**Después de** + *INFINITIVE*
**Después de** estar en la biblioteca, fui a mi casa.

**Antes de ir a Santiago fuimos a Valparaíso.**

**¿Y luego?**

BIOGRAFÍAS
**a los** cinco años...
**de** niño / joven / soltero / estudiante / mayor...

### 10–10 Dos poetas chilenos

Estos dos chilenos universalmente famosos tuvieron muchas cosas en común. Coméntalas con tu compañero/a.

**EJEMPLO:**

**E1:** No **usaron** sus nombres reales.
**E2:** Sí, es verdad, los dos **usaron** pseudónimos.

| | Gabriela Mistral | Pablo Neruda |
|---|---|---|
| Nombre verdadero: | Lucía Godoy | Neftalí Ricardo Reyes Basualto |
| Profesiones: | Periodista, maestra, escritora | Maestro, escritor |
| Género literario: | Poesía | Poesía |
| Países de residencia: | México, Puerto Rico, Italia, Guatemala, Brasil, Portugal, Estados Unidos | Birmania, Ceilán, Singapur, España, Francia, México, Francia, Italia |
| Premio Nobel de Literatura: | 1945 | 1971 |
| Otros trabajos: | Cónsul | Cónsul, Embajador |
| Otros premios: | Premio Nacional de Literatura, Chile | Premio Nacional de Literatura, Chile |
| Muere en: | Nueva York, Estados Unidos | Santiago (Chile) |
| Obra más famosa: | *Desolación* | *Veinte poemas de amor y una canción desesperada* |

¿Y ustedes? ¿Qué tienen en común? Hablen con su compañero/a para ver qué cosas tienen en común. Después compartan la información.

### 10–11 El detective privado

Un detective privado está siguiendo a un hombre llamado Valerio Guzmán. Ayer Valerio hizo estas cosas.

*7:45 Sale de su casa. Entra en su casa otra vez.*
*8:00 Sale otra vez a la calle. Camina durante 15 minutos.*
*8:15 Un carro con una mujer para a su lado. Él sube.*
*8:35 Baja en la Plaza de Armas. Sigue a pie.*
*8:50 Entra en un edificio de oficinas.*

Escribe tú ahora el informe del detective usando el pretérito y expresiones de secuencia.

**INTERACCIONES**

10-32 to
10-33

### ESTRATEGIAS PARA LA COMUNICACIÓN ORAL

**Using approximation and circumlocution**

Having a conversation in Spanish can be challenging for an English speaker due to a lack of vocabulary. There are many strategies available to you that can keep the conversation flowing. Asking for the Spanish equivalent of a word is an easy strategy you can employ (*Perdona, ¿cómo se dice "envelope" en español?*). There are two other strategies:

1. Approximation: You can try a Spanish word that, although you know is not quite right, has a related meaning. It could be a more general word or a synonym. For example, you may not know the verb *limpiar* (to clean), but you may use *lavar* (to wash) instead. They are not interchangeable, but they are close. Your interlocutor might even provide you with the correct word.
2. Circumlocution: You can "work around" the word or concept that you don't know without switching to English. For example, if you don't know the word *cuchara* (spoon), you may say *la cosa que usas para comer sopa*.

Avoiding conversation or giving up entirely on conveying your message are poor strategies. Likewise, switching back and forth between Spanish and your first language may not be productive if your interlocutor doesn't speak your first language. Approximation and circumlocution, which are strategies that only involve the target language, can be successfully used with any Spanish speaker.

 **10–12  ¿Quién lo inventó?**

Observen estos seis inventos. Su profesor/a les va a dar el nombre de tres inventos a cada uno. Un/a estudiante describe un invento y otro/a estudiante debe tratar de averiguar qué es. Luego pregunten quién lo inventó, cuándo y dónde.

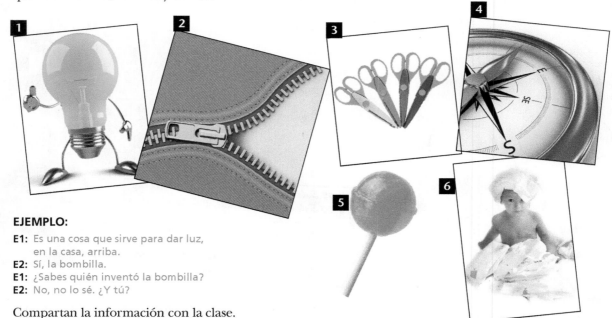

**EJEMPLO:**

**E1:** Es una cosa que sirve para dar luz, en la casa, arriba.
**E2:** Sí, la bombilla.
**E1:** ¿Sabes quién inventó la bombilla?
**E2:** No, no lo sé. ¿Y tú?

Compartan la información con la clase.

**10–13 ¿Qué hicieron?**

Aquí tienen un listado de personas famosas. Háganse preguntas el uno al otro para saber por qué son famosas. Si no saben algunas palabras, usen aproximaciones o circunloquios.

**EJEMPLO:**

**E1:** ¿Qué hizo Cristóbal Colón?
**E2:** Inició la colonización de América.

| | | | |
|---|---|---|---|
| Louis Pasteur | Isaac Newton | Gabriel García Márquez | Diego de Almagro |
| Miguel de Cervantes | Alexander Graham Bell | Bernardo O'Higgins | Bill Gates |
| Dom Perignon | Vincent Van Gogh | Albert Einstein | Alexander Fleming |

 **10–14 Un concurso**

La clase se va a dividir en cuatro equipos. Primero juegan dos equipos y después los otros dos.

**REGLAS DEL CONCURSO**

- Hay dos equipos. Cada equipo prepara, por escrito, seis preguntas sobre hechos del pasado de su país (fechas, personajes, acontecimientos importantes). Luego le hace las preguntas al otro equipo.
- Cada pregunta bien construida vale un punto. Sólo valen las preguntas de las que se conocen las respuestas. El/la profesor/a las va a corregir antes de empezar el concurso. Deben usar interrogativos.
- Cada respuesta correcta vale dos puntos.
- Gana el equipo que obtiene más puntos.

| | | |
|---|---|---|
| ¿Quién...? | ¿En qué siglo...? | ¿Cuál...? |
| ¿Cuándo...? | ¿Con quién...? | ¿Desde cuándo...? |
| ¿En qué año...? | ¿Por qué...? | |

**EJEMPLO:**

**E1:** ¿Quién fue el primer presidente de Estados Unidos?

 **10–15 Situaciones: *un robo en el dormitorio***

There was a robbery in a dorm last night. A detective is interrogating two students who seem suspicious. S/he is asking questions about their whereabouts the night before.

**ESTUDIANTE A**

You are a student living in the dorm where the robbery occurred. A detective wants to ask you some questions about the night before. Answer all his/her questions with as much detail as possible, so that s/he can rule you out as a suspect. Don't forget to mention that you were with Student B between 7:00 p.m. and 9:00 p.m.

**ESTUDIANTE B**

You are a student living in the dorm where the robbery occurred. A detective wants to ask you some questions about the night before. Answer all his/her questions with as much detail as possible, so that s/he can rule you out as a suspect. Don't forget to mention that you were alone in your room between 8:00 p.m. and 9:00 p.m.

**ESTUDIANTE C**

You are a dectective investigating this robbery. Ask the two suspects what they did the day before from the moment they woke up. The robbery occurred sometime between 7 p.m. and 9 p.m.

# TAREA

**Gente en acción**

**Escribir la biografía de un personaje famoso a partir de datos previos.**

### PREPARACIÓN

Elige cuál de estos dos personajes de Chile te interesa más. Luego, busca a tres compañeros/as interesados/as en el mismo personaje. Juntos van a escribir una biografía y después la van a presentar a la clase.

## Dos vidas apasionantes

**El primer presidente socialista de Chile**
**SALVADOR ALLENDE**
Colaboró en la fundación del Partido Socialista de Chile en 1933. Fue el primer marxista elegido presidente por voto popular en la historia del mundo occidental.

**El marino que incorporó la isla de Pascua a Chile**
**POLICARPO TORO : 1851–1921**
Su vida estuvo unida al mar y gracias a él la isla de Pascua se convirtió en territorio de Chile en 1888.

**Paso 1** Escuchen a estos estudiantes chilenos que comentan dos acontecimientos o datos importantes en la vida de cada uno de estos personajes. Tomen nota del año también.

Toro  1: En _____, _____

     2: En _____, _____

Allende  1: En _____, _____

     2: En _____, _____

**Paso 2** Ahora busquen en las cajas de la página siguiente los fragmentos que se refieren a su personaje.

**Paso 3** Preparen una ficha con toda la información que tienen. Ordenen la información. Muestren el orden a su profesor/a para comprobar que es correcto.

**Paso 4** Incorporen a su narración varios de estos **marcadores de secuencia** para dar fluidez a su narración.

(Número) + día(s) / mes(es) / año(s) después…
Después de (número) día(s) / mes(es) / año(s)…
Ese / aquel día / mes / año…
Más tarde…
Entonces, luego, después,…
Después de + *infinitivo*…
Antes de + *infinitivo*…
Poco / mucho tiempo después…

**Paso 5** Preparen una presentación oral para la clase. Cada miembro del grupo presenta una parte, en orden cronológico.

┤ **AYUDA** ├

**a los**… años…
**De** 1986 a 1990
**Desde** 1986 **hasta** 1990 vivió en París.
Vivió en París **durante** cuatro años.
El año **en el que**…
La época **en la que**…

▸ Fue senador entre 1945 y 1969 y durante esos años se postuló tres veces a la presidencia de Chile sin éxito. La cuarta vez que se postuló ganó las elecciones.

▸ En 1972, asistió a la Asamblea de las Naciones Unidas, donde denunció la agresión internacional hacia su país. Al final de su discurso, la Asamblea lo ovacionó de pie durante varios minutos.

▸ Nació en 1851 en Melipilla, Chile, e ingresó en la Escuela Naval a los 19 años.

▸ Estudió Medicina y recibió su título de médico cirujano en 1932.

▸ En 1870 llegó a la isla de Pascua o Rapa Nui, ubicada a 3.760 km de la costa chilena. Éste era un territorio desconocido para el resto del mundo hasta su descubrimiento el 5 de abril de 1722 por el holandés Roeggeween, en la época de Pascua de Resurrección.

▸ Recorrió las costas de la Patagonia, llegando hasta el río Santa Cruz. Al estallar la guerra ruso-turca se enroló en la Marina británica y recorrió el Mediterráneo y el Medio Oriente.

▸ En 1973 dijo: "...mucho más temprano que tarde, se abrirán las grandes alamedas, por donde pasará el hombre libre para construir una sociedad mejor. ¡Viva Chile, viva el pueblo, vivan los trabajadores!"

▸ En 1887 comenzó las gestiones para la incorporación a Chile de la isla de Pascua. Redactó un documento de estudio sobre el lamentable estado de la población. Negoció con las autoridades francesas y suscribió un compromiso de compraventa. Tomó posesión de Rapa Nui el 9 de septiembre de 1888.

▸ Vivió sus últimos años en Santiago, ciudad donde falleció en 1921.

▸ Gobernó desde 1970 hasta 1973, ya que el 11 de septiembre de 1973 se produjo el golpe de estado que lo destituyó.

**Paso 6** Foco lingüístico.

NUESTRA GENTE

## GENTE QUE LEE

### ESTRATEGIAS PARA LEER

**Following a chronology**

When reading biographical or historical texts, you should be able to follow the sequence of events. Writers not always present data in chronological order, and this may lead to misunderstandings. It is important to be familiar with:

(a) time expressions (*la semana pasada, el año siguiente, de niño, en esa época, antes, después,* etc.)
(b) cohesive markers, especially demonstratives (*éste, ése, aquel...*), object pronouns (*lo, la...*), and relative pronouns (*el que, la que...*).

Take a look at this example:

> *Diego de Almagro llegó a América en 1514. Viajó a Perú con Pizarro en 1532 y **a los tres años** partió hacia Chile.*

You need to know that *a los tres años* means "three years later" to understand the sequence of events (first he was in Peru, then in Chile).

Now take a look at this example:

> *Almagro llegó a Chile en 1535. A **éste** le sucedió Valdivia.*

It is important to know that *éste* refers to Almagro (and also that Valdivia is the subject of the sentence) in order to understand that, chronologically, Almagro arrived to Chile before Valdivia.

### ANTES DE LEER

### 10–16 Islas

¿Conoces estas islas? ¿Dónde están? ¿Son países o partes de un país? ¿Cuáles están en Sudamérica?

| | | | | |
|---|---|---|---|---|
| Groenlandia | Gran Bretaña | Hawai | Islas Canarias | Granada |
| Cuba | Malvinas | Japón | La Española | Puerto Rico |

### 10–17 Activando estrategias

1. Mira el título de la lectura y las fotos. ¿De qué trata este texto?
2. Identifica la frase temática de cada párrafo. ¿Qué tipo de información vas a encontrar?
3. Busca en el texto fechas (días, años, siglos). ¿Sobre qué período histórico crees que vas a leer?

### DESPUÉS DE LEER

### 10–18 ¿Comprendes?

1. ¿Cuáles son las dos hipótesis sobre el origen de los pobladores de esta isla?
2. ¿Qué originó las guerras tribales en los siglos XVII y XVIII?
3. ¿Qué causó la disminución de población entre 1859 y 1877?
4. ¿Qué representan los moais?

*A LEER*

## LA ISLA RAPA NUI

La isla de Pascua está ubicada en la Polinesia, en medio del océano Pacífico. Tiene una superficie de 163,6 km² y una población de unos 3.800 habitantes. El nombre tradicional que recibe esta isla es Rapa Nui, que significa "isla grande" en el idioma rapanui.

Según la tradición oral, el pueblo rapanui llegó a esta isla desde una **mítica** isla llamada Hiva, guiados por Hotu Matu'a, su primer rey, hacia el siglo IV. De acuerdo con algunas investigaciones arqueológicas, esta etnia proviene de la Polinesia, pero otros postulan un origen **preincaico**. Esta sociedad **tribal** estableció centros religiosos, políticos y ceremoniales, y construyó los moai, unas gigantescas cabezas **talladas** en piedra volcánica que representan a sus ancestros deificados. Todavía no se sabe cómo se realizó la construcción y **desplazamiento** de aquellas esculturas, <u>de las que</u> existen cerca de mil distribuidas por toda la isla. La población de Rapa Nui sufrió una crisis de **sobrepoblación** en los siglos XVII y XVIII, <u>lo que</u> provocó guerras entre las tribus. Estas guerras causaron la destrucción de muchos moais.

El capitán de la Armada de Chile, Policarpo Toro, llegó a la isla en 1870. Sin embargo, muchos años antes, en 1722, el holandés Jakob Roggeveen **realizó** el primer contacto europeo. Más tarde varias expediciones europeas visitaron la isla, que se

convirtió en un punto de escala de viajes hacia Oceanía. Entre 1859 y 1863, unos veinte barcos se llevaron alrededor de 2.000 **isleños** a trabajar como esclavos a las haciendas de Perú, matando a gran número <u>de los que</u> no pudieron llevarse. El exterminio de la clase sacerdotal significó una enorme **pérdida**. Años más tarde, en 1877, las epidemias de tuberculosis y **viruela**, redujeron la población a un mínimo de 110 personas.

Dieciocho años después de llegar a la isla, Policarpo Toro <u>la</u> incorporó a Chile. El 9 de septiembre de 1888, Chile consiguió la firma de un tratado con los nativos, representados por su rey Atamu Tekena. Se redactó un documento en español y otro en rapanui. La tradición oral cuenta que el rey Atamu Tekena tomó un **trozo** de **pasto** con **tierra**; luego le entregó el pasto a los **emisarios** chilenos y se quedó con (*kept*) la tierra. La antropóloga Paloma Hucke dice que con ese acto Atamu Tekena <u>le</u> dio la soberanía a Chile, pero se reservó el derecho sobre sus tierras. El gobierno chileno reservó una zona en la costa occidental para la población indígena y utilizó el resto del terreno para el pastoreo de ovejas y vacas. Los isleños no tuvieron derechos de ciudadanía hasta 1966.

### 10–19 Activando estrategias

1. Di qué significan estas palabras del texto (en negrita), y de qué palabras vienen: "preincaico", "tribal", "sobrepoblación", "isleños". ¿Son nombres o adjetivos?

2. Busca en el diccionario las siguientes palabras: "mítica", "talladas", "desplazamiento", "trozo", "pasto" y "emisarios".

3. Busca la palabra "tierra". ¿Cuántos significados tiene? ¿Cuál es el más adecuado en este contexto?

4. Identifica en los párrafos 3 y 4 todas las expresiones usadas para marcar la secuencia de acontecimientos. ¿Puedes hacer una línea temporal?

5. ¿A qué o a quién se refieren las expresiones subrayadas en el texto?

### 10–20 Expansión

1. Reflexionen sobre los efectos de la anexión de la isla de Pascua sobre las poblaciones originarias.

2. Piensen en otros ejemplos de islas que ahora son parte de otros países. ¿Cómo fue el proceso de anexión? ¿Qué efectos tuvo en la población?

## GENTE QUE ESCRIBE

10-36 to
10-38

### ESTRATEGIAS PARA ESCRIBIR

**Writing a narrative (I): past actions and events**

When you write a narrative, you are telling a story, recounting an event or a series of events in the past. These are some important factors to consider:

1. The actions and events of a narrative may be told in any order, but the most straightforward way is to narrate them in chronological order.
2. The time expressions and cohesive markers are the elements that help you (and your reader) to establish a coherent chronological sequence.
3. You can tell a story about yourself or about someone else. Be sure to pay close attention to the verb forms (first vs. third person) when narrating so that you don't confuse the reader.
4. A narrative consists of (a) past actions or events, and (b) situations and descriptions of the backgrounds in which those actions happened. For now, we will concentrate on actions: what happened and when. In the next chapter we will work on situations and backgrounds.

### MÁS ALLÁ DE LA FRASE

**Use of time markers in narratives**

Time markers are used to give coherence and carry the story forward. Besides the ones you have already learned (Tarea section), you can use the following ones:

| | |
|---|---|
| ***Hace*** *(número) día(s) / mese(s) / año(s)...* | (number) Day(s) / month(s) / year(s) ago... |
| ***El*** *mes / año / siglo* ***pasado...*** | Last month / year / century... |
| ***La*** *semana* ***pasada...*** | Last week... |
| ***A l*** *día /mes / año* ***siguiente...*** | The following day / month / year... |
| ***A los*** *(número) días / meses / años...* | (number) Day(s) / month(s) / year(s) later... |
| ***Desde entonces...*** | Since then... |
| ***Desde ese / aquel*** *día / año /*| Since that day / year / moment / instant... |
| *momento / instante...* | |
| ***En ese/aquel momento*** */ instante...* | At that moment / instant... |
| ***De repente...*** | Suddenly... |

### 10–21 Una biografía

Escribe la biografía de una persona que conoces (puede ser un miembro de tu familia, un amigo de la universidad o de tu ciudad, un profesor) o de un personaje famoso.

Piensa en lo que esta persona hizo y en acontecimientos relevantes de su vida y haz una lista. Luego decide la estructura: piensa en los párrafos y las frases temáticas y ordena la información de forma relevante.

 ***¡ATENCIÓN!***

Para escribir esta biografía debes seguir los Pasos 1 a 8. Presta atención a la organización cronológica. Usa una variedad de marcadores de tiempo y otros recursos cohesivos. No olvides revisar las formas del pretérito.

## COMPARACIONES

### 10–22 Héroes americanos

¿Qué es un héroe? ¿Cuáles son los héroes de la historia de tu país? ¿De qué época son?

Ahora lee este texto sobre un héroe mapuche. Luego responde a las preguntas.

Lautaro (*Levtraru* en la lengua mapuche) fue un destacado líder militar mapuche en la guerra de Arauco durante la primera fase de la conquista española. Fue prisionero de los españoles durante seis años y en ese tiempo aprendió sus tácticas militares. En 1552 se escapó y regresó a su pueblo. Poco después dirigió una gran sublevación militar contra los españoles. Con la muerte de Lautaro, desapareció una figura notable de la guerra de Arauco.

Escucha ahora a Joaquín, quien nos da más datos sobre la historia de Lautaro. Anota dos datos importantes.

—¿Cuál fue la causa de Lautaro? ¿Crees que es una causa justa? ¿Por qué?
—¿Qué características del héroe tiene Lautaro?

### 10–23 Héroes indígenas

¿Conocen a alguno de estos héroes indígenas? Relacionen los nombres con los datos. ¿En qué se parecen a Lautaro? Expliquen las similitudes y diferencias.

A. Toro sentado     B. Caupolicán
C. Atahualpa       D. Tupac Amaru II

1. Jefe indio de la tribu de los sioux Hunkpapa. Vivió entre los años 1831 y 1890. Luchó contra el Séptimo de Caballería, bajo las órdenes del general Custer, en la batalla de Little Big Horn. Esta batalla fue ganada por los nativo-americanos el 25 de junio de 1876.
2. Fue un caudillo mapuche de la guerra de Arauco y sucesor de Lautaro. Junto con Lautaro fue uno de los conductores de los araucanos en las guerras del siglo XVI.
3. Vivió entre 1502 y 1533 y fue gobernante del imperio incaico entre 1532 y 1533. Fue apresado por Pizarro y condenado a muerte.
4. Su verdadero nombre fue José Gabriel Condorcanqui. A finales del siglo XVIII condujo una rebelión indígena contra la burocracia colonial española. Es considerado uno de los precursores de la independencia del Perú.

## CULTURA

La comunidad chilena en Estados Unidos es bastante pequeña (unas 110.000 personas). La mayoría reside en Florida, California, Nueva York o Nueva Jersey. Una parte de esta población salió de Chile por motivos políticos (dictadura de Pinochet); otros vinieron para realizar estudios universitarios de posgrado y otros por motivos económicos. California tiene una presencia chilena desde la época de la "fiebre del oro" y varias calles en San Francisco y otras ciudades del norte de California tienen nombres chilenos.

Posiblemente los dos hispanos de ascendencia chilena más conocidos en Estados Unidos sean la escritora Isabel Allende y el académico Arturo Valenzuela. Isabel Allende, ciudadana de Estados Unidos desde 2003, es considerada la más popular novelista iberoamericana y sus novelas están traducidas a más de 27 idiomas. Entre las más importantes están *La casa de los espíritus* (1982) y *Cuentos de Eva Luna* (1989).

Arturo Valenzuela es un experto en análisis político y socioeconómico de Chile, México y el Cono Sur. Es director del Centro de Estudios Latinoamericanos de la Universidad de Georgetown y consejero del *National Council of La Raza*. Fue consejero de Bill Clinton para asuntos de Latinoamérica. El interés de Valenzuela por la consolidación de las democracias en América Latina se manifiesta en su trabajo como asesor, y en varios artículos y textos publicados a lo largo de su carrera.

 VOCABULARIO

## Biografías *(Biographies)*

| | |
|---|---|
| la amistad | *friendship* |
| el amor | *love* |
| el crecimiento | *growth* |
| el destino | *destiny* |
| la generación | *generation* |
| la infancia | *childhood* |
| la juventud | *youth* |
| la muerte | *death* |
| la niñez | *childhood* |
| el nacimiento | *birth* |
| el pensamiento | *thought* |
| el sentimiento | *feeling* |
| la vejez | *old age* |
| la vida | *life* |

## Conceptos históricos y socio-políticos
*(Socio-political and historical concepts)*

| | |
|---|---|
| el acontecimiento | *event* |
| el acuerdo | *agreement* |
| el asesinato | *murder* |
| la conquista | *conquest* |
| el conquistador | *conqueror* |
| la costumbre | *custom* |
| los derechos civiles | *civil rights* |
| el descubrimiento | *discovery* |
| el discurso | *speech* |
| el ejército | *military* |
| las elecciones | *elections* |
| la esclavitud | *slavery* |
| el/la explorador/a | *explorer* |
| la firma | *signature* |
| el golpe de estado | *coup d'état* |
| la guerra | *war* |
| el/la indígena | *native* |
| la leyenda | *legend* |
| la libertad | *freedom* |
| la manifestación | *demonstration* |
| el mito | *myth* |
| el movimiento | *movement* |
| la patria | *homeland* |
| la paz | *peace* |
| el premio | *award* |
| el pueblo | *people, nation* |
| la riqueza | *wealth* |
| el territorio | *territory* |
| el tratado | *treaty* |

## Verbos *(Verbs)*

| | |
|---|---|
| anunciar | *to announce* |
| aumentar | *to increase* |
| casarse | *to get married* |
| casarse con alguien | *to marry someone* |
| comprometerse | *to get engaged* |
| conseguir (i) | *to achieve* |
| crecer (zc) | *to grow up* |
| darse cuenta de | *to realize* |
| desarrollar | *to develop* |
| descubrir | *to discover* |
| dimitir | *to resign* |
| divorciarse | *to divorce* |
| elegir (i) | *to choose, to elect* |
| enamorarse de | *to fall in love* |
| fundar | *to found* |
| ganar | *to win* |
| interrumpir | *to interrupt* |
| liberar | *to free* |
| llegar | *to arrive* |
| morir (ue) | *to die* |
| nacer (zc) | *to be born* |
| ocurrir | *to happen* |
| partir | *to depart* |
| perder (ie) | *to loose* |
| pertenecer zc) | *to belong* |
| preocuparse | *to worry* |
| regresar | *to come back* |
| suceder | *to happen, to follow* |
| trasladarse | *to move* |
| unirse a | *to join* |

## Adjetivos *(Adjectives)*

| | |
|---|---|
| conocido/a | *known* |
| conservador/a | *conservative* |
| desconocido/a | *unknown* |
| extraño/a | *strange* |
| feliz | *happy* |
| progresista | *progressive* |
| sorprendente | *surprising* |

# CONSULTORIO GRAMATICAL

## 1 The Preterite Tense

*Regular verbs:*

|  | **-AR** | **-ER** | **-IR** |
|---|---|---|---|
|  | TERMINAR | CONOCER | VIVIR |
| (yo) | terminé | conocí | viví |
| (tú) | termin**aste** | conoc**iste** | viv**iste** |
| (él, ella, usted) | termin**ó** | conoc**ió** | viv**ió** |
| (nosotros/as) | termin**amos** | conoc**imos** | viv**imos** |
| (vosotros/as) | termin**asteis** | conoc**isteis** | viv**isteis** |
| (ellos, ellas, ustedes) | termin**aron** | conoc**ieron** | viv**ieron** |

*Two of the most frequently used irregular verbs:*

|  | SER | IR |
|---|---|---|
| (yo) | **fui** | **fui** |
| (tú) | **fuiste** | **fuiste** |
| (él, ella, usted) | **fue** | **fue** |
| (nosotros/as) | **fuimos** | **fuimos** |
| (vosotros/as) | **fuisteis** | **fuisteis** |
| (ellos, ellas, ustedes) | **fueron** | **fueron** |

*In many irregular verbs, the stressed syllable in the preterite is shifted from the final syllable to the stem. This occurs in the first person singular (**yo**) and in the third person singular (**él, ella, usted**).*

**tu**ve, **tu**vo
**vi**ne, **vi**no

*Verbs that are irregular in the preterite adopt a different stem and usually have these endings:*

|  |  |
|---|---|
| (yo) | **-e** |
| (tú) | **-iste** |
| (él, ella, usted) | **-o** |
| (nosotros/as) | **-imos** |
| (vosotros/as) | **-isteis** |
| (ellos, ellas, ustedes) | **-ieron** |

| PODER: | **pud-** | VENIR: | **vin-** |
|---|---|---|---|
| PONER: | **pus-** | ESTAR: | **estuv-** |
| QUERER: | **quis-** | SABER: | **sup-** |
| TENER: | **tuv-** |  |  |

|  | HACER | DECIR | DAR |
|---|---|---|---|
| (yo) | **hice** | **dije** | **di** |
| (tú) | **hiciste** | **dijiste** | **diste** |
| (él, ella, usted) | **hizo** | **dijo** | **dio** |
| (nosotros/as) | **hicimos** | **dijimos** | **dimos** |
| (vosotros/as) | **hicisteis** | **dijisteis** | **disteis** |
| (ellos, ellas, ustedes) | **hicieron** | **dijeron*** | **dieron** |

*Almost all **-er** and **-ir** verbs take **-ieron** in the third person plural; **decir** and some other verbs that end in **-cir** take **-eron**.

## 2 Use of the Preterite Tense

*The preterit tense presents information as an event.*

Ayer **llovió.**
**It rained** yesterday.

Ayer por la noche **estuvimos** en un restaurante muy bueno.
Last night **we were** in a very good restaurant.

Ayer Ana **fue** a una tienda y **se compró** un par de zapatos. Luego **volvió** a casa en taxi.
Yesterday Ana went to a store and **bought** a pair of shoes. Then **went back** home by taxi.

*These types of markers often accompany the preterit:*

**ayer**
(yesterday)

**anteayer**
(the day before yesterday)

**anoche**
(last night)

**el otro día**
(the other day)

**el lunes / martes...**
(on Monday / Tuesday...)

**el (día) 6 / 21 /...**
(on [day] the 6th, the 21st...)

**la semana pasada**
(last week)

**el mes pasado**
(last month)

**el año pasado**
(last year)

## 3 Talking about Dates

- ¿Qué día nació su hija?          —On what day was your daughter born?
- **El (día)** 14 de agosto de 1992.   —**On** August 14, 1992.

- ¿Cuándo llegaste a Chile?        —When did you arrive in Chile?
- **En** marzo de 1992.              —**In** March of 1992.

- ¿Cuándo terminó Juan sus estudios?  —When did Juan finish his studies?
- **En el** 94.                      —**In** '94.

- ¿En qué año se casó?             —In what year did he get married?
- **En** 1985.                       —**In** 1985.

## 4 Sequencing Past Events

*To indicate order, use* **antes (de)**, **después (de)** y **luego.**

Fui a la facultad, pero **antes** estuve en la biblioteca.
I went to the school, but **before that** I went to the library.

Estuve en la biblioteca y **después** fui a la facultad; **luego** volví a casa.
*I was at the library and **afterwards** I went to the school; **then** I went back home.*

**Antes de** + *INFINITIVE*

**Antes de** ir a la facultad, estuve en la biblioteca.

**Después de** + *INFINITIVE*

**Después de** estar en la biblioteca, fui a la facultad.
***After** being at the library, I went to the school.*

**Entonces** *is a very common connector that is used...*

● *to refer to a time period that has already been mentioned:*

Me fui a vivir a Italia en el 71. **Entonces** yo era muy joven.
*I went to live in Italy in '71. I was very young **then**.*

● *to refer to what happened next:*

Juan fue a la bibioteca pero no pudo encontrar a su amigo. **Entonces** fue al apartamento pero tampoco lo encontró.

*Juan went to the library but couldn't find his friend. **Then** he went to the apartment but couldn't find him there either.*

> To sequence actions or events in chronological order:
>
> **antes** = *before*
> **después** = *after/afterwards*
>
> Note that in Spanish the words for *after* and *before* are followed by an infinitive rather than by an *-ing* form:
> Después de **ver** el partido fuimos a cenar. (= *After **watching** the match, we went to get dinner.*)

## TAREA

Escribir el relato de un episodio o período de la historia de nuestro país.

### 11–1 Historia de Nicaragua

| | |
|---|---|
| 1821 | 1. Centroamérica fue una república federal (Costa Rica, El Salvador, Nicaragua, Honduras y Guatemala). |
| 1824–1838 | 2. Ocurrieron las primeras elecciones democráticas. |
| 1838 | 3. Ocurrió la revolución sandinista. |
| 1927–1933 | 4. Augusto Sandino luchó contra la ocupación estadounidense. |
| 1934–1979 | 5. Fue un período de gobiernos militares. |
| 1979 | 6. Se declaró la independencia de Nicaragua. |
| 1990 | 7. Nicaragua se separó de la República Federal de Centroamérica. |
| 2006 | 8. Daniel Ortega, del Frente Sandinista de Liberación Nacional, ganó las elecciones. |

### NUESTRA GENTE

Nicaragua
Hispanos/latinos en Estados Unidos

¿Con qué conceptos asocias cada período o acontecimiento?

*dictadura*   *independencia*   *libertad*   *paz*
*democracia*   *héroe*   *guerra*   *gobierno*182

## CULTURA

Nicaragua es un país centroamericano con una población de cinco millones y medio de habitantes, compuesta por: un 69% de mestizos, un 17% de descendientes de europeos, un 9% de descendientes de africanos y un 5% de población indígena. La lengua oficial es el español, pero en la costa atlántica se habla inglés criollo, miskito y otras lenguas nativas.

Su capital es Managua, una ciudad rodeada de lagunas volcánicas.

## CULTURA

La ciudad de Managua, la capital de Nicaragua, no tiene un centro porque el terremoto de 1972 lo destruyó. En los años sesenta, Managua era una de las principales capitales de America Latina. Sin embargo, tras el terremoto quedó totalmente devastada. Fueron afectados el 90% de sus edificios y 320.000 personas perdieron sus casas. El total de muertos fue de más de 10.000.

## ACERCAMIENTOS

### 11–2 Geografía de Nicaragua

Mira el mapa en la página anterior y lee estos textos. Después identifica los lugares que se mencionan. ¿Qué información te parece más interesante? Escribe dos frases, cada una con una fecha específica.

En la época colonial, la zona del Pacífico era española, pero la zona del Caribe era inglesa. Las ciudades más importantes de aquella época, fundadas por los españoles, eran León y Granada. Los ingleses tenían influencia en la Costa de Mosquitos, un área que abarcaba toda la costa este de Nicaragua. La ciudad más importante del territorio era Bluefields. Los británicos mantuvieron su influencia sobre el área hasta 1860, cuando reconocieron la soberanía de Nicaragua.

Los Cayos Miskitos son un archipiélago situado en la costa nordeste caribeña de Nicaragua. La reserva biológica Cayos Miskitos es una de las 78 áreas protegidas de Nicaragua desde 1991.

Las Islas del Maíz están ubicadas a unos 70 kms de la costa caribeña de Nicaragua. Son dos islas descubiertas por Cristóbal Colón en su cuarto viaje a las Indias en el año 1504. Las Islas del Maíz fueron un protectorado británico desde 1655 hasta 1894, y después Estados Unidos tuvo el derecho al uso de las islas hasta 1971.

**EJEMPLO:**

**E1:** Cristóbal Colón descubrió las Islas del Maíz en 1504.

### 11–3 Ometepe, la isla del fin del mundo

Lee ahora este texto sobre otra isla de Nicaragua.

La Isla de Ometepe es la más grande del mundo situada dentro de un lago de agua dulce, el Cocibolca, en pleno centro de Nicaragua. Tiene unos 35.000 habitantes, descendientes de toltecas, mayas, aztecas, nahuas, olmecas y chibchas, además de pueblos indígenas que poblaron la isla, que ya estaba habitada desde 1500 a.C. Cuando llegaron a la isla los colonizadores españoles, los indios que la habitaban se refugiaron en las cumbres de los volcanes Concepción y Madera, considerados durante generaciones el hogar de los dioses, y dejaron atrás los petroglifos de sus antepasados, llenos de imágenes misteriosas, que datan aproximadamente del año 300 d.C.

1. El origen y significado de los petroglifos de Ometepe está lleno de misterios e incógnitas. Aunque todo parece indicar que los petroglifos son ejemplos del desarrollo de las civilizaciones indígenas, algunas personas piensan que estos dibujos y grabados fueron hechos por extraterrestres. ¿Qué opinas?

2. ¿Conoces ejemplos similares a los de los petroglifos de Ometepe en otros países de América?

VOCABULARIO EN CONTEXTO

11-01 to
11-04

### 11–4 Los miskitos

Lean estos textos sobre una etnia de la región de Nicaragua. Después traten de identificar qué palabras faltan.

Los miskitos son un grupo étnico indígena de Centroamérica. Su _____ , que se extiende desde el sur de Honduras hasta el sur de Nicaragua, es muy inaccesible y por eso estuvieron aislados de la _____ española del área. Su origen étnico no está claro pero se cree que provienen de la mezcla de caribes (la población autóctona) y africanos. El rey miskito y los británicos llegaron a un _____ de amistad y alianza en 1740 y después, en 1749, la nación miskita se convirtió en un protectorado. El reino de los miskitos ayudó durante las _____ revolucionarias americanas atacando _____ españolas, y consiguieron numerosas victorias junto a los británicos. Aún así, después de la _____ del tratado de _____ en 1783, los británicos tuvieron que ceder el control sobre la costa.

tratado     firma     guerras     paz     conquista     territorio     colonias

Los colonos españoles comenzaron a llegar a las tierras miskitas en 1787, pero los miskitos continuaron dominando la región debido a su superioridad numérica y a su experiencia _____ . Los miskitos nunca se sintieron controlados por el _____ nicaragüense, y muchos miskitos aún hoy día no se consideran nicaragüenses. El _____ miskito desapareció en 1894, cuando Nicaragua lo ocupó. El 16 de abril de 2009 el pueblo miskito, una comunidad de unas 500.000 personas, se declaró independiente de Nicaragua en una ceremonia en la que nombraron a su máximo _____ , el "wihta tara" o rey de la comunidad. Su objetivo es crear una _____ miskitia.

gobierno     líder     nación     estado     militar

### 11–5 ¿Cómo eran?

¿Recuerdas algunos de estos personajes que estudiamos en la *Lección 10*? ¿Cómo crees que eran? Usa el banco de adjetivos para describirlos.

| | | | |
|---|---|---|---|
| valiente | misterioso | honrado | comprometido |
| cobarde | delgado | atractivo | innovador |
| conservador | malvado | fuerte | misterioso |
| liberal | bueno | débil | convincente |

1. Simón Bolívar
2. Cristóbal Colón
3. Abraham Lincoln

**EJEMPLO:**

**E1:** Creo que Lincoln era un hombre muy valiente y comprometido.

**E2:** Sí, estoy de acuerdo. Y físicamente era muy delgado y no muy alto.

4.

Toro Sentado

5.

Tupac Amaru II

### 11–6 Augusto Sandino

Mira la foto y lee la descripción de Augusto César Sandino (1895–1934), revolucionario nicaragüense y uno de los personajes más destacados de la historia reciente de Nicaragua.

Sandino era alto y delgado. Tenía una cara ovalada pero angulosa. En sus ojos oscuros brillaba con frecuencia una simpatía, pero también reflejaban gravedad y reflexión. Su voz era suave, convincente; no dudaba de sus conceptos, y sus palabras eran precisas. Sandino era un ferviente nacionalista y era considerado un buen militar y estadista. Se dice que era muy humano y popular, y que le gustaba mucho hablar con la gente.

¿Puedes pensar ahora en un familiar o amigo muy querido que ya no está vivo o al que no ves desde hace mucho tiempo?

- ¿Cómo se llamaba? _____
- ¿De dónde era? _____
- ¿Qué era (profesión, ocupación)? _____
- ¿Cómo era físicamente? _____
- ¿Cómo era (personalidad)? _____
- ¿Qué aficiones tenía? _____

Ahora comparte esta información con tu compañero/a.

### 11–7 Antes y ahora

Completen estas frases para cada uno de estos momentos de la historia de su país.

1. Antes de la llegada de los conquistadores…

2. Antes de la Declaración de Independencia…

3. Antes de la Declaración de Emancipación…

4. A principios del Siglo XX…

5. En la época de la Gran Depresión…

6. Después de la segunda Guerra Mundial…

1. _____(no) había / existía(n)_____. Ahora _____.

2. _____(no) tenía(n)_____. Ahora _____.

3. _____(no) era(n) / estaba(n) / existía(n) _____. Ahora _____.

**EJEMPLO:**

**E1:** Antes de la conquista de América había muchos indígenas. Ahora hay pocos.
**E2:** Sí, y Estados Unidos no existía. Ahora sí.

### CULTURA

El primer explorador que recorrió Nicaragua fue Gil González de Avila. La leyenda dice que cuando González de Avila llegó a Nicaragua, el cacique Nicarao gobernaba la región y el nombre "Nicaragua" se deriva del nombre de Nicarao; sin embargo muchos historiadores creen que en realidad deriva del idioma náhuatl, dialecto hablado por sus primitivos pobladores en épocas precolombinas.

**GRAMÁTICA EN CONTEXTO**

11-05 to
11-28

 **11-8  La vida antes de Internet**

Escucha esta entrevista con tres jóvenes nicaragüenses. Hablan sobre los efectos de Internet en su vida cotidiana. Escribe una de las cosas que estas personas **hacían** antes de Internet y que ahora no hacen.

1. Antes _____ y ahora _____ .

2. Antes _____ y ahora _____ .

3. Antes _____ y ahora _____ .

Ahora lee la entrevista e identifica los verbos **en el pasado**. Haz dos grupos: (1) verbos que se refieren a las **circunstancias o el contexto de un acontecimiento o actividad**, y (2) verbos que se refieren a **actividades o acontecimientos habituales** en el pasado.

**11-9  Leyenda de Oyanka**

Escucha y lee al mismo tiempo esta leyenda nicaragüense. Después clasifica los verbos en pasado de acuerdo a su significado y uso.

### Oyanka, la princesa que se convirtió en montaña

Allá por 1590, en el Valle de Sébaco, habitaba una nación de indígenas matagalpas que trabajaba el oro. Su líder era el cacique Yamboa. Mientras tanto en Córdoba, España, vivía José López de Cantarero. José era un joven guapo y muy ambicioso que quería ir a Nicaragua a buscar aventuras y tesoros en aquella tierra misteriosa. Un día se fue al puerto de Cádiz y allá tomó un barco a América. Cuando llegó a Nicaragua se instaló en Sébaco y allá conoció a la hija del cacique, que se llamaba Oyanka. Oyanka era bellísima y llevaba siempre muchas joyas de oro. José se enamoró de ella y ella de él. Pero José era muy ambicioso y quería saber de dónde extraía Yamboa el oro. Entonces Oyanka condujo a José hasta las montañas, donde había una cueva escondida. José, viendo todo aquel oro, se guardó siete pepitas grandes en su bolso. Cuando salían de la cueva, el caquique los encontró; vendió a José a otra tribu indígena y encerró a la princesa. Oyanka se deprimió tanto que no quiso comer más. Su padre trató de convencerla, pero Oyanka no podía vivir sin José, así que se durmió en un sueño profundo esperando el regreso de José. Pero José nunca regresó. Oyanka se convirtió en montaña y hoy puede verse, al norte del valle de Sébaco, el cerro de Oyanka.

| SIGNIFICADO / USO | VERBOS |
|---|---|
| Circunstancias / contexto | habitaba |
| Descripción | |
| Actividad / acontecimiento habitual | trabajaba |
| Acción puntual | se fue |
| Acción en progreso (*ongoing*) | |

---

**EL PRETÉRITO IMPERFECTO**

Verbos regulares:

| ESTAR | TENER, VIVIR |
|---|---|
| estaba | tenía |
| estabas | tenías |
| estaba | tenía |
| estábamos | teníamos |
| estabais | teníais |
| estaban | tenían |

Verbos irregulares:

| SER | IR |
|---|---|
| era | iba |
| eras | ibas |
| era | iba |
| éramos | íbamos |
| erais | ibais |
| eran | iban |

**USOS DEL IMPERFECTO**

Imperfecto: contraste **ahora / antes**

Ahora
Actualmente } todo el mundo tiene Internet.

Antes
Cuando yo era niño/a
Entonces
En esa/aquella época } no **teníamos** Internet.

Imperfecto: **actividades** o **acontecimientos habituales**

De niño/a
En esa/aquella época } **jugaba** con trenes eléctricos.
} **visitaba** con frecuencia a mis abuelos.

Cuando yo era rico tenía más problemas.

Sí, yo también.

Imperfecto: **circunstancias, descripciones**

**Era** Navidad.
**Hacía** frío.
No **había** nadie en la calle.
**Estaba** muy cansado.

Pretérito: información presentada como **acontecimientos o acciones puntuales**, con marcadores como:

Ayer...
Anteayer...
Anoche...
El otro día...
El lunes / martes...
El día 6...
La semana pasada...
El mes / año pasado...
Entre 2006 y 2009...
Por / durante tres meses / años / días...

} **estuve** en Nicaragua.

Imperfecto: información presentada como **circunstancias** en que una acción (pretérito) ocurre

No **tenía** dinero.

{ Por eso
Así que }

no pudo comer en el restaurante.

No llevaba corbata y por eso no me dejaron entrar en el club.

Cuando me encontré con Elvira **llovía** mucho.

Imperfecto: **acción en proceso** cuando otra acción (pretérito) ocurre

**Caminaba** por la calle cuando vi a Elvira.

Imperfecto: acción repetida o habitual en el pasado, no puntual

Antes **hacía** ejercicio todos los días.

Pretérito: acción repetida o habitual en el pasado durante un límite de tiempo específico

**Hice** ejercicio cada día durante tres meses.

 **11–10  Historia de William Walker**

Lean este episodio de la historia de Nicaragua. Después pongan los verbos en pretérito o imperfecto según su uso: (1) acciones o acontecimientos, (2) estados o descripciones, (3) circunstancias y (4) acciones habituales en el pasado.

A mediados del Siglo XIX **COMENZAR** la "fiebre del oro" en California. En aquella época la mayor parte de los viajeros **IR** de la costa este a la costa oeste por mar. Normalmente **VIAJAR** a través de Nicaragua, que **SER** una ruta muy común. Esto **ATRAER** a muchos aventureros, como por ejemplo el estadounidense William Walker. William Walker **SER** un aventurero de Tennessee que **LLEGAR** a Nicaragua en 1855 con 56 hombres, llamados *filibusteros,* para participar en una guerra contra los conservadores. William Walker **QUERER** establecer un estado y controlar la ruta de tránsito a California, y por eso **APODERARSE** del país y **PROCLAMARSE** presidente. Entre 1855 y 1857 **OCURRIR** en Nicaragua la guerra nacional contra William Walker. En aquella época el idioma oficial **SER** el español pero bajo el dominio de Walker **DECLARARSE** el inglés como idioma oficial de Nicaragua. El 19 de marzo de 1857, cuando Walker **ESTAR** en La Hacienda Santa Rosa con sus hombres, las tropas nicaragüenses los **ATACAR** y los **EXPULSAR** del país.

**11–11  El detective privado (II)**

¿Recuerdas a Valerio Guzmá, en la Lección 10? Esto es lo que Valerio hizo.

7:45 Salió de su casa. Entró en su casa otra vez.
8:00 Salió otra vez a la calle. Caminó durante 15 minutos.
8:15 Un carro con una mujer se detuvo a su lado. Él se subió.
8:35 Se bajó en la Plaza de Armas. Siguió a pie.
8:50 Entró en un edificio de oficinas.

Ahora escucha lo que Valerio explica a sus colegas a las 9:00 de la mañana. ¿Puedes completar el informe del detective?

|  ACCIÓN  |  CIRCUNSTANCIAS |
| --- | --- |

1. **Salió** de casa sin darse cuenta de que _____.
   No _____.

2. **Salió** a la calle otra vez pero _____ y _____.

3. Entonces **vio** a su amiga Elvira que _____.

|  CIRCUNSTANCIAS  |  ACCIÓN |
| --- | --- |

4. _____ y por eso Elvira y Valerio **tardaron** veinte minutos.

5. _____, así que Valerio **llegó** mojado a la oficina.

**INTERACCIONES**

11-29 to
11-31

## ESTRATEGIAS PARA LA COMUNICACIÓN ORAL

**Collaboration in conversation (II)**
When narrating a story or event, the speaker applies certain strategies to make sure that the listener is following the narration. Likewise, the listener uses expressions to show that s/he is understanding. We saw this in *Lección 9*.

As a listener, you may also want to show interest, surprise, and other reactions, with expressions like this:

| | |
|---|---|
| *¡No me digas!* | No way! |
| *¿De verdad?* | Really? Is that right? |
| *¿En serio?* | Seriously? |
| *¿Sí?* | Really? |
| *¡Qué bien!* | Great! |
| *¡Qué horror!* | How awful! |
| *¡Qué miedo!* | How scary! |
| *¡Qué pena / lástima!* | What a shame! |
| *¡Qué suerte!* | How lucky! |
| *¡Qué interesante / aburrido / divertido!* | How interesting / boring / fun! |
| *¡Qué gracioso / chistoso!* | How funny! |
| *¡Qué desastre!* | What a disaster! |
| *!No lo puedo creer!* | I can't believe it! |
| *!No te creo!* | I don't believe you! |
| *¡Qué mala suerte!* | How unlucky! |

**11–12 Imprevistos, sorpresas, anécdotas**

Piensa en tres sorpresas, anécdotas o cosas imprevistas que te ocurrieron en algún momento. Completa este cuadro.

| | ¿CUÁNDO? | ¿DÓNDE? | ¿EN QUÉ CINCUNSTANCIAS? | ¿QUÉ PASÓ? |
|---|---|---|---|---|
| 1. | | | | |
| 2. | | | | |
| 3. | | | | |

 Comparte ahora estas historias con tu compañero/a.

**EJEMPLO:**

**E1:** Un verano, cuando era pequeño, mi hermano y yo estábamos en una barca en un lago, en un pueblo pequeño donde vivían mis abuelos. Yo remaba y mi hermano pequeño se cayó al agua. ¡Y yo no sabía nadar!
**E2:** ¿De verdad? ¡Qué susto! ¿No? ¿Y qué hiciste?
**E1:** Pues lo agarré por la camiseta y lo subí a la barca.
**E2:** ¡Qué horror!

Ahora algunos/as voluntarios/as cuentan sus propias historias a la clase. Los demás deben reaccionar con expresiones de interés, sorpresa, etc.

### 11-13  Antes y ahora

Usa este esquema para describir ciertos aspectos de tu vida que contrastan entre antes y ahora.

|  | ANTES | FRECUENCIA | AHORA | FRECUENCIA |
|---|---|---|---|---|
| La comida |  |  |  |  |
| El ejercicio |  |  |  |  |
| Las bebidas |  |  |  |  |
| La lectura |  |  |  |  |
| Los restaurantes |  |  |  |  |
| Las aficiones |  |  |  |  |
| La ropa |  |  |  |  |
| Los viajes / las vacaciones |  |  |  |  |

 Ahora compara tus datos con los de tu compañero/a.

**EJEMPLO:**

**E1:** Yo antes **comía** muchas frutas, cada día, pero ahora casi nunca las como.
**E2:** Sí, yo también. Yo **comía** mejor que ahora. Ahora como mal.

 ### 11-14  Entrevista

Prepara una lista de cinco preguntas para tu compañero/a sobre una de estas etapas de su vida. Luego entrevista a tu compañero/a.

1. Cuando eras niño.

2. Cuando estabas en la escuela secundaria.

3. Antes de llegar a la universidad.

**EJEMPLO:**

¿Qué hacías cuando eras niño? ¿Quiénes eran tus mejores amigos?

### 11-15  Situaciones: *Viaje al futuro*

A historical figure travels to the future where a journalist interviews him/her. The journalist wants to focus on two main events in the life of this person.

**ESTUDIANTE 1**

You are a journalist who has the opportunity to travel through time and interview an important figure from the past. Prepare some questions for him/her related to two events or episodes in his/her life.

**ESTUDIANTE 2**

You are _____ . You have traveled to the future and are now being interviewed by a journalist. Think about two important events in your life: what happened, what did you do, when, where, and under what circumstances.

# TAREA

**Gente en acción**

**Escribir el relato de un episodio o período de la historia de nuestro país.**

## PREPARACIÓN

Para comenzar vamos a conocer un período importante de la historia de otro país: Nicaragua.

Primero miren la foto y comenten con su profesor/a la relevancia de este personaje en la historia de Nicaragua.

Lean este breve esquema que resume un período de la historia de Nicaragua. El esquema presenta acontecimientos puntuales.

### La revolución sandinista (1962–1979)

**1962:** Se funda el Frente Sandinista de Liberación Nacional (FSLN) para luchar contra la dictadura de los Somoza.

**1963:** Daniel Ortega se une al FSLN.

**1974:** El FSLN toma como rehenes a unos funcionarios del gobierno. Consigue la liberación de algunos presos políticos. Se difunde la causa del FSLN en todo el mundo.

**1976:** El Frente Sandinista se divide en varias tendencias. El apoyo popular crece.

**1979:** El FSLN lanza la ofensiva final. Somoza renuncia el 17 de julio y huye a Estados Unidos. El 19 de julio los sandinistas celebran el triunfo de su revolución.

Daniel Ortega

Ahora lean estos párrafos descriptivos y colóquenlos en el lugar apropiado del esquema anterior.

- Hay una dictadura militar muy represiva en el país desde 1933. El país es muy pobre y tiene muchos problemas sociales y económicos. La gente quiere un cambio.

- El presidente Luis Somoza es hijo de Anastasio Somoza, primer dictador de la dinastía. Es un hombre sin escrúpulos y trata muy mal a su pueblo.

Finalmente, escriban una narración incluyendo los datos anteriores. Decidan qué verbos deben estar en pretérito y cuáles en imperfecto. Usen varios de estos conectores para dar fluidez a su narración.

**Acontecimientos puntuales**
- Un mes / año antes (después)…
- Al mes / año siguiente…
- A los dos meses / años…
- Después de un mes / año / tiempo…
- Entonces, luego, (inmediatamente) después…
- Ese / aquel mes / año…
- A partir de + entonces / aquel mes / aquel año / aquel momento…

**Circunstancias / contexto**
- En aquella época…
- Entonces…

**Paso 1** En grupo, decidan qué episodio o período de la historia de su país quieren narrar. Luego preparen una lista de los datos (acontecimientos o acciones) principales de forma cronológica.

**Título (fechas)**                          **Acontecimientos**
Fecha 1: _____
Fecha 2: _____
Fecha 3: _____
Fecha 4: _____
_____: _____

**Paso 2** Escriban ahora sobre las circunstancias relacionadas con cada acontecimiento específico de su lista. Piensen también en descripciones de lugares o personas importantes.

**Circunstancias / contextos / descripciones**
■ _____
■ _____
■ _____
■ _____

**Paso 3** Piensen en algunas relaciones de causa y consecuencia.

┤ AYUDA ├

**Causa y consecuencia**

● Pretérito + **porque** + imperfecto
  **Se fue** porque le **dolía** la cabeza.

● Imperfecto + **y por eso / así que** +
  pretérito
  Le **dolía** la cabeza así que / y por eso
  **se fue.**

■ _____ porque _____.
■ _____ y por eso _____.

**Paso 4** Escriban su relato usando toda la información anterior de forma organizada. No olviden incluir conectores.

**Paso 5** Cada miembro del grupo presenta una parte, en orden cronológico, a la clase.

**Paso 6** Foco lingüístico.

**NUESTRA GENTE**

11-32 to
11-33

## GENTE QUE LEE

### ESTRATEGIAS PARA LEER

**Summarizing a text**

Summarizing a passage that you have read in Spanish can help you synthesize its most important ideas. When reading a text, try to underline the main ideas and circle the key words and phrases. Then approach the task of summarizing it by asking the following five questions:

| | | | |
|---|---|---|---|
| *¿Quién? o ¿Quiénes?* | (Who?) | *¿Dónde?* | (Where?) |
| *¿Qué?* | (What?) | *¿Por qué? o ¿Cómo?* | (Why? or How?) |
| *¿Cuándo?* | (When?) | | |

This is especially useful when reading stories or accounts of events that happened in the past.

*ANTES DE LEER*

### 11–16 Heroínas

¿Qué es una heroína? Mira esta lista de nombres. ¿Son heroínas? Justifica tus respuestas. Luego piensa en otras y justifica por qué son heroínas. ¿Conoces otras?

1. Harriet Tubman (1820–1913)    2. Clara Barton (1821–1912)

3. Madre Teresa de Calcuta (1910–1997)    4. Juana de Arco (1412–1431)

### 11–17 Activando estrategias

1. Mira el título y la foto del texto que vas a leer. ¿Qué información te dan sobre este texto? ¿Qué tipo de texto es?

2. Lee la primera frase del texto. ¿Confirma el tipo de texto? ¿De qué período histórico es?

*DESPUÉS DE LEER*

### 11–18 ¿Comprendes?

1. ¿Cuántos días duró la lucha?

2. ¿En qué año ocupó la fortaleza el capitán Nelson?

3. Responde a las preguntas y después haz un breve resumen.

¿Qué? _____

¿Quién? _____

¿Dónde? _____

¿Cuándo? _____

¿Por qué? _____

*A LEER*

## RAFAELA HERRERA, UNA HEROÍNA NICARAGÜENSE

**A**mediados del siglo XVIII, Nicaragua era el principal objetivo de los ataques ingleses a causa de su importancia estratégica y las facilidades que presentaba para la comunicación **interoceánica**. Por eso, en 1762, el gobernador de Jamaica decidió invadir la provincia de Nicaragua por el río San Juan.

El 29 de julio llegó la armada inglesa para apoderarse de la **fortaleza** El Castillo, un lugar que los nicaragüenses usaban para defenderse de los piratas ingleses. El Castillo estaba situado sobre una colina a la orilla derecha del río San Juan. La fortaleza tenía muchos cañones para defenderse de los ataques enemigos. La armada de los invasores británicos contaba con 50 barcos y 2.000 hombres. El día de la invasión la situación en El Castillo no era buena: el comandante Don Pedro Herrera, que estaba gravemente enfermo, murió poco antes de la llegada de los ingleses.

Inmediatamente después de su llegada, el gobernador de Jamaica pidió las llaves de la fortaleza El Castillo a un soldado, pero en ese momento la hija de Don Pedro, Rafaela Herrera, que tenía sólo 19 años, tomó el mando de la fortaleza. Cuenta la historia que Rafaela Herrera dirigió la lucha contra la expedición de soldados británicos y miskitos, logrando detenerlos después de sostener un combate de varios días. Inmediatamente después de tomar el mando, Rafaela dijo la célebre frase: "Que los **cobardes** se rindan y que los **valientes** se queden a morir conmigo". Después disparó varios **cañonazos** que provocaron el pánico y la huida de muchos de los piratas. Durante varios días y noches combatieron a los ingleses hasta que éstos finalmente se retiraron el tres de agosto. Ocho años después la fortaleza cayó en manos del capitán inglés Horacio Nelson, el cual se hizo famoso en la batalla de Trafalgar. Así fue como Rafaela Herrera pasó a la categoría de heroína. La historia de este personaje está llena de misterios sobre su origen y no se sabe mucho sobre su vida. Sin embargo, hoy es un símbolo de **valentía** y **patriotismo** para las mujeres nicaragüenses.

### 11–19 Activando estrategias

1. Di qué significan estas palabras del texto y de qué palabras provienen: "interoceánica" y "patriotismo".
2. Busca la palabra "fortaleza" en el diccionario. ¿Cuántos significados tiene? ¿Cuál es el apropiado en este contexto?
3. Si la palabra "cobardes" significa *cowards*, ¿qué significa la palabra "valientes"? ¿Son nombres o adjetivos? ¿Y la palabra "valentía" es un nombre o un adjetivo?
4. Si la palabra "cañón" significa *cannon*, ¿qué significa la palabra "cañonazos"? ¿Cómo se forma esta palabra?
5. ¿A qué o a quién se refieren las palabras subrayadas "detenerlos" y "éstos"?
6. Identifica el sujeto, el verbo y los complementos de la frase subrayada en el texto.

### 11–20 Expansión

1. ¿Te parece que Rafaela fue una heroína? ¿Por qué?
2. ¿Una persona que defiende su país es siempre un héroe o heroína? Justifica tu opinión.

## GENTE QUE ESCRIBE

11-34 to
11-36

### ESTRATEGIAS PARA ESCRIBIR

**Writing a narrative (II): including circumstances that surround events**

A basic narrative is divided into three parts: (a) the introduction, which sets the scene (situación, contexto, circunstancias) and informs the reader about the events or actions leading up to the main plot of the story; (b) the main events or actions, or high point of the story; (c) the outcome or consequences of the principal events. As you already know, in Spanish this narrative structure is closely related to the effective use of the imperfect or preterit tenses.

1. Identifica las tres partes de la narración en la lectura de la página 193 sobre Rafaela Herrera.
2. Justifica la elección del autor de los tiempos verbales (pretérito o imperfecto) en el primer párrafo y en el segundo.

### MÁS ALLÁ DE LA FRASE

**Use of time markers in narratives (II)**

As you know past tenses are often introduced by specific time markers. A few markers are exclusive to one tense or the other, but most can be used with both.

These markers require the imperfect tense:

| | |
|---|---|
| *En esa / aquella época…* | (*En esa época viajaba mucho; ahora no.*) |
| *Antes…* | (*Antes me gustaba la tele; ahora no.*) |

While these ones require the preterit tense:

| | |
|---|---|
| *de repente…* | (*…de repente oí un ruido.*) |
| *entonces\*, luego…* | (*No tenía sueño; entonces me puse a ver la tele.*) |

\*Note that "entonces" can be used either to mark the consequence of an actiòn (as in the example above), or to refer to a period of time in the past:

| | |
|---|---|
| *Entonces no había Internet.* | (Back then, there was no Internet.) |

The choice of the imperfect or the preterit tenses and the selection of time markers are determined by the way the writer presents the narrative.

## 11–21 Un acontecimiento memorable

Escribe una narración sobre algo memorable que te ocurrió a ti: un accidente en casa o en la carretera, una sorpresa muy agradable, una primera cita que fue un desastre, la primera vez que hiciste algo, etc. Ten en cuenta las tres partes de la narración y escribe los párrafos correspondientes.

 **¡ATENCIÓN!**

Presta atención a la organización cronológica y a la cohesión de los párrafos y del texto. Usa una variedad de marcadores de tiempo y otros recursos cohesivos. Revisa el uso de los tiempos del pasado teniendo en cuenta qué función tienen en la narración: combina contextos y descripciones (uso del imperfecto) con acciones (uso del pretérito).

## COMPARACIONES

### 11-22 Mark Twain en Nicaragua

Lee este texto sobre el viaje del escritor estadounidense Mark Twain a Nicaragua. Después comenta los temas con la clase.

Entre 1866 y 1867 Mark Twain, el periodista y escritor estadounidense autor de clásicos como *Las aventuras de Tom Sawyer* y *Las aventuras de Huckleberry Finn*, recorrió parte de Nicaragua en su viaje desde San Francisco a Nueva York, o sea, del oeste al este de Estados Unidos.

Twain salió de San Francisco en barco el 15 de diciembre de 1866 siguiendo la Ruta del Tránsito, que comunicaba el Atlántico y el Pacífico. Desembarcó en el puerto de San Juan del Sur, en el Pacífico nicaragüense, y desde allá viajó en diligencia hasta el puerto de La Virgen, en la costa suroeste del Lago de Nicaragua. En este puerto abordó un vapor con destino al puerto de San Carlos, situado en la costa sureste del lago. Desde San Carlos viajó por el río en lancha hasta el puerto de San Juan del Norte (o Greytown, como lo bautizaron los ingleses), en la costa atlántica de Nicaragua, donde tomó otro barco rumbo a Nueva York.

Durante su travesía por Nicaragua, Mark Twain elogió las bellezas naturales de la nación centroamericana. Según cuenta en el libro *Mark Twain's Travels with Mr. Brown*, a Twain le impresionó la belleza de la isla de Ometepe, situada en el centro del Lago de Nicaragua, el más grande de Centroamérica. En ese libro, el famoso escritor estadounidense dice de Ometepe:

"En el centro del bello Lago de Nicaragua se levantan dos magníficas pirámides, revestidas por el más suave y concentrado verdor, salpicadas de sombras y por los rayos del sol, cuyas cumbres penetran las ondulantes nubes. Se ven tan aisladas del mundo y su alboroto, tan tranquilas, tan maravillosas, tan sumidas en el sueño y el eterno reposo. [...] Monos aquí y allá; pájaros gorjeando; bellas aves emplumadas. El paraíso mismo, el reino imperial de la belleza —nada que desear para hacerla perfecta".

Volcanes Concepción y Madera

1. ¿Qué era la Ruta del Tránsito y por qué era famosa principalmente? ¿Por qué iba la gente, como Mark Twain, de la costa oeste a la costa este siguiendo esta ruta?
2. ¿Sabes por qué Twain viajaba con mucha frecuencia?
3. En el texto, Twain habla de dos pirámides. ¿A qué se refiere?

### 11-23 Viajeros ilustres

Todos estos famosos personajes viajaron por el continente americano con diferentes propósitos. ¿Sabes por dónde viajaron y por qué razón?

1. Lewis (1774–1809) y Clark (1770–1838)
2. Charles Darwin (1809–1882)
3. Francisco de Orellana (1511–1546)
4. Fernando de Magallanes (1480–1521)

## CULTURA

En Estados Unidos viven alrededor de 290.000 personas de ascendencia nicaragüense, la mayor parte de ellas en el sur de Florida y California. La inmigración a Estados Unidos comenzó en los años sesenta y estaba motivada por razones económicas. Sin embargo durante los ochenta, y debido a la revolución sandinista, muchas familias de clase alta abandonaron Nicaragua y se establecieron en Estados Unidos. Más tarde, la revolución contra el gobierno sandinista provocó la llegada de más inmigrantes. En 1998 el huracán Mitch asoló el país y dejó a más de dos millones de nicaragüenses sin casa. Por ello muchos recibieron residencia temporal o permanente en Estados Unidos.

Sin duda la mujer latina de ascendencia nicaragüense más influyente en Estados Unidos es Hilda Solís, secretaria de trabajo de Estados Unidos desde 2009. Nació en Los Ángeles y es hija de dos inmigrantes: su papá es mexicano y su mamá es nicaragüense. Hilda fue la primera persona de su familia que asistió a la universidad y pagó su educación con la ayuda de becas federales y con empleos a tiempo parcial. Antes de ser secretaria de trabajo fue congresista por California.

 VOCABULARIO

## Acontecimientos y conceptos históricos y político-sociales (*Socio-political and historical concepts and events*)

| | |
|---|---|
| el apoyo | *support* |
| el/la aventurero/a | *adventurer* |
| la bandera | *flag* |
| el castillo | *castle* |
| la colonia | *colony* |
| la colonización | *colonization, settlement* |
| el/la colonizador/a | *colonist* |
| el colono | *settler* |
| el dictador | *dictator* |
| la dictadura | *dictatorship* |
| el estado | *state* |
| la fortaleza | *fortress* |
| el/la funcionario/a | *government official* |
| el gobierno | *government* |
| la independencia | *independence* |
| la lucha | *fight* |
| la nación | *nation* |
| el/la pirata | *pirate* |
| la pobreza | *poverty* |
| la revolución | *revolution* |
| la riqueza | *richess, wealth* |
| la ruta | *rute* |
| el/la soldado | *soldier* |
| el terremoto | *earthquake* |
| el triunfo | *triumph* |
| el/la viajero/a | *traveler* |

## Verbos (*Verbs*)

| | |
|---|---|
| alimentarse | *to feed (oneself)* |
| apoderarse (de) | *to take possession of* |
| apoyar | *to support* |
| atacar | *to attack* |
| convertirse en | *to become* |
| datar de | *to date back to* |
| desembarcar | *to disembark* |
| desolar | *to ruin* |
| embarcar | *to embark, to board* |
| encerrar | *to lock down, to lock up* |
| expulsar | *to throw out, to expel* |

| | |
|---|---|
| firmar | *to sign* |
| formar parte (de) | *to be part of* |
| gobernar | *to govern* |
| habitar | *to inhabit, to dwell* |
| huir | *to escape, to run away* |
| invadir | *to invade* |
| luchar | *to fight* |
| ocasionar | *to cause* |
| ocurrir | *to take place* |
| recorrer | *to travel through* |
| refugiarse | *to take shelter* |
| retirarse | *to retreat, to withdraw* |
| romper | *to break* |

## Adjetivos (*Adjectives*)

| | |
|---|---|
| cobarde | *cowardly* |
| conservador/a | *conservative* |
| defensor/a | *defender* |
| escondido/a | *hidden* |
| honrado/a | *honest, decent* |
| independiente | *independent* |
| malvado/a | *wicked* |
| militar | *military* |
| nómada | *nomadic* |
| revolucionario/a | *revolutionary* |
| valiente | *brave* |

# CONSULTORIO GRAMATICAL

## 1 The Imperfect Tense

|  | -AR HABLAR | -ER TENER | -IR VIVIR |  |
|---|---|---|---|---|
| (yo) | hablaba | tenía | vivía |  |
| (tú) | hablabas | tenías | vivías |  |
| (él, ella, usted) | hablaba | tenía | vivía | REGULAR |
| (nosotros/as) | hablábamos | teníamos | vivíamos |  |
| (vosotros/as) | hablabais | teníais | vivíais |  |
| (ellos, ellas, ustedes) | hablaban | tenían | vivían |  |

|  | SER | IR |  |
|---|---|---|---|
| (yo) | era | iba |  |
| (tú) | eras | ibas |  |
| (él, ella, usted) | era | iba | IRREGULAR |
| (nosotros/as) | éramos | íbamos |  |
| (vosotros/as) | erais | ibais |  |
| (ellos, ellas, ustedes) | eran | iban |  |

## 2 Uses of the Imperfect Tense

The imperfect tense is used to portray various aspects of the background of a story.

■ Details about the context in which the story takes place, such as the time, date, place, weather, etc.

**Eran** las nueve.
*It was nine o'clock.*

**Era** de noche.
*It was evening.*

**Hacía** mucho frío y **llovía**.
*It was very cold and raining.*

**Estábamos** cerca de Managua.
*We were near Managua.*

■ The condition and description of the people in the story.

**Estaba** muy cansado.
*I was very tired.*

Me **sentía** mal.
*I felt sick.*

Yo no **llevaba** anteojos.
*I wasn't wearing glasses.*

■ The existence of things that pertain to the story we are telling.

**Había** mucho tráfico.
*There was a lot of trafic.*

**Había** un camión parado en la carretera.
*There **was** a truck parked on the road.*

■ *To contrast the way things are now and the way they used to be.*

Ahora hablo español y portugués. Antes solo **hablaba** inglés.
*Now I speak Spanish and Portuguese. **I used to speak** only English.*

Antes **tenía** muchos amigos. Ahora sólo tengo dos o tres.
***I used to have** a lot of friends. Now I only have two or three.*

■ *To talk about habitual actions in the past.*

Cuando era niño, **íbamos** a la escuela a pie porque no había autobuses escolares.
*When I was a child, **we used to go** to school by foot because there weren't any school buses.*

Antes no **salía** nunca de noche; no me **gustaba**.
*In the past **I did not go** out at night; **I did not like** it.*

## 3   Contrasting the Preterit and the Imperfect Tenses

■ *The preterit tense presents information as an event.*

Ayer **llovió**.
***It rained** yesterday.*

Ayer por la noche **estuvimos** en un restaurante muy bueno.
*Last night **we were** in a very good restaurant.*

■ *The imperfect tense sets the background to an action that is expressed in the preterit tense.*

**Fuimos** al cine por la noche y al salir, **llovía**.
***We went to** the movies in the evening, and **it was raining** when we came out.*

**Estábamos** en un restaurante muy bueno y **llegó** Rogelio.
***We were** in a very good restaurant and Rogelio **arrived**.*

■ *These types of markers often accompany the preterit tense:*

ayer
anoche
el lunes / martes...
la semana pasada
el año pasado
anteayer
el otro día
el (día) 6
el mes pasado

## 4 Relating Past Events: Cause and Consequence

*To demonstrate the consequences of an action we can use* **así que** *and* **por eso**.

Mónica tuvo que trabajar para pagarse los estudios **porque** su familia no <u>tenía mucho</u> dinero.
*Monica had to work to pay her studies* **because** *her family didn't have a lot of money.*

Su familia no <u>tenía</u> mucho dinero, **así que** Mónica tuvo que trabajar para pagarse los estudios.
*Her family didn't have a lot of money,* **so** *Monica had to work to pay her studies.*

Se fue a casa **porque** le <u>dolía</u> la cabeza.
*S/he went home* **because** *he/she had a headache.*

Le <u>dolía</u> la cabeza, **por eso** se fue a casa.
*S/he had a headache* **so** *s/he went home.*

# 12 GENTE SANA

## 12-1 Para llevar una vida sana (*healthy*)...

¿Qué hay que hacer para llevar una vida sana? Den algunas recomendaciones.

**EJEMPLO:**

Para llevar una vida sana (no) hay que...

## 12-2 En Costa Rica

¿Qué sabes de Costa Rica? Lee este texto y mira los datos para saber más.

Los datos de la Organización Mundial de la Salud (OMS) indican que Costa Rica es el país con mayor esperanza de vida de América Latina (80,1 años). El sistema de salud de Costa Rica es el segundo mejor sistema de América Latina, superado solo por Chile. A nivel mundial está en el puesto 26.

☑

## TAREA

Crear una campaña para la prevención de accidentes o problemas de salud.

## NUESTRA GENTE

Costa Rica
Hispanos/latinos en Estados Unidos

|  | FUENTE (SOURCE) | POSICIÓN MUNDIAL | POSICIÓN EN LATINOAMÉRICA |
|---|---|---|---|
| Desempeño Ambiental (2008) | Universidad de Yale | 5 | 1 |
| Grado de Democracia (2006) | *The Economist* | 25 | 1 |
| Paz Global (2008) | *The Economist* | 34 | 3 |
| Calidad de vida (2005) | *The Economist* | 35 | 3 |
| Índice de Prosperidad (2009) | Instituto Legatum | 38 | 4 |
| Desarrollo humano* (2007) | Naciones Unidas | 54 | 6 |
| Índice de satisfacción de vida | Banco Interamericano de desarrollo | – | 1 |

*El índice de desarrollo humano (IDH) es un indicador social estadístico compuesto de tres parámetros: vida larga y saludable, educación y nivel de vida digno.

Marca las afirmaciones correctas.

1. En Costa Rica se cuida mucho el medioambiente (*environment*).

2. Costa Rica tiene una de las democracias más estables del mundo.

3. Costa Rica es un país muy pacifista.

4. La calidad de vida en Costa Rica es la más alta de Latinoamérica.

5. Costa Rica es el segundo país más próspero de Latinoamérica.

6. Costa Rica tiene un sistema educativo muy bueno.

7. En general la gente de Costa Rica está contenta con su vida.

## ACERCAMIENTOS

### 12–3 Consejos para un corazón sano

Un periódico costarricense publicó estos consejos para prevenir problemas de corazón. Léelos y decide si te estás cuidando bien.

# ¿Qué tal su corazón? ¡Cuídelo!

**¡Cuídelo!**

**¿FUMA?**
Si fuma, **déjelo.**
No será fácil. Al 50% de los fumadores les cuesta mucho.
Hay tratamientos que ayudan (chicles, parches, acupuntura, etc.), sin embargo la voluntad es lo más importante.

**¿TIENE LA TENSIÓN ALTA?**
Si las cifras de tensión son superiores a 140 de máxima y 90 de mínima, **visite** al médico.
La hipertensión es peligrosa. No causa molestias pero poco a poco va deteriorando las arterias y el corazón. Si está tomando medicinas, **no deje** el tratamiento.

**¿TIENE EL COLESTEROL ALTO?**
Si tiene el colesterol superior a 240 mg/dl, **reduzca** el consumo de grasas animales y **aumente** el de frutas y verduras.

**¿BEBE ALCOHOL?**
Un poco de vino es bueno para el corazón, pero más de dos vasos al día dejan de ser saludables. Y **no tome** más de cuatro: pueden ser peligrosos.

**¿TIENE EXCESO DE PESO?**
**Divida** su peso en kilos por el cuadrado de su altura.
Si el resultado está entre 25 y 29, **reduzca** su peso. Si está por encima de 30, debe visitar a un especialista. Si desea adelgazar, **no haga** dietas extremas.

**Ejemplo: usted mide 1,73 metros y pesa 78 kilos.**
**Operaciones:**
1. **El cuadrado de su altura: $1,73 \times 1,73 = 3$.**
2. **El peso dividido entre el cuadrado de su altura: $78 : 3 = 26$.**
   **Conclusión: Usted debe reducir peso.**

**¿HACE EJERCICIO?**
**Dé** un paseo diario de 45 minutos: Es el mejor ejercicio a partir de una cierta edad.
**Tenga** cuidado con los deportes violentos: pueden tener efectos negativos para su corazón.

**¿TIENE ALGÚN RIESGO COMBINADO?**
Si tiene varios de los factores de riesgo anteriores, debe vigilarlos mucho más.

UN FUMADOR DE 40 AÑOS QUE DEJA DE FUMAR GANA CINCO AÑOS DE VIDA CON RESPECTO A OTRO QUE SIGUE FUMANDO. A LOS DOS AÑOS DE DEJARLO, SU CORAZÓN ES COMO EL DE UN NO FUMADOR.

☐ Cuido bien mi corazón.          ☐ ¡Tengo que cambiar urgentemente de vida!
☐ Tengo que cuidarme un poco más.

Ahora pregunta a tu compañero/a y decide si cuida bien su corazón. ¿Qué tiene que hacer para cuidarse más? Dale algún consejo.

**EJEMPLO:**
**E1:** ¿Fumas?
**E2:** Sí, un poco.
**E1:** Tienes que dejar de fumar. Es muy malo para el corazón.

VOCABULARIO EN CONTEXTO

12-01 to
12-09

### 12–4 **Un verano tranquilo**

Una compañía de seguros elaboró esta campaña informativa para evitar los problemas típicos del verano a sus clientes. Lee los textos y completa estas frases con recomendaciones y consejos.

---

**ASEGÚRESE UN VERANO TRANQUILO**

Aquí tiene una serie de consejos para evitar problemas de salud frecuentes en esta época del año.

---

**LESIONES PROVOCADAS POR EL SOL**

Tomar el sol moderadamente es beneficioso: el sol proporciona vitamina D. Sin embargo, si se toma en exceso, el sol se puede convertir en un peligro.

**¿QUÉ HACER?**

**Quemaduras**

Para calmar el dolor es conveniente aplicar agua fría, usar crema hidratante sin grasa y no poner nada en contacto con la piel durante unas horas.

**Insolación**

Si es ligera, apliquese paños húmedos por el cuerpo y la cabeza, beba tres o cuatro vasos de agua salada, uno cada cuarto de hora, y descanse en un lugar fresco. Si es grave, llame al médico. Para prevenir quemaduras es aconsejable utilizar cremas con filtros solares, ponerse un gorro o buscar zonas de sombra, especialmente en las horas del mediodía.

---

**INFECCIONES ALIMENTARIAS**

El calor hace proliferar frecuentemente gérmenes en algunos alimentos, lo que puede provocar diarreas, vómitos y fiebre. No tome alimentos con huevo crudo o poco cocido. Controle también las fechas de caducidad de los productos emvasados y enlatados.

**¿QUÉ HACER?**

Tras una intoxicación de este tipo, haga dieta absoluta el primer día. Tome únicamente limonada alcalina (1litro de agua hervida, 3 limones exprimidos, una pizca de sal, una pizca de bicarbonato y 3 cucharadas soperas de azúcar). El segundo día puede tomar ciertos alimentos en pequeñas cantidades: arroz blanco, yogur, plátano, manzana, zanahoria, etc.

---

### PICADURAS

En verano son frecuentes las picaduras. Las más comunes son las picaduras de abeja y avispa, que pueden provocar reacciones alérgicas, y las de mosquito. Los síntomas más frecuentes son inflamación, dolor y escozor. En algunos casos pueden aparecer diarreas, vómitos, dificultad al tragar, convulsiones, etc. En este caso, hay que llevar al paciente al servicio de emergencias más próximo.

---

1. Si tomas el sol...
   tienes que _____ una gorra y _____ cremas.
2. Si te quemaste muchísimo...
3. Si comes en un restaurante en verano...

4. Si te pica una abeja...
5. Si tienes diarrea...
6. Si, después de una picadura, tienes vómitos...
7. Si tienes síntomas muy graves...

### 12–5 **Y a ellos, ¿qué les pasa?**

| ¿Qué le pasa? | ¿Por qué? | ¿Qué tiene que hacer? |
|---|---|---|
| 1. _____ | _____ | _____ |
| 2. _____ | _____ | _____ |
| 3. _____ | _____ | _____ |

### 12–6 Problemas en vacaciones

¿Has tenido tú alguno de estos problemas durante las vacaciones? ¿Dónde estabas? ¿Con quién estabas? ¿Qué te pasó? ¿Qué síntomas tenías? Cuéntaselo a tus compañeros/as.

**EJEMPLO:**

Yo una vez estaba en la costa de vacaciones con unos amigos, comimos langosta y a las dos horas me puse enfermísimo... Me dolía mucho el estómago.

### 12–7 ¿Qué le duele?

Una serie de personas llegan al hospital por razones diferentes. ¿A qué sección deben ir? ¿A qué especialista deben ver?

**EJEMPLO:**

José Luis tiene que ir a **odontología** en el quinto piso. Tiene que ver al **odontólogo**.

1. A Francisco le duele mucho la garganta, la nariz y los oídos. Está resfriado.
2. Marisa necesita anteojos nuevos.
3. Mercedes trajo a sus hijos a una revisión médica y a ponerles unas vacunas.
4. A José Luis le duelen las muelas.
5. Bartolomé se lesionó jugando al fútbol.
6. Reinaldo tuvo un infarto hace dos meses.
7. Rodrigo tiene depresión y está en tratamiento desde hace seis meses.
8. Rosalinda está embarazada y espera su bebé para noviembre.
9. Marcos está muy enfermo. Tiene cáncer de pulmón.

## HOSPITAL SANTA MARÍA MILAGROSA
## SAN JOSÉ, COSTA RICA

| | |
|---|---|
| Cardiología (3er piso) | Odontología (5º piso) |
| Cirugía general (4º piso) | Oftalmología (5º piso) |
| Cuidados intensivos (4º piso) | Oncología (4º piso) |
| Emergencias médicas (1er piso) | Ortopedia (1er piso) |
| Gastroenterología (4º piso) | Otorrinolaringología (3er piso) |
| Ginecología (2º piso) | Pediatría (2º piso) |
| Medicina del deporte (1er piso) | Psiquiatría (3er piso) |
| Medicina familiar (2º piso) | Radiología (1er piso) |

### 12–8 Síntomas

¿Conoces estas enfermedades? Elige una que conozcas y describe los síntomas, lo que hay que hacer y lo que no se debe hacer. Tu compañero/a tratará de adivinar cuál es.

**EJEMPLO:**

**E1:** Cuando tienes esto te duelen los ojos. No hay que tomar el sol, y hay que lavarse bien los ojos.

**E2:** ¡La conjuntivitis!

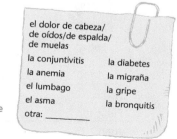

el dolor de cabeza/
de oídos/de espalda/
de muelas

la conjuntivitis     la diabetes

la anemia     la migraña

el lumbago     la gripe

el asma     la bronquitis

otra: _____

GRAMÁTICA EN CONTEXTO

12-10 to
12-36

 **12–9  La historia clínica**

Juan José Morales tuvo que ir a emergencias porque se cayó. El enfermero completó esta ficha.

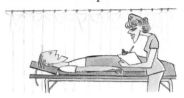

**Nombre:** Juan José    **Apellidos:** Morales Ramos
**Edad:** 31 años    **Peso:** 85 kilos    **Estatura:** 1,81metros
**Grupo sanguíneo:** A+
**Enfermedades:** meningitis, hepatitis
**Operaciones:** apendicitis, menisco
**Alergias:** ninguna
**Observaciones:** paciente hipertenso, fumador
**Medicación actual:** cápsulas contra la hipertensión
**Motivo de la visita:** dolor agudo en la rodilla izquierda producido por una caída

Ahora escuchen este diálogo entre el enfermero y una paciente. Completen una ficha similar.

| | |
|---|---|
| Nombre: | Apellidos: |
| Edad: | Peso: |
| Grupo sanguíneo: | Estatura: |
| Operaciones: | Enfermedades: |
| Observaciones: | Alergias: |
| Medicación actual: | |
| Motivo de la visita: | |
| Diagnóstico preliminar: | |

**EJEMPLO:**

**E1:** ¿Es alérgico a algo?
**E2:** Sí, tiene alergia a la penicilina.

**12–10  ¡Pobrecitos!**

Mira las fotos de Javier, Félix y Juan. Escribe qué les pasa y qué crees que deben y no deben hacer. Usa formas de imperativo y algunos adverbios terminados en -*mente*.

**Javier**          **Félix**          **Juan**

| | ¿QUÉ LE PASA? | RECOMENDACIONES |
|---|---|---|
| Javier | | **¡Camina** muy **lentamente!** |
| Félix | | |
| Juan | | |

**LA SALUD**

¿Cuánto pesa/s?
¿Cuánto mide/s?
¿Cuál es su/tu grupo sanguíneo?
¿Es/eres alérgico/a a algo?
¿Ha/s tenido alguna enfermedad grave?
¿Lo/la/te han operado alguna vez?
¿De qué lo/la/te han operado?
¿Toma/s algún medicamento?
¿Qué le/te pasa?

**Estoy** cansado / enfermo / mareado / resfriado...
**No me encuentro bien.**
**No me siento bien.**

**Me siento / encuentro** { cansado.
                             débil.

**Tengo** { un resfriado.
           una indigestión.
           gripe.
           diarrea.

**Tengo dolor de** { muelas.
                     cabeza.
                     barriga.

**Me / te / le duele** { la cabeza.
                         el estómago.
                         una muela.
                         aquí.

**Me / te / le duelen** { los ojos.
                          los pies.

*TÚ* IMPERSONAL

Si **comes** demasiado, **engordas.**
Cuando **tienes** gripe, **te sientes** mal.

## EL IMPERATIVO (MANDATOS)

*Formas Regulares*

TOMAR

| | | |
|---|---|---|
| tú | **toma** | no **tomes** |
| usted | **tome** | no **tome** |

COMER

| | | |
|---|---|---|
| tú | **come** | no **comas** |
| usted | **coma** | no **coma** |

VIVIR

| | | |
|---|---|---|
| tú | **vive** | no **vivas** |
| usted | **viva** | no **viva** |

*Formas Irregulares*

HACER

| | | |
|---|---|---|
| tú | **haz** | no **hagas** |
| usted | **haga** | no **haga** |

IR

| | | |
|---|---|---|
| tú | **ve** | no **vayas** |
| usted | **vaya** | no **vaya** |

## RECOMENDACIONES Y ADVERTENCIAS

### IMPERSONALES

Cuando se tiene la tensión alta...

...**no hay que comer** sal.

...**no es conveniente comer** sal.

...**no se debe comer** sal.

Tener la tensión alta **puede** ser peligroso para el corazón.

### PERSONALES

Si tienes la tensión alta...

...**no comas** sal.

...**no debes comer** sal.

...**puedes** enfermarte.

No coma mucha sal.

## ADVERBIOS (–MENTE)

| | | |
|---|---|---|
| moderada | → | moderada**mente** |
| excesiva | → | excesiva**mente** |
| frecuente | → | frecuente**mente** |
| regular | → | regular**mente** |
| lenta | → | lenta**mente** |

 **12–11  A dieta**

Estas amigas comentan dos dietas para adelgazar. ¿En qué consisten? ¿Cuál te parece mejor?

| | TIENES QUE... | NO PUEDES... | HAY QUE... |
|---|---|---|---|
| dieta del "sirope" | | | |
| dieta del astronauta | | | |

¿Tienes tú otras sugerencias para adelgazar?

**12–12  Disfrute de la naturaleza en Costa Rica**

Lee este texto sobre las actividades relacionadas con la naturaleza que ofrece Costa Rica. Después completa el cuadro.

- Playas: ideales para la práctica de actividades enfocadas en la naturaleza y el mar, como la pesca deportiva y el buceo, y también para disfrutar del sol y los paseos a orillas del mar. Las playas de la costa del Pacífico son preferidas para la práctica del surf.

- Aventura: Costa Rica es tierra de volcanes, bosques húmedos, enormes cataratas y ríos caudalosos. Esta naturaleza facilita una variada oferta de actividades, que incluye rafting, windsurf, buceo, kayaking, pesca deportiva, o surf.

- Ecoturismo: El país está dividido en 20 parques naturales, ocho reservas biológicas y una serie de áreas protegidas que cautivan a los amantes de las actividades ecoturísticas. La oferta de excursiones es muy variada: desde paseos a caballo hasta caminatas por senderos montañosos y salidas guiadas para la observación de aves. El Parque Nacional Tortuguero es famoso por sus tortugas marinas.

| | IMPERATIVO NEGATIVO | IMPERATIVO | TÚ IMPERSONAL |
|---|---|---|---|
| Si vas a las playas... | **no vayas** sin bronceador | **practica** el surf y la pesca | **puedes** bucear / **necesitas** bronceador |
| Si quieres aventura... | | | |
| Si te gusta el ecoturismo... | | | |
| Si quieres conocer algún parque natural... | | | |
| Si te gustan los animales... | | | |
| Si te gusta el deporte... | | | |

## INTERACCIONES

12-37 to
12-39

### ESTRATEGIAS PARA LA COMUNICACIÓN ORAL

**Verbal courtesy (II)**

As we have seen in *Lección 8* and in this lesson, the command forms have many more functions than just giving orders or commands. We can use them to give advice, recommendations and warnings. Other uses of the command forms are:

1. To attract someone's attention:
   - *Oye / oiga, ¿me puede decir qué hora es?*
   - *Disculpa / disculpe, ¿dónde está la oficina del doctor Rosales?*
   - *Mira / mire, éste es el parque donde quiero ir de vacaciones.*
2. To encourage the listener:
   - *Pasa / pase y siéntate / siéntese, por favor.*
   - *No te preocupes / se preocupe. Todo va a salir bien.*
   - *¿Te importa si uso este libro?*
   - *Sí, claro, úsalo.*
3. In fixed expressions:
   - *¡No me digas!* (You're kidding!)
   - *¡Ven! Vamos a caminar.* (Come on! Let's go for a walk.)

 **12–13 Con cortesía**

Pide a tu compañero/a permiso para hacer estas cosas. Tu compañero/a te debe responder usando imperativos para animarte (*encourage you*).

1. Quieres usar su coche.
2. Has perdido el bolígrafo que tu compañero te prestó. Necesitas otro.
3. Quieres ponerte su abrigo porque tienes frío.
4. Tocas la puerta. Quieres entrar en su cuarto.
5. Quieres comer más pizza.
6. Quieres poner la tele porque hay un partido de fútbol.
7. Has roto el iPod de tu amigo/a. Quieres comprarle otro.

**EJEMPLO:**

**E1:** Disculpa, ¿puedo usar tu carro? Tengo que ir al aeropuerto.
**E2:** Sí, claro, úsalo.

**12–14 Hacer deporte para estar sano**

Completen individualmente el cuadro con información sobre los deportes que practican. Luego intercambien la información. Háganse preguntas para saber más de estos deportes.

| DEPORTE | PROPÓSITO | TRES RECOMENDACIONES |
|---------|-----------|----------------------|
| 1. | Para hacer/jugar a...<br>Si quieres hacer/jugar... | |
| 2. | | |
| 3. | | |

**EJEMPLO:**

**E1:** Yo hago surf. Para hacer surf **hay que** tener mucho equilibrio, **tienes que** concentrarte mucho y **debes** nadar muy bien. **Puede** ser peligroso.
**E2:** Si quiero aprender, ¿qué me recomiendas?
**E1:** Mira, te recomiendo tres cosas: **compra** una buena tabla, **ve** a una buena playa y **practica** mucho.

12–15 **A la aventura**

Ustedes están de vacaciones en Costa Rica. Uno de ustedes es experto en windsurfing y el otro en rafting. Den tres recomendaciones (basadas en la información de los textos) a su compañero/a.

### Windsurfing

 Los vientos que cruzan Costa Rica durante los meses secos crean las condiciones necesarias en la parte noroeste del país para realizar este deporte. En esta región se encuentra el lago Arenal, uno de los puntos más reconocidos y premiados mundialmente. Durante la estación seca el viento alcanza velocidades promedio de 33 millas por hora, algo que solamente pueden manejar los expertos del windsurfing. Durante los meses lluviosos los vientos se calman y es el lugar perfecto para aprender este deporte. La Costa Pacífica (Golfo de Papagayo) es la mejor área para surfeadores con menos experiencia, ya que hay aguas más tranquilas y vientos menos intensos.

### Descenso de rápidos (rafting)

 En Costa Rica se encuentran algunos de los mejores ríos del mundo para correr rápidos.

- Pacuare: Este río está en la lista de los 10 mejores del mundo para rafting y kayaking. Su curso atraviesa una serie de increíbles y densos bosques, y tiene al menos 20 cascadas. Su recorrido se puede hacer desde mediados de mayo hasta mediados de marzo.
- Sarapiqui: Un bellísimo río ideal para principiantes, disponible de mayo a mediados de marzo. Tiene salvajes viajes al principio, un suave flotar al final y una sección de interminables rápidos en el medio. Ideal para los amantes de la naturaleza.

**EJEMPLO:**

**E1:** ¿Cuándo me recomiendas aprender a hacer windsurf?
**E2:** Si quieres aprender a hacer windsurf **hazlo** durante los meses de lluvia, porque hay menos viento.

 12–16 **Situaciones: *En la clínica estudiantil***

Two students are at the student health clinic. They are in the doctor's office.

**ESTUDIANTE A**

When you were coming out of the dorm, you tripped and fell down the stairs. As a result, you are now in a lot of pain. Explain your symptoms to the doctor. Answer the doctor's questions as accurately as possible.

**ESTUDIANTE B**

After having lunch in the cafeteria, you got sick. Several hours passed but you didn't get better, so you decided to go to the doctor. Explain your symptoms to the doctor. Answer the doctor's questions as accurately as possible.

**ESTUDIANTE C**

You are a doctor at the student health clinic. Two students with different health problems come to see you. Listen to them, ask them questions, make diagnoses, and give them some recommendations.

# TAREA  Gente en acción

**Crear una campaña para la prevención de accidentes o problemas de salud.**

## PREPARACIÓN

¿Cuál de los siguientes temas te parece más interesante? Ordénalos de más a menos interesante.

- ☐ los accidentes de tráfico
- ☐ los trastornos alimenticios (anorexia, obesidad, etc.)
- ☐ la adicción al tabaco
- ☐ las drogadicciones
- ☐ la vida sedentaria

 Ahora observen estas fotos de campañas publicitarias. Relacionen cada una con los temas anteriores. Comenten los mensajes que transmiten y cómo los transmiten. Elijan el tema de su campaña y el dibujo que les sirve como inspiración.

**Paso 1** Elaboren una lista de palabras o expresiones relacionadas con el tema que eligieron para su campaña. Usen el dibujo para pensar en palabras. Después piensen en otras imágenes o gráficos que podrían incluir en su campaña.

**Paso 2** Para obtener más información, lean la noticia relacionada con el tema que han elegido. ¿Qué datos quieren incluir en su campaña?

### 1. Aumento de la anorexia

Según la ONU, Argentina es el segundo consumidor mundial de "anorexígenos". Una de cada 10 adolescentes argentinas sufre alguna patología alimentaria y unas 400.000 argentinas optan por consumir diariamente drogas para quitar el hambre. El aumento de su consumo es considerado un síntoma más de la excesiva obsesión por la figura que se vive en muchos países de América Latina. México, Colombia, Perú y Chile también están sufriendo una explosión de casos.

### 3. Aumenta el alcoholismo en menores

El número de niños y adolescentes que beben en exceso ha aumentado dramáticamente en los últimos años en Latinoamérica. Las estadísticas muestran un aumento del 20% en el número de menores de 18 años admitidos en hospitales por trastornos como envenenamiento de alcohol y un aumento del consumo de alcohol, especialmente en menores de 21 años. Los expertos afirman que parte del problema es el desconocimiento de los peligros del consumo de alcohol.

### 2. Fumar altera el cerebro "como las drogas"

Según un estudio publicado en el *Journal of Neuroscience*, fumar cigarrillos causa el mismo daño al cerebro que el uso de drogas ilícitas, como la cocaína, produciendo cambios en el cerebro que son evidentes años después de que alguien deja de fumar.

### 4. Más ejercicio, más felices

Según los científicos, el ejercicio físico intenso libera endorfinas en el cerebro, lo que explicaría la euforia que sienten las personas que lo practican. El ejercicio aumenta la sensación de bienestar y de felicidad.

### 5. Consumo de drogas en aumento

El aumento global en el consumo de drogas sintéticas supone una carga para toda la sociedad, ya que estas drogas están afectando a los sistemas de salud, que deben costear el tratamiento y la rehabilitación de los pacientes. Los efectos de las drogas sintéticas no son inmediatos, pero su excesivo consumo afecta a ciertas partes del cerebro que controlan los movimientos y la memoria. Estos daños son, en muchos casos, permanentes.

**Paso 3** Escriban su campaña, incluyendo

1. la descripción del problema, sus causas y consecuencias principales,
2. una serie de recomendaciones y consejos para evitarlo y combatirlo, y
3. un eslogan.

**Paso 4** Presentación de la campaña.
Presenten su folleto en forma de cartel y expongan ante la clase su campaña. La clase decide qué campaña es la mejor.

**Paso 5** Foco lingüístico.

---

**AYUDA**

**Relacionar ideas**

La nicotina tiene efectos muy nocivos; **sin embargo**, muchas personas fuman.

La gente bebe mucho por la noche y **por eso** hay tantos accidentes de tráfico.

**Adverbios en -*mente***
moderad**amente**
excesiv**amente**
especial**mente**
frecuente**mente**

**NUESTRA GENTE**

12-40 to
12-41

## GENTE QUE LEE

---

### ESTRATEGIAS PARA LEER

**Considering the type of text**

One important pre-reading strategy is to consider the type of text that you will be reading. For example, when you are about to read a newspaper article, you can anticipate certain structures (based on headlines or titles, subtitles, etc.), and a specific writing style. What could you expect to find if you were about to read the following types of texts?

1. a schedule
2. a chart or graphic
3. a short story
4. a children's story

5. a brochure
6. a letter
7. an interview

8. a poem
9. a restaurant menu
10. an e-mail

---

### ANTES DE LEER

### 12–17 El sistema de salud ideal

Ordena, de más a menos importante, las características de un buen sistema de salud en cualquier país.

☐ acceso gratuito para los ciudadanos con menos recursos

☐ médicos que te prestan mucha atención y que son muy amables

☐ hospitales muy acogedores

☐ bajos precios de los servicios médicos

☐ rapidez en la atención médica (cirugías, urgencias…)

☐ acceso para todo el mundo (visitantes, inmigrantes…)

☐ médicos muy bien preparados

¿Conoces el sistema de salud de tu país? ¿Qué características tiene? Señala los aspectos positivos y los negativos.

### 12–18 Activando estrategias

1. Considera el título del texto. ¿Es informativo?
2. Mira por encima (*skim*) el texto durante 30 segundos. ¿Qué información has obtenido?
3. Busca la siguiente información en el texto usando la técnica del escaneado (*scanning*):

   A. Número de hospitales y clínicas en Costa Rica.

   B. Porcentaje de visitantes que van a Costa Rica para obtener servicios médicos.

### DESPUÉS DE LEER

### 12–19 ¿Comprendes?

1. Costa Rica es el tercer país en esperanza de vida. Da dos razones que expliquen esto.
2. En Costa Rica no hay ejército. ¿Qué consecuencia positiva tiene este hecho?
3. ¿Por qué muchos médicos de Costa Rica hablan más de un idioma?
4. ¿Cuánto tiene que pagar un extranjero residente para tener acceso al sistema de salud?
5. ¿Por qué muchas personas van a Costa Rica para tener cirugía plástica?

*A LEER*

## CUIDADO MÉDICO DE CALIDAD PARA TODO EL MUNDO

Según un informe de la Organización Mundial de la Salud (OMS), Costa Rica es el tercer país del mundo en esperanza de vida, detrás de Japón y Francia, y delante de Gran Bretaña y Estados Unidos. <u>Esto</u> es **especialmente** relevante si se considera que su renta per cápita es una décima parte de la de <u>esos países</u>. Ciertamente, algunas razones de <u>este fenómeno</u> se pueden encontrar en la forma de vida menos frenética de los costarricenses: los alimentos frescos, saludables y sin **conservantes**, el clima tropical…; <u>sin embargo</u>, la razón principal es que su gobierno continúa un **compromiso** de muchos años: el de ofrecer a cada uno de sus ciudadanos servicio **asequible** en uno de los mejores sistemas sanitarios del mundo.

El sistema médico de Costa Rica es el segundo de América latina y figura entre los 30 mejores del mundo. La ausencia de ejército y el énfasis del gobierno en el bienestar social y educativo de sus ciudadanos han dado como resultado un sistema de salud **altamente** desarrollado. El Dr. Soto, jefe de cirugía del Hospital México, dice que Costa Rica es única en su posición mundial con respecto a la sanidad. "He estudiado todos los sistemas de salud en las Américas y puedo asegurarle que en ninguna parte se puede encontrar lo que ofrece Costa Rica a sus ciudadanos". Con una red estatal de 29 hospitales y de más de 250 clínicas a través del país, el sistema público de salud tiene la responsabilidad de proporcionar servicios médicos de bajo costo a toda la gente de Costa Rica y a cualquier residente extranjero o visitante. Los extranjeros residentes sólo tienen que pagar una pequeña tasa anual basada en sus ingresos.

Generalmente los doctores y dentistas de Costa Rica reciben su entrenamiento médico en Costa Rica. <u>Después</u> viajan al extranjero para formarse en especialidades diversas y <u>lo</u> hacen en excelentes universidades de Europa o Estados Unidos. <u>Por eso</u> no es extraño encontrar médicos que hablan dos o más idiomas. <u>Muchos de ellos</u> trabajan por la mañana en el sistema público y <u>luego</u> en su **consulta** privada.

Se calcula que alrededor del 14% de todos los visitantes que llegan a Costa Rica <u>lo</u> hacen con el propósito de recibir algún tipo de atención médica. Gente de todo el mundo llega para visitar dentistas, tener cirugías de diversos tipos o pasar una temporada en uno de los balnearios del país. Costa Rica <u>también</u> es destino para aquellos que buscan la fuente de la eterna juventud; los cirujanos plásticos de este país atienden diariamente a cientos de visitantes para llevar a cabo reconstrucciones faciales, reducciones o aumentos de pecho, lipoesculturas, eliminación permanente del **vello** no deseado, injertos capilares, borrado de cicatrices, y muchos otros tratamientos de belleza. <u>Además</u>, el costo de estos tratamientos y cirugías suele ser un tercio más bajo que el de otros países como los Estados Unidos, llegando a veces a costar la mitad.

### 12–20 Activando estrategias

1. Observa las tres palabras del primer párrafo marcadas en negrita: "especialmente", "conservantes" y "compromiso". ¿Crees que son cognados o falsos cognados? Usa el diccionario si no sabes la respuesta.

2. Usa el contexto para adivinar el significado de las palabras "asequible" y "consulta".

3. Si "alto" significa *tall*, ¿qué significa "altamente"? ¿Qué categoría gramatical es y cómo se forma? Busca dos palabras más en el texto de la misma categoría y formación.

4. Busca en el diccionario la palabra "vello". Identifica primero la categoría y dale el significado adecuado al contexto. ¿Sabes un sinónimo?

### 12–21 Expansión

¿Qué opinas del sistema de salud de Costa Rica? Menciona aspectos positivos y negativos, ¿Conoces otros países con sistemas de salud como éste o mejores?

**GENTE QUE ESCRIBE**

12-42 to
12-43

## ESTRATEGIAS PARA ESCRIBIR

**The good foreign language writer**

Good writers use similar strategies:

1. They have a plan, but are willing to change it as they write, coming up with new ideas.
2. They are willing to revise, and consider early drafts to be tentative.
3. They delay editing and worry about formal correctness only after they are satisfied with the ideas and the organization.
4. They stop frequently and reread what they have written.
5. They write a bit every day and take breaks. This strategy produces better writing.

## MÁS ALLÁ DE LA FRASE

**Reviewing your text for cohesion**

In order to go beyond the sentence level, you need mechanisms to give cohesion to your text. When reviewing the text, make sure you have used a variety of connectors (to organize, to add and sequence ideas, to introduce examples, to clarify information, or to express relations of cause and effect). The use of referent words that carry information about previous elements (pronouns such as *él, la, ello, lo, la, los, las*, or demonstratives such as *éste, esto*, etc.) will eliminate excessive repetition. To make sure you do not repeat information, revise your draft and look for information that can be replaced with these referents.

1. Find in the text about Costa Rica (A leer section) the following underlined words : "esto", "esos países", "este fenómeno", "muchos de ellos" y "lo". What or who are they referring to? How do they help you as a reader to understand the text?
2. Now find the underlined connectors "sin embargo", "después", "por eso", "luego", "también" y "además". What is their function?

### 12–22 Artículo informativo

El periódico en español de tu escuela necesita un artículo. Con recomendaciones y consejos para llevar una vida saludable durante el año académico. Escribe tu artículo después de reflexionar sobre los posibles significados de este gráfico.

 **¡ATENCIÓN!**

Para generar ideas, piensa en el propósito de tu artículo y las personas que van a leerlo. Luego desarrolla un esquema y decide cómo quieres organizar la información. Sigue los Pasos 1 a 8 y revisa los mecanismos que has usado para conseguir cohesión textual.

## COMPARACIONES

### 12–23 Salud y biodiversidad

¿Qué es la biodiversidad? ¿Crees que tiene relación con la salud? Da algunos ejemplos. Luego lee el texto y responde a las preguntas.

**Biodiversidad en Costa Rica**

Recientes investigaciones sobre biodiversidad y salud humana demuestran que la salud del ser humano depende completamente de la salud del ecosistema. Costa Rica es uno de los mejores ejemplos de un país que se preocupa por su biodiversidad. Está dividido en 20 parques naturales, 8 reservas biológicas y una serie de áreas protegidas. Su excelente sistema de conservación garantiza la supervivencia de las especies autóctonas.

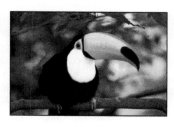

El Parque Internacional La Amistad, patrimonio de la humanidad debido a su excepcional valor universal, tiene un gran número de extraordinarios hábitats. Una mezcla de bosques muy altos y húmedos cubre la mayor parte del territorio. Se han observado más de 263 especies de anfibios y reptiles, así como también mamíferos como pumas, jaguares, monos, etc. Hay más de 400 especies de aves.

La Isla del Coco, en el Océano Pacífico, es un laboratorio natural para el estudio de la evolución de las especies. Hay unas 235 especies de plantas, 85 de aves, 200 de peces y 18 de corales. También es común encontrar tiburones blancos y aves marinas como la gaviota y el pingüino. Las leyes de conservación mantienen el balance entre los ecosistemas de la isla y ayudan a preservar los organismos marinos en peligro de extinción.

1. ¿Existe en tu país una preocupación por la biodiversidad y la salud del medio ambiente? ¿Crees que es suficiente? ¿Hay parques nacionales y espacios naturales protegidos? Da algunos ejemplos.

 2. Hagan una lista de seis recomendaciones para el gobierno de su país con el objetivo de mejorar la salud del ecosistema y, consecuentemente, la de todos.

## CULTURA

La población de origen costarricense en Estados Unidos asciende a aproximadamente 117.000 personas y se ubica principalmente en California, Florida, Texas y el área de Nueva York. Los costarricenses que emigraron en el pasado a Estados Unidos no lo hicieron por problemas políticos o económicos. Por ello, sólo unos 60.000 costarricenses han emigrado a Estados Unidos desde 1930.

Óscar Arias es el costarricense más conocido a nivel internacional. Recibió el Premio Nobel de la Paz en 1987 gracias a sus esfuerzos para conseguir la paz en América Central. Fue presidente de Costa Rica desde 2006 hasta 2010, y también desde 1986 a 1990.

Franklin Chang-Díaz es un astronauta y físico costarricense de nacimiento, nacionalizado estadounidense. Completó su doctorado en ingeniería nuclear en MIT. Fue el primer latinoamericano en la NASA y ha realizado siete misiones en transbordador espacial. En 2005 fundó un laboratorio llamado Ad Astra Rocket en Costa Rica. Su investigación se concentra en la construcción de un motor de plasma que permita la realización de viajes espaciales más rápidos y económicos.

Óscar Arias

Franklin Chang-Díaz

## 🔊 VOCABULARIO

### Medicina: síntomas y enfermedades
### (Medicine: symptoms and illnesses)

| | |
|---|---|
| la alergia | *allergy* |
| el ataque al corazón | *heart attack* |
| el cansancio | *tiredness* |
| el cigarrillo | *cigarette* |
| el/la cirujano/a | *surgeon* |
| la cirugía | *surgery* |
| la consulta | *(doctor's) office* |
| el dolor | *pain* |
| el dolor de cabeza | *headache* |
| el dolor de espalda | *backache* |
| el dolor de estómago | *stomachache* |
| el dolor de muelas | *toothache* |
| el dolor de oídos | *earache* |
| la enfermedad | *illness, sickness* |
| la fiebre | *fever* |
| el/la fumador/a | *smoker* |
| la gripe | *flu* |
| la inflamación | *swelling, inflammation* |
| la insolación | *sunstroke* |
| el insomnio | *sleeplessness, insomnia* |
| la intoxicación | *food poisoning* |
| el jarabe | *syrup* |
| la lesión | *injury* |
| el mareo | *dizziness* |
| el masaje | *massage* |
| la medicina | *medicine* |
| el/la médico | *doctor* |
| la operación | *surgery* |
| la pastilla | *pill* |
| el peso | *weight* |
| la picadura | *sting, bite* |
| la píldora | *pill* |
| la quemadura | *burn* |
| la receta | *prescription* |
| el régimen | *diet* |
| el resfriado | *cold* |
| el riesgo | *risk* |
| la salud | *health* |
| el seguro médico | *health insurance* |
| el servicio de emergencias | *emergency room* |
| el síntoma | *symptom* |
| la tensión | *blood pressure* |
| la tos | *cough* |
| el tratamiento | *treatment* |

### Adjetivos (Adjectives)

| | |
|---|---|
| adicto/a | *addicted* |
| alérgico/a | *allergic* |
| grave | *severe, serious* |
| inconsciente | *unconscious* |
| mareado/a | *dizzy* |
| peligroso/a | *dangerous* |
| recomendable | *advisable* |

### Verbos (Verbs)

| | |
|---|---|
| adelgazar | *to loose weight* |
| advertir (ie) (de) | *to notice, to warn* |
| aumentar | *to increase* |
| caerse | *to fall* |
| cansarse | *to get tired* |
| cuidarse | *to take care of oneself* |
| dejar de | *to stop doing something* |
| descansar | *to rest* |
| desmayarse | *to faint* |
| doler | *to hurt* |
| enfermarse | *to get sick* |
| engordar | *to gain weight* |
| estirarse | *to stretch* |
| evitar | *to avoid* |
| fumar | *to smoke* |
| lesionarse | *to get hurt, to get injured* |
| marearse | *to get dizzy* |
| medir (i) | *to measure* |
| operar | *to operate on* |
| operarse (de) | *to have surgery* |
| padecer (zc) | *to suffer* |
| pesar | *to weight* |
| picar | *to itch, to sting* |
| prevenir | *to prevent* |
| quemarse | *to get burned* |
| recetar | *to prescribe* |
| tumbarse | *to lie down* |
| resfriarse | *to get a cold* |
| romperse (algo) | *to break (something)* |
| sudar | *to sweat* |
| toser | *to cough* |
| vomitar | *to vomit* |

### Otras palabras y expresiones
### (Other words and expressions)

| | |
|---|---|
| la advertencia | *warning* |
| el consumo | *consumption* |
| enfermarse | *to get sick* |
| estar resfriado/a | *to have a cold* |
| hacerse daño | *to hurt oneself* |
| ponerse enfermo / enfermarse | *to get sick* |
| tener exceso de peso | *to be overweight* |
| tener un accidente | *to have an accident* |

# CONSULTORIO GRAMATICAL

## 1 Commands Forms

Command forms in Spanish have affirmative and negative forms. In Lección 6 we studied affirmative forms. In this lesson we will review those, and also study negative commands.

(Please see the Consultorio gramatical in Lección 6 for a review of affirmative command forms, and the multiple uses of command forms in Spanish).

### REGULAR FORMS

|  | TOMAR | BEBER | VIVIR |
|---|---|---|---|
| (tú) | toma no tomes | bebe no bebas | vive no vivas |
| (usted) | tome no tome | beba no beba | viva no viva |

 **¡ATENCIÓN!**

When asking others not to do something, the imperative form may come across as aggressive, and therefore it is only used in very casual situations or when softened by other expressions.

Por favor, **no se siente** ahí. Esa silla está rota.   Carlitos, **no comas** tan deprisa......
Please, **don't sit** there. That chair is broken.   Carlitos, **don't eat** so quickly...

### IRREGULAR FORMS

| HACER | (tú) | **haz** | no **hagas** |  | SALIR | (tú) | **sal** | no **salgas** |
|---|---|---|---|---|---|---|---|---|
|  | (usted) | **haga** | no **haga** |  |  | (usted) | **salga** | no **salga** |
| PONER | (tú) | **pon** | no **pongas** |  | DECIR | (tú) | **di** | no **digas** |
|  | (usted) | **ponga** | no **ponga** |  |  | (usted) | **diga** | no **diga** |
| SER | (tú) | **sé** | no **seas** |  |  |  |  |  |
|  | (usted) | **sea** | no **sea** |  |  |  |  |  |
| IR | (tú) | **ve** | no **vayas** |  |  |  |  |  |
|  | (usted) | **vaya** | no **vaya** |  |  |  |  |  |
| VENIR | (tú) | **ven** | no **vengas** |  |  |  |  |  |
|  | (usted) | **venga** | no **venga** |  |  |  |  |  |
| TENER | (tú) | **ten** | no **tengas** |  |  |  |  |  |
|  | (usted) | **tenga** | no **tenga** |  |  |  |  |  |

Ve a clase. Es tarde.

¡No vayas; espera! ¡Ven aquí!

## Use of negative commands

Negative commands are used primarily to make recommendations, give warnings, and give advice.

**No fumes** tanto; tienes tos.
**Don't smoke** so much; you have a cough.

**No ponga** sal en el pollo y **no beba** alcohol.
**Don't put** salt on the chicken and **don't drink** alcohol.

**No salgas** ahora; hay mucho tráfico.
**Don't go out** now; there is too much traffic.

## Pronoun placement

In contrast to what happens with the affirmative imperative, in the negative form the direct object, the indirect object, and reflexive pronouns precede the verb.

Di**le** a Luisa la verdad.
Tell Luisa the truth.

No **le** digas nada a Luisa.
Don't tell anything to Luisa.

Esas pastillas, tóma**las** en ayunas.
Those pills, take them before breakfast.

Esas pastillas, no **las** tomes en ayunas.
Those pills, don't take them before breakfast.

Pónga**se** la chaqueta.
Put the jacket on.

No **se** ponga la chaqueta.
Don't put the jacket on.

¿Me la dejas?

De acuerdo, pero cuídala bien.

## 2 Recommendations, Advice, and Warnings

As we saw in Lección 5, there are many ways to give recommendations and advice.
These ways can be more or less personal.

IMPERSONAL

Cuando tienes la tensión alta,
Si **tienes** la tensión alta,

{ no se debe
{ no hay que
{ no es bueno        comer sal.
{ no es aconsejable

When you have high blood pressure,
If you have high blood pressure,

{ you mustn't
{ you shouldn't
{ it is not good to        eat salt.
{ it is not recommended to

Algunos deportes **pueden** ser peligrosos para el corazón.
Some sports **can** be dangerous for your heart.

PERSONAL

Si tienes dolor de estómago,

{ no comas sal.
{ hay que tomar té.
{ debes tomar té.

If you have a stomachache,

{ don't eat salt.
{ you should have tea.
{ you must have tea.

Si tomas tanto sol, te **puedes** quemar.
If you get so much sun, you can get sunburned.

*Speech bubble:* Tienes que dejar de fumar. Y debes ir al médico, no tienes buena cara.

## 3 Impersonal *Tú*

The second person of a verb can have an impersonal meaning in Spanish. It can also serve as a way to talk about oneself indirectly, without saying yo.

Si **comes** demasiado, **engordas.**          Cuando **tienes** dolor de estómago, es bueno tomar té.
(= anybody, everybody)                 (= anybody, everybody)
If **you eat** too much, **you get fat.**       When **you have** a stomachache, it is good to have tea.

**Sales, te acuestas** tarde y luego **te sientes** muy mal.
**You go out, you go to bed** late and then **you feel** very sick.

Remember that we can also express impersonal with **se** and the third person of the verb (see Lección 8).

Si **se come** demasiado, **se engorda.**          Cuando **se tiene** dolor de estómago, es bueno tomar té.
If **one eats** too much, **one gets fat.**       When **one has** a stomachache, it is good to have tea.

## 4 Talking about Health

### Questions at the doctor's office

**¿Cuál es tu / su grupo sanguíneo?**
What's your blood type?

**¿Es/eres alérgico a algo?**
Are you allergic to anything?

**¿Ha/s tenido alguna enfermedad?**
Have you ever had an illness?

**¿Lo / la / te han operado alguna vez?**
Have you ever had surgery?

**¿De qué lo / la / te han operado?**
What kind of surgery have you had?

**¿Toma/s algún medicamento?**
Do you take any medication?

**¿Cuánto mide/s?**
How tall are you?

**¿Cuánto pesa/s?**
What's your weight?

**¿Cómo se/te siente/s?**
How do you feel?

**¿Qué le/te pasa?**
What's the problem?

## To describe physical condition

**Estoy / estás / está......**    cansado/a (tired)
          enfermo/a (sick)
          mareado/a (dizzy)
          resfriado/a (have a cold)

**Tengo / tienes / tiene...**    un resfriado (a cold)
          una indigestión (an indigestion)
          gripe (a cold)
          diarrea (diarrea)

**Tengo / tienes / tiene... dolor de**    muelas (toothache)
          cabeza (headache)
          barriga (stomachache)

**Me / te / le... duele**    la cabeza (my/your/his/her head hurts)
          el estómago (my/your/his/her stomach hurts)
          una muela (my/your/his/her tooth hurts)
          acá (it hurts here)

**Me / te / le... duelen**    los ojos (my eyes hurt)
          los pies (my feet hurt)

**Me encuentro / me siento...**    cansado (I feel tired)
          débil (I feel weak)
          bien/mal (I feel good/bad)

 **¡ATENCIÓN!**

The verb doler is similar to gustar. The subject is the part of the body that hurts, not the person who expresses the condition.

 **¡ATENCIÓN!**

The verbs sentirse and encontrarse are reflexive verbs. The subject is the person who experiences the sensation or condition.

|  | ENCONTRARSE | SENTIRSE |
|---|---|---|
| (yo) | me encuentro | me siento |
| (tú) | te encuentras | te sientes |
| (él, ella, usted) | se encuentra | se siente |
| (nosotros/as) | nos encontramos | nos sentimos |
| (vosotros/as) | os encontráis | os sentís |
| (ellos/as, ustedes) | se encuentran | se sienten |

## 5 Adverbs Ending in *-Mente*

These adverbs are formed from the feminine form of an adjective and are commonly used in Spanish to express the way in which something is done.

         FEMININE ADJECTIVE + **mente**

moderada   ⟶   modera**damente**
excesiva   ⟶   excesiva**mente**
frecuente   ⟶   frecuente**mente**
lenta   ⟶   lenta**mente**
rápida   ⟶   rápida**mente**

Seguramente es una fractura de fémur.

Sí, ocurre frecuentemente con jugadores de fútbol.

 **¡ATENCIÓN!**

The meaning of the adverb created by adding **-mente** is not always the same as that of the adjective from which it was formed.

Yo **personalmente** pienso que eso no es verdad. (≠ de forma personal)
I **personally** think that isn't true.

Hola, Juan, **precisamente** estábamos hablando de ti. (≠ de forma precisa)
Hello, Juan, we were **just** speaking about you.

**Seguramente** iremos de vacaciones a París. (≠ de forma segura)
We will **most likely** go on vacation to Paris.

¡Hola! **justamente** quería llamarte. (≠ de forma justa)
Hi! I was **just** going to call you.

# Verb Charts

## REGULAR VERBS: SIMPLE TENSES

| Infinitive Present Participle Past Participle | Indicative | | | | | Subjunctive | | Imperative |
|---|---|---|---|---|---|---|---|---|
| | Present | Imperfect | Preterit | Future | Conditional | Present | Imperfect | Commands |
| hablar hablando hablado | hablo hablas habla hablamos habláis hablan | hablaba hablabas hablaba hablábamos hablabais hablaban | hablé hablaste habló hablamos hablasteis hablaron | hablaré hablarás hablará hablaremos hablaréis hablarán | hablaría hablarías hablaría hablaríamos hablaríais hablarían | hable hables hable hablemos habléis hablen | hablara hablaras hablara habláramos hablarais hablaran | habla (tú), no hables hable (usted) hablemos hablad (vosotros), no habléis hablen (Uds.) |
| comer comiendo comido | como comes come comemos coméis comen | comía comías comía comíamos comíais comían | comí comiste comió comimos comisteis comieron | comeré comerás comerá comeremos comeréis comerán | comería comerías comería comeríamos comeríais comerían | coma comas coma comamos comáis coman | comiera comieras comiera comiéramos comierais comieran | come (tú), no comas coma (usted) comamos comed (vosotros), no comáis coman (Uds.) |
| vivir viviendo vivido | vivo vives vive vivimos vivís viven | vivía vivías vivía vivíamos vivíais vivían | viví viviste vivió vivimos vivisteis vivieron | viviré vivirás vivirá viviremos viviréis vivirán | viviría vivirías viviría viviríamos viviríais vivirían | viva vivas viva vivamos viváis vivan | viviera vivieras viviera viviéramos vivierais vivieran | vive (tú), no vivas viva (usted) vivamos vivid (vosotros), no viváis vivan (Uds.) |

# REGULAR VERBS: PERFECT TENSES

|  | Indicative | | | | | Subjunctive | |
| --- | --- | --- | --- | --- | --- | --- | --- |
|  | Present Perfect | Past Perfect | Preterite Perfect | Future Perfect | Conditional Perfect | Present Perfect | Past Perfect |
|  | he hablado | había hablado | hube hablado | habré hablado | habría hablado | haya hablado | hubiera hablado |
|  | has comido | habías comido | hubiste comido | habrás comido | habrías comido | hayas comido | hubieras comido |
|  | ha vivido | había vivido | hubo vivido | habrá vivido | habría vivido | haya vivido | hubiera vivido |
|  | hemos | habíamos | hubimos | habremos | habríamos | hayamos | hubiéramos |
|  | habéis | habíais | hubisteis | habréis | habríais | hayáis | hubierais |
|  | han | habían | hubieron | habrán | habrían | hayan | hubieran |

# IRREGULAR VERBS

| Infinitive / Present Participle / Past Participle | Indicative | | | | | Subjunctive | | Imperative |
| --- | --- | --- | --- | --- | --- | --- | --- | --- |
|  | Present | Imperfect | Preterit | Future | Conditional | Present | Imperfect | Commands |
| andar<br>andando<br>andado | ando<br>andas<br>anda<br>andamos<br>andáis<br>andan | andaba<br>andabas<br>andaba<br>andábamos<br>andabais<br>andaban | anduve<br>anduviste<br>anduvo<br>anduvimos<br>anduvisteis<br>anduvieron | andaré<br>andarás<br>andará<br>andaremos<br>andaréis<br>andarán | andaría<br>andarías<br>andaría<br>andaríamos<br>andaríais<br>andarían | ande<br>andes<br>ande<br>andemos<br>andéis<br>anden | anduviera<br>anduvieras<br>anduviera<br>anduviéramos<br>anduvierais<br>anduvieran | anda (tú),<br>no andes<br>ande (usted)<br>andemos<br>andad (vosotros),<br>no andéis<br>anden (Uds.) |
| caer<br>cayendo<br>caído | caigo<br>caes<br>cae<br>caemos<br>caéis<br>caen | caía<br>caías<br>caía<br>caíamos<br>caíais<br>caían | caí<br>caíste<br>cayó<br>caímos<br>caísteis<br>cayeron | caeré<br>caerás<br>caerá<br>caeremos<br>caeréis<br>caerán | caería<br>caerías<br>caería<br>caeríamos<br>caeríais<br>caerían | caiga<br>caigas<br>caiga<br>caigamos<br>caigáis<br>caigan | cayera<br>cayeras<br>cayera<br>cayéramos<br>cayerais<br>cayeran | cae (tú),<br>no caigas<br>caiga (usted)<br>caigamos<br>caed (vosotros),<br>no caigáis<br>caigan (Uds.) |
| dar<br>dando<br>dado | doy<br>das<br>da<br>damos<br>dais<br>dan | daba<br>dabas<br>daba<br>dábamos<br>dabais<br>daban | di<br>diste<br>dio<br>dimos<br>disteis<br>dieron | daré<br>darás<br>dará<br>daremos<br>daréis<br>darán | daría<br>darías<br>daría<br>daríamos<br>daríais<br>darían | dé<br>des<br>dé<br>demos<br>deis<br>den | diera<br>dieras<br>diera<br>diéramos<br>dierais<br>dieran | da (tú),<br>no des<br>dé (usted)<br>demos<br>dad (vosotros),<br>no deis<br>den (Uds.) |

# IRREGULAR VERBS (CONTINUED)

| Infinitive Present Participle Past Participle | Indicative Present | Imperfect | Preterit | Future | Conditional | Subjunctive Present | Imperfect | Imperative Commands |
|---|---|---|---|---|---|---|---|---|
| decir diciendo dicho | digo dices dice decimos decís dicen | decía decías decía decíamos decíais decían | dije dijiste dijo dijimos dijisteis dijeron | diré dirás dirá diremos diréis dirán | diría dirías diría diríamos diríais dirían | diga digas diga digamos digáis digan | dijera dijeras dijera dijéramos dijerais dijeran | di (tú), no digas diga (usted) digamos decid (vosotros), no digáis digan (Uds.) |
| estar estando estado | estoy estás está estamos estáis están | estaba estabas estaba estábamos estabais estaban | estuve estuviste estuvo estuvimos estuvisteis estuvieron | estaré estarás estará estaremos estaréis estarán | estaría estarías estaría estaríamos estaríais estarían | esté estés esté estemos estéis estén | estuviera estuvieras estuviera estuviéramos estuvierais estuvieran | está (tú), no estés esté (usted) estemos estad (vosotros), no estéis estén (Uds.) |
| haber habiendo habido | he has ha hemos habéis han | había habías había habíamos habíais habían | hube hubiste hubo hubimos hubisteis hubieron | habré habrás habrá habremos habréis habrán | habría habrías habría habríamos habríais habrían | haya hayas haya hayamos hayáis hayan | hubiera hubieras hubiera hubiéramos hubierais hubieran | |
| hacer haciendo hecho | hago haces hace hacemos hacéis hacen | hacía hacías hacía hacíamos hacíais hacían | hice hiciste hizo hicimos hicisteis hicieron | haré harás hará haremos haréis harán | haría harías haría haríamos haríais harían | haga hagas haga hagamos hagáis hagan | hiciera hicieras hiciera hiciéramos hicierais hicieran | haz (tú), no hagas haga (usted) hagamos haced (vosotros), no hagáis hagan (Uds.) |
| ir yendo ido | voy vas va vamos vais van | iba ibas iba íbamos ibais iban | fui fuiste fue fuimos fuisteis fueron | iré irás irá iremos iréis irán | iría irías iría iríamos iríais irían | vaya vayas vaya vayamos vayáis vayan | fuera fueras fuera fuéramos fuerais fueran | ve (tú), no vayas vaya (usted) vamos, no vayamos id (vosotros), no vayáis vayan (Uds.) |

# IRREGULAR VERBS (CONTINUED)

| Infinitive / Present Participle / Past Participle | Indicative | | | | | Subjunctive | | Imperative |
|---|---|---|---|---|---|---|---|---|
| | Present | Imperfect | Preterit | Future | Conditional | Present | Imperfect | Commands |
| oír<br>oyendo<br>oído | oigo<br>oyes<br>oye<br>oímos<br>oís<br>oyen | oía<br>oías<br>oía<br>oíamos<br>oíais<br>oían | oí<br>oíste<br>oyó<br>oímos<br>oísteis<br>oyeron | oiré<br>oirás<br>oirá<br>oiremos<br>oiréis<br>oirán | oiría<br>oirías<br>oiría<br>oiríamos<br>oiríais<br>oirían | oiga<br>oigas<br>oiga<br>oigamos<br>oigáis<br>oigan | oyera<br>oyeras<br>oyera<br>oyéramos<br>oyerais<br>oyeran | oye (tú),<br>no oigas<br>oiga (usted)<br>oigamos<br>oíd (vosotros),<br>no oigáis<br>oigan (Uds.) |
| poder<br>pudiendo<br>podido | puedo<br>puedes<br>puede<br>podemos<br>podéis<br>pueden | podía<br>podías<br>podía<br>podíamos<br>podíais<br>podían | pude<br>pudiste<br>pudo<br>pudimos<br>pudisteis<br>pudieron | podré<br>podrás<br>podrá<br>podremos<br>podréis<br>podrán | podría<br>podrías<br>podría<br>podríamos<br>podríais<br>podrían | pueda<br>puedas<br>pueda<br>podamos<br>podáis<br>puedan | pudiera<br>pudieras<br>pudiera<br>pudiéramos<br>pudierais<br>pudieran | |
| poner<br>poniendo<br>puesto | pongo<br>pones<br>pone<br>ponemos<br>ponéis<br>ponen | ponía<br>ponías<br>ponía<br>poníamos<br>poníais<br>ponían | puse<br>pusiste<br>puso<br>pusimos<br>pusisteis<br>pusieron | pondré<br>pondrás<br>pondrá<br>pondremos<br>pondréis<br>pondrán | pondría<br>pondrías<br>pondría<br>pondríamos<br>pondríais<br>pondrían | ponga<br>pongas<br>ponga<br>pongamos<br>pongáis<br>pongan | pusiera<br>pusieras<br>pusiera<br>pusiéramos<br>pusierais<br>pusieran | pon (tú),<br>no pongas<br>ponga (usted)<br>pongamos<br>poned (vosotros),<br>no pongáis<br>pongan (Uds.) |
| querer<br>queriendo<br>querido | quiero<br>quieres<br>quiere<br>queremos<br>queréis<br>quieren | quería<br>querías<br>quería<br>queríamos<br>queríais<br>querían | quise<br>quisiste<br>quiso<br>quisimos<br>quisisteis<br>quisieron | querré<br>querrás<br>querrá<br>querremos<br>querréis<br>querrán | querría<br>querrías<br>querría<br>querríamos<br>querríais<br>querrían | quiera<br>quieras<br>quiera<br>queramos<br>queráis<br>quieran | quisiera<br>quisieras<br>quisiera<br>quisiéramos<br>quisierais<br>quisieran | quiere (tú),<br>no quieras<br>quiera (usted)<br>queramos<br>quered (vosotros),<br>no queráis<br>quieran (Uds.) |
| saber<br>sabiendo<br>sabido | sé<br>sabes<br>sabe<br>sabemos<br>sabéis<br>saben | sabía<br>sabías<br>sabía<br>sabíamos<br>sabíais<br>sabían | supe<br>supiste<br>supo<br>supimos<br>supisteis<br>supieron | sabré<br>sabrás<br>sabrá<br>sabremos<br>sabréis<br>sabrán | sabría<br>sabrías<br>sabría<br>sabríamos<br>sabríais<br>sabrían | sepa<br>sepas<br>sepa<br>sepamos<br>sepáis<br>sepan | supiera<br>supieras<br>supiera<br>supiéramos<br>supierais<br>supieran | sabe (tú),<br>no sepas<br>sepa (usted)<br>sepamos<br>sabed (vosotros),<br>no sepáis<br>sepan (Uds.) |
| salir<br>saliendo<br>salido | salgo<br>sales<br>sale<br>salimos<br>salís<br>salen | salía<br>salías<br>salía<br>salíamos<br>salíais<br>salían | salí<br>saliste<br>salió<br>salimos<br>salisteis<br>salieron | saldré<br>saldrás<br>saldrá<br>saldremos<br>saldréis<br>saldrán | saldría<br>saldrías<br>saldría<br>saldríamos<br>saldríais<br>saldrían | salga<br>salgas<br>salga<br>salgamos<br>salgáis<br>salgan | saliera<br>salieras<br>saliera<br>saliéramos<br>salierais<br>salieran | sal (tú),<br>no salgas<br>salga (usted)<br>salgamos<br>salid (vosotros),<br>no salgáis<br>salgan (Uds.) |

# IRREGULAR VERBS (CONTINUED)

| Infinitive Present Participle Past Participle | Indicative | | | | | Subjunctive | | Imperative |
|---|---|---|---|---|---|---|---|---|
| | Present | Imperfect | Preterit | Future | Conditional | Present | Imperfect | Commands |
| ser siendo sido | soy eres es somos sois son | era eras era éramos erais eran | fui fuiste fue fuimos fuisteis fueron | seré serás será seremos seréis serán | sería serías sería seríamos seríais serían | sea seas sea seamos seáis sean | fuera fueras fuera fuéramos fuerais fueran | sé (tú), no seas sea (usted) seamos sed (vosotros), no seáis sean (Uds.) |
| tener teniendo tenido | tengo tienes tiene tenemos tenéis tienen | tenía tenías tenía teníamos teníais tenían | tuve tuviste tuvo tuvimos tuvisteis tuvieron | tendré tendrás tendrá tendremos tendréis tendrán | tendría tendrías tendría tendríamos tendríais tendrían | tenga tengas tenga tengamos tengáis tengan | tuviera tuvieras tuviera tuviéramos tuvierais tuvieran | ten (tú), no tengas tenga (usted) tengamos tened (vosotros), no tengáis tengan (Uds.) |
| traer trayendo traído | traigo traes trae traemos traéis traen | traía traías traía traíamos traíais traían | traje trajiste trajo trajimos trajisteis trajeron | traeré traerás traerá traeremos traeréis traerán | traería traerías traería traeríamos traeríais traerían | traiga traigas traiga traigamos traigáis traigan | trajera trajeras trajera trajéramos trajerais trajeran | trae (tú), no traigas traiga (usted) traigamos traed (vosotros), no traigáis traigan (Uds.) |
| venir viniendo venido | vengo vienes viene venimos venís vienen | venía venías venía veníamos veníais venían | vine viniste vino vinimos vinisteis vinieron | vendré vendrás vendrá vendremos vendréis vendrán | vendría vendrías vendría vendríamos vendríais vendrían | venga vengas venga vengamos vengáis vengan | viniera vinieras viniera viniéramos vinierais vinieran | ven (tú), no vengas venga (usted) vengamos venid (vosotros), no vengáis vengan (Uds.) |
| ver viendo visto | veo ves ve vemos veis ven | veía veías veía veíamos veíais veían | vi viste vio vimos visteis vieron | veré verás verá veremos veréis verán | vería verías vería veríamos veríais verían | vea veas vea veamos veáis vean | viera vieras viera viéramos vierais vieran | ve (tú), no veas vea (usted) veamos ved (vosotros), no veáis vean (Uds.) |

# STEM-CHANGING AND ORTHOGRAPHIC-CHANGING VERBS

| Infinitive / Present Participle / Past Participle | Indicative | | | | | Subjunctive | | Imperative |
|---|---|---|---|---|---|---|---|---|
| | Present | Imperfect | Preterit | Future | Conditional | Present | Imperfect | Commands |
| almorzar (z, c) almorzando almorzado | almuerzo almuerzas almuerza almorzamos almorzáis almuerzan | almorzaba almorzabas almorzaba almorzábamos almorzabais almorzaban | almorcé almorzaste almorzó almorzamos almorzasteis almorzaron | almorzaré almorzarás almorzará almorzaremos almorzaréis almorzarán | almorzaría almorzarías almorzaría almorzaríamos almorzaríais almorzarían | almuerce almuerces almuerce almorcemos almorcéis almuercen | almorzara almorzaras almorzara almorzáramos almorzarais almorzaran | almuerza (tú) no almuerces almuerce (usted) almorcemos almorzad (vosotros) no almorcéis almuercen (Uds.) |
| buscar (c, qu) buscando buscado | busco buscas busca buscamos buscáis buscan | buscaba buscabas buscaba buscábamos buscabais buscaban | busqué buscaste buscó buscamos buscasteis buscaron | buscaré buscarás buscará buscaremos buscaréis buscarán | buscaría buscarías buscaría buscaríamos buscaríais buscarían | busque busques busque busquemos busquéis busquen | buscara buscaras buscara buscáramos buscarais buscaran | busca (tú) no busques busque (usted) busquemos buscad (vosotros) no busquéis busquen (Uds.) |
| corregir (g, j) corrigiendo corregido | corrijo corriges corrige corregimos corregís corrigen | corregía corregías corregía corregíamos corregíais corregían | corregí corregiste corrigió corregimos corregisteis corrigieron | corregiré corregirás corregirá corregiremos corregiréis corregirán | corregiría corregirías corregiría corregiríamos corregiríais corregirían | corrija corrijas corrija corrijamos corrijáis corrijan | corrigiera corrigieras corrigiera corrigiéramos corrigierais corrigieran | corrige (tú) no corrijas corrija (usted) corrijamos corregid (vosotros) no corrijáis corrijan (Uds.) |
| dormir (ue, u) durmiendo dormido | duermo duermes duerme dormimos dormís duermen | dormía dormías dormía dormíamos dormíais dormían | dormí dormiste durmió dormimos dormisteis durmieron | dormiré dormirás dormirá dormiremos dormiréis dormirán | dormiría dormirías dormiría dormiríamos dormiríais dormirían | duerma duermas duerma durmamos durmáis duerman | durmiera durmieras durmiera durmiéramos durmierais durmieran | duerme (tú), no duermas duerma (usted) durmamos dormid (vosotros), no durmáis duerman (Uds.) |

# STEM-CHANGING AND ORTHOGRAPHIC-CHANGING VERBS (CONTINUED)

| Infinitive / Present Participle / Past Participle | Indicative — Present | Imperfect | Preterit | Future | Conditional | Subjunctive — Present | Imperfect | Imperative — Commands |
|---|---|---|---|---|---|---|---|---|
| incluir (y) / incluyendo / incluido | incluyo / incluyes / incluye / incluimos / incluís / incluyen | incluía / incluías / incluía / incluíamos / incluíais / incluían | incluí / incluiste / incluyó / incluimos / incluisteis / incluyeron | incluiré / incluirás / incluirá / incluiremos / incluiréis / incluirán | incluiría / incluirías / incluiría / incluiríamos / incluiríais / incluirían | incluya / incluyas / incluya / incluyamos / incluyáis / incluyan | incluyera / incluyeras / incluyera / incluyéramos / incluyerais / incluyeran | incluye (tú), no incluyas / incluya (usted) / incluyamos / incluid (vosotros), no incluyáis / incluyan (Uds.) |
| llegar (g, gu) / llegando / llegado | llego / llegas / llega / llegamos / llegáis / llegan | llegaba / llegabas / llegaba / llegábamos / llegabais / llegaban | llegué / llegaste / llegó / llegamos / llegasteis / llegaron | llegaré / llegarás / llegará / llegaremos / llegaréis / llegarán | llegaría / llegarías / llegaría / llegaríamos / llegaríais / llegarían | llegue / llegues / llegue / lleguemos / lleguéis / lleguen | llegara / llegaras / llegara / llegáramos / llegarais / llegaran | llega (tú), no llegues / llegue (usted) / lleguemos / llegad (vosotros), no lleguéis / lleguen (Uds.) |
| pedir (i, i) / pidiendo / pedido | pido / pides / pide / pedimos / pedís / piden | pedía / pedías / pedía / pedíamos / pedíais / pedían | pedí / pediste / pidió / pedimos / pedisteis / pidieron | pediré / pedirás / pedirá / pediremos / pediréis / pedirán | pediría / pedirías / pediría / pediríamos / pediríais / pedirían | pida / pidas / pida / pidamos / pidáis / pidan | pidiera / pidieras / pidiera / pidiéramos / pidierais / pidieran | pide (tú), no pidas / pida (usted) / pidamos / pedid (vosotros), no pidáis / pidan (Uds.) |
| pensar (ie) / pensando / pensado | pienso / piensas / piensa / pensamos / pensáis / piensan | pensaba / pensabas / pensaba / pensábamos / pensabais / pensaban | pensé / pensaste / pensó / pensamos / pensasteis / pensaron | pensaré / pensarás / pensará / pensaremos / pensaréis / pensarán | pensaría / pensarías / pensaría / pensaríamos / pensaríais / pensarían | piense / pienses / piense / pensemos / penséis / piensen | pensara / pensaras / pensara / pensáramos / pensarais / pensaran | piensa (tú), no pienses / piense (usted) / pensemos / pensad (vosotros), no penséis / piensen (Uds.) |
| producir (zc) / produciendo / producido | produzco / produces / produce / producimos / producís / producen | producía / producías / producía / producíamos / producíais / producían | produje / produjiste / produjo / produjimos / produjisteis / produjeron | produciré / producirás / producirá / produciremos / produciréis / producirán | produciría / producirías / produciría / produciríamos / produciríais / producirían | produzca / produzcas / produzca / produzcamos / produzcáis / produzcan | produjera / produjeras / produjera / produjéramos / produjerais / produjeran | produce (tú), no produzcas / produzca (usted) / produzcamos / producid (vosotros), no produzcáis / produzcan (Uds.) |

# STEM-CHANGING AND ORTHOGRAPHIC-CHANGING VERBS (CONTINUED)

| Infinitive Present Participle Past Participle | Indicative | | | | | Subjunctive | | Imperative |
|---|---|---|---|---|---|---|---|---|
| | Present | Imperfect | Preterit | Future | Conditional | Present | Imperfect | Commands |
| reír (i, i) riendo reído | río ríes ríe reímos reís ríen | reía reías reía reíamos reíais reían | reí reíste rio reímos reísteis rieron | reiré reirás reirá reiremos reiréis reirán | reiría reirías reiría reiríamos reiríais reirían | ría rías ría riamos riáis rían | riera rieras riera riéramos rierais rieran | ríe (tú), no rías ría (usted) riamos reíd (vosotros), no riáis rían (Uds.) |
| seguir (i, i) (ga) siguiendo seguido | sigo sigues sigue seguimos seguís siguen | seguía seguías seguía seguíamos seguíais seguían | seguí seguiste siguió seguimos seguisteis siguieron | seguiré seguirás seguirá seguiremos seguiréis seguirán | seguiría seguirías seguiría seguiríamos seguiríais seguirían | siga sigas siga sigamos sigáis sigan | siguiera siguieras siguiera siguiéramos siguierais siguieran | sigue (tú), no sigas siga (usted) sigamos seguid (vosotros), no sigáis sigan (Uds.) |
| sentir (ie, i) sintiendo sentido | siento sientes siente sentimos sentís sienten | sentía sentías sentía sentíamos sentíais sentían | sentí sentiste sintió sentimos sentisteis sintieron | sentiré sentirás sentirá sentiremos sentiréis sentirán | sentiría sentirías sentiría sentiríamos sentiríais sentirían | sienta sientas sienta sintamos sintáis sientan | sintiera sintieras sintiera sintiéramos sintierais sintieran | siente (tú), no sientas sienta (usted) sintamos sentid (vosotros), no sintáis sientan (Uds.) |
| volver (ue) volviendo vuelto | vuelvo vuelves vuelve volvemos volvéis vuelven | volvía volvías volvía volvíamos volvíais volvían | volví volviste volvió volvimos volvisteis volvieron | volveré volverás volverá volveremos volveréis volverán | volvería volverías volvería volveríamos volveríais volverían | vuelva vuelvas vuelva volvamos volváis vuelvan | volviera volvieras volviera volviéramos volvierais volvieran | vuelve (tú), no vuelvas vuelva (usted) volvamos volved (vosotros), no volváis vuelvan (Uds.) |

# SPANISH TO ENGLISH VOCABULARY

## A

abajo *below* (5)
abandonar *to abandon* (11)
abarcar *to include* (11)
abeja *bee* (12)
abierto/a *open-minded* (20)
abobado/a *amazed; spellbound* (17)
abogado/a *lawyer* (2)
abolición *abolition* (10)
abordar *to tackle, to approach* (11)
abrazar *to embrace* (20)
abrebotellas *bottle opener* (8)
abrelatas *can opener* (8)
abrigo *coat* (4)
abril *April* (3)
abrir *to open* (7)
absurdo *absurd* (14)
abuelo/a *grandfather/grandmother* (2)
abuelos *grandparents* (2)
abundancia *abundance* (17)
aburrido/a *boring* (1) (7)
aburrirse *to get bored* (9)
abusar *to abuse* (20)
abuso *abuse* (20)
acá *here* (12)
acabar de *to have just* (7)
acampar *to go camping* (7)
a causa de que *due to* (20)
acceder *to access* (3)
accidente *accident* (10)
acción *action* (11)
aceite *oil* (8)
acelga *Swiss chard* (8)
acercamiento *approach* (3)
aclamar *to acclaim; applaud* (17)
aclarar *to clarify* (17)
acogedor/a *welcoming; friendly; warm* (9)
acomodarse *to make oneself comfortable* (17)
acompañante *companions* (7)
aconsejable *advisable* (20)
acontecimiento *event* (10)
a continuación *next* (8)
acordarse (ue) de *to remember* (13)
acostarse (ue) *to go to bed* (5)
acostumbrarse *to become accustomed* (17)
actividad *activity* (5)
actor *actor* (2)
actriz *actress* (2)
actuación *acting; performance* (15)
actualmente *currently* (2)
actuar *to perform; act* (14)
acuario *aquarium* (15)
acudir (a) *to attend; turn up* (15)
acuerdo *agreement* (10); *agreemente* (3)
acumulación *accumulation* (20)
acumular *to accumulate* (16)
adecuado/a *appropriate* (4)

adelanto científico *scientific advance* (19)
adelgazamiento *thinning* (16)
adelgazar *to lose weight* (5)
ademán *gesture* (17)
además *besides; moreover* (4)
a diario *daily activity* (8)
adicción *addiction* (5)
adicto/a *addicted* (12)
a diferencia de *in contrast to* (7)
adivinar *to guess* (1)
adjetivo *adjective* (1)
admirar *to admire* (14)
adolescente *adolescent* (20)
adquirir (ie) *to acquire* (4)
advertencia *warning* (19)
advertir (ie) (de) *to notice; warn* (12)
aeropuerto *airport* (1)
a favor *in favor of* (19)
afectar *to affect* (11)
afición *interest* (2)
aficionado/a *fan* (5)
afirmar *affirm* (8)
afluencia *affluence* (20)
afortunado/a *fortunate* (14)
afuera *outside* (16)
agarrar *to get hold of; take* (11)
agenda electrónica *electronic agenda* (16)
ágil *agile; flexible* (5)
agobiar *to oppress; put down* (20)
agosto *August* (3)
agotarse *to run out; to be used up* (19)
agradable *agreeable* (5); *pleasant; nice* (2)
agradecer (zc) *to thank* (15)
agravar *to make worse* (19)
agrícola *agricultural* (9)
agricultura *agriculture* (18)
agropecuario/a *agricultural; farming* (18)
agua *water* (1)
aguacate *avocado* (8)
agua mineral *mineral water* (4)
aguantar a *to put up with* (20)
aguardiente *brandy; hard liquor* (5)
agudo/a *acute* (12)
agujero *hole* (19)
ahora *now* (11)
ahorrar *to save* (4)
ahorro *savings* (16)
aire *air* (9)
aire acondicionado *air conditioning* (3)
aislado/a *isolated* (3)
ajeno/a *distant; alien* (7)
ajo *garlic* (8)
ajustar *to adjust to* (15)
alabar *to praise* (20)
a la derecha *to the right* (6)
a la izquierda *to the left* (6)
alameda *tree-lined avenue* (10)
albañil *builder* (6)

albergar *to house* (9)
albergue *lodging* (3)
alcalde/esa *mayor* (9)
alcaldía *city hall* (3)
alcance *reach; scope* (16)
alcanzar *to be enough; reach* (7)
al contrario *on the contrary* (14)
alegre *happy* (2)
alegría *happiness* (14)
alemán *German* (13)
Alemania *Germany* (18)
alergia *allergy* (12)
alérgico/a *allergic* (12)
alfabetización *literacy* (16)
al final *finally* (8)
algo *something* (11)
algodón *cotton* (16)
alguien *someone* (17)
alguno/a *some* (10)
alianza *alliance* (11)
alimentación *food* (18)
alimentar *to feed* (5)
alimentarse *to feed (oneself)* (11)
alimento *food* (8)
alistar *to get ready* (17)
allá *there* (4)
allí *there* (2)
alma *soul* (1)
almacén *warehouse; storage room; store* (18)
almacenar *to warehouse; store* (18)
al menos *at least* (5)
almíbar *syrup* (8)
almirante *admiral* (10)
al mismo tiempo *at the same time* (15)
aló *hello* (6)
alojamiento *lodging* (3)
alojarse (en) *to lodge* (3)
a lo mejor *maybe* (15)
alquilar *to rent* (3)
alquiler *rent* (6)
alrededor *around; about* (10)
alrededores *outskirts; surroundings* (9)
altibajos *ups and downs* (14)
alto/a *high* (1)
altura *height* (12)
amabilidad *friendliness* (18)
amable *nice; kind* (2)
amanecer (zc) *to dawn* (15)
amante *lover* (12)
amar *to love; to like a lot* (20)
amargura *bitterness* (14)
amarillo/a *yellow* (4)
ambicioso/a *ambitious* (11)
ambiental *environmental* (9)
ambiente *atmosphere* (8)
ambos *both* (13)
ambulante *traveling* (18)
ambulatorio *outpatient department* (9)

a mediados de *about the middle of* (11)
amenazar *to threaten* (19)
a menudo *often* (5)
amigo/a *friend* (2)
amistad *friendship* (10)
amor *love* (10)
ampliación *extension* (18)
amplio/a *ample* (6)
amueblado/a *furnished* (6)
amueblar *to furnish* (6)
añadir *to add* (8)
anaranjado/a *orange* (4)
anécdota *anecdote* (11)
añejo/a *old* (19)
anexión *annexation* (10)
anfiteatro *amphitheater* (7)
anguloso/a *angular* (11)
angustia *anguish* (20)
angustiar *to distress* (14)
anillo *ring* (8)
animación *animation; liveliness* (15)
animado/a *lively* (15)
animar *to encourage* (12)
anímico/a *of the mind* (5)
aniquilar *to annihilate* (16)
anís *anise* (8)
año *year* (12)
anoche *last night* (10)
anochecer *sunset; nightfall* (15)
anotar *to note* (5)
ansiedad *anxiety* (5)
anteayer *day before yesterday* (7)
antena parabólica *satellite dish* (7)
anteojos *eyeglasses* (4)
antepasado *ancestor* (11)
anteponer *to place before; to prefer* (14)
antes (de) *before* (3)
antes de ayer *day before yesterday* (7)
antibalas *bulletproof* (14)
anticipar *to anticipate* (18)
anticuado/a *antiquated; out-of-date* (18);
   *old-fashioned* (20)
antigüedad *antique* (4)
antiguo/a *old* (3)
antipático/a *unpleasant; unfriendly* (2)
antirrobo *anti-theft* (14)
antropólogo/a *anthropologist* (10)
anunciar *to announce* (10)
anuncio *ad* (3)
apagar *to turn off* (16)
aparato *device* (16)
aparcamiento *parking lot* (9)
aparejar *to prepare; equip* (18)
apariencia *appearance* (14)
apartamento *apartment* (3)
apellido *last name* (1)
aperitivo *appetizer* (8)
apertura *opening* (8)
apetecer *to feel like doing* (15)
a pie *by foot* (11)
apio *celery* (8)

aplicación *application* (16)
aplicar *to apply* (9)
apoderarse (de) *to take possession of* (11)
aporte *contribution* (9)
apoyar *to support* (11)
apoyo *support* (11)
apreciación *appreciation* (13)
apreciar *to notice; appreciate* (7)
aprender *to learn* (1)
aprendiz *learner* (13)
aprendizaje *learning* (13)
a principios de *at the beginning of* (20)
aprobar *to approve* (14)
apropiado/a *adequate* (13)
a propósito *by the way* (17)
aprovechar *to benefit from* (13)
aprovecharse de *to take advantage of* (13)
aproximadamente *approximately* (2)
apuntar *to point; write down* (18)
a punto *ready* (18)
a punto de *on the verge of* (18)
apurado/a *in a hurry* (5)
árabe *arabic* (13)
árbol *tree* (2)
archipiélago *archipelago* (11)
archivo *file* (16)
arder *to burn* (17)
argentino/a *Argentinian* (2)
argumento *plot* (15)
aritmética *arithmetic* (9)
arma *arm; weapon* (1)
armada *navy* (11)
armario *closet* (6)
arqueológico/a *archeological* (8)
arquitecto *architect* (2)
arquitectura *architecture* (2)
arrancar *to start; pull out* (17)
arrastrar *to sweep along* (19)
arreglar *to repair; fix* (16)
arrepentirse (ie) *to regret* (15)
arrojar *to throw* (17)
arroyo *stream* (20)
arroz *rice* (8)
arte *art* (2)
artesanía *craft; artisan work* (4)
artes gráficas *graphic arts* (18)
artista *artist* (2)
asado *roast* (8)
asado/a *roasted* (8)
asamblea *assembly* (10)
asar *to roast* (8)
ascendencia *descent; extraction; ancestry* (2)
ascender *to ascend; climb; promote* (9)
ascenso *ascent* (5)
ascensor *elevator* (6)
asegurar *to assure* (12)
asentamiento *settlement* (6)
asequible *affordable* (12)
asesinar *to murder* (10)
asesinato *assassination; killing* (10)
asesor/a *advisor; consultant* (10)

asesoría *consulting service* (18)
asiento *seat* (14)
asilo *asylum* (17)
asimismo *likewise* (14)
así pues *therefore* (15)
así que *so* (3)
asistencia *assistance; care* (19)
asistente *assistant* (6)
asistir *to attend; be present at* (2)
asma *asthma* (12)
asociar *to associate* (20)
asunto *affair* (19)
asunto de interés mundial *world affairs* (19)
asustado/a *scared* (20)
asustar *to frighten* (17)
atacar *to attack* (11)
ataque *attack* (10)
ataque al corazón *heart attack* (12)
atentamente *attentively* (13)
aterrizar *to land* (7)
a tiempo completo *full-time* (6)
a tiempo parcial *part-time* (6)
atmósfera *atmosphere* (16)
átomo *atom* (20)
atracción *attraction* (8)
atractivo/a *attractive* (9)
atraer(se) *to attract* (4)
atravesar *to cross* (12)
a tráves de *across; through* (5)
atreverse *to dare* (19)
atropellar *to run down; knock down;*
   *assault* (20)
aula *classroom* (13)
aumentar *to increase* (10)
aumento *increase* (18)
aunque *although* (18)
ausencia *absence* (7)
austero/a *austere* (2)
autobús *bus* (3)
autóctono/a *indigenous; native* (11)
autoevaluación *self-assessment* (13)
automatizar *to automate* (16)
automóvil *car* (6)
autopista *highway* (6)
autor/a *author* (11)
autoridad *authority* (17)
autoritario/a *authoritarian* (14)
autorizar *to authorize* (19)
avalancha *avalanche* (8)
avance *advance* (14)
avanzar *to move forward; make progress* (17)
avaricia *greed* (14)
avaro/a *miserly; avaricious* (14)
ave *bird* (6)
avellana *hazelnut* (8)
aventurero/a *adventurous* (11)
avergonzado/a *ashamed* (17)
averiarse *to break down* (16)
averiguar *to find out* (2)
aviario *aviary* (15)
avión *plane* (3)

avisar *to warn; inform* (16)
avispa *wasp* (12)
ayer *yesterday* (7)
ayudar *to help* (6)
ayunas *breakfast* (12)
ayuntamiento *city hall* (7)
azafato/a *flight attendant* (17)
azúcar *sugar* (5)
azucarar *to sweeten* (8)
azul *blue* (4)

**B**

bailar *to dance* (2)
baile *dance* (1)
bajar *download* (16); *to go down; get out* (13)
bajo/a *low; below* (6)
ballena *whale* (17)
balneario *spa* (12)
baloncesto *basketball* (3)
banca *banking* (18)
banco *bank* (3)
banda sonora *soundtrack* (15)
bandeja *tray* (8)
bandera *flag* (11)
baño *bathroom; toilet* (6)
banquero/a *banker* (19)
barato/a *cheap* (4)
barco *boat; ship* (3)
barra *bar* (12)
barrera *barrier* (14)
barriga *stomach* (12)
barrio *neighborhood* (9)
barroco/a *Baroque* (14)
bastante *enough* (5); *quite a lot* (8)
basura *garbage* (9); *junk food* (5)
batalla *battle* (11)
batería *battery* (16)
batir *to beat* (8)
bautizar *to baptize* (11)
beber *to drink* (5)
bebida *drink* (5)
beca *scholarship* (11)
béisbol *baseball* (5)
belleza *beauty* (3)
bello/a *beautiful* (3)
beneficiar *to benefit* (18)
beneficioso/a *beneficial* (12)
berenjena *eggplant* (8)
besar *to kiss* (14)
biblioteca *librar* (2)
bicicleta *bicycle* (3)
bien *well; good* (11)
bienes de consumo *consumer goods* (19)
bienestar *well-being* (2)
bien/mal situado/a *well/badly located* (9)
bigote *mustache* (8)
bilingüe *bilingual* (6)
biodiversidad *biodiversity* (12)
biografía *biography* (10)
biólogo/a *biologist* (16)

biométrico/a *biometric* (19)
bistec *steak* (8)
blanco/a *white* (4)
blando/a *soft* (8)
blanquecino/a *whitish* (17)
blusa *blouse* (4)
boca *mouth* (5)
boca abajo *face down* (7)
bodega *wine store* (4)
boleto *ticket* (3)
boleto de ida *one-way ticket* (7)
boleto de ida y vuelta *round-trip ticket* (7)
bolígrafo *pen* (12)
boliviano/a *Bolivian* (2)
bolsa *stock market* (20)
bolsillo *pocket* (10)
bolso *purse* (4)
bombero/a *fireman/woman* (6)
bombilla *lightbulb* (4)
bombo *drum* (4)
bombón *candy* (18)
bondad *goodness* (14)
boquiabierto/a *astonished; speechless* (14)
bordado *embroidery* (20)
borrado *removal* (12)
borrar *to delete; to erase* (14)
bosque *forest* (3)
bota *boot* (4)
botar *to throw away* (19)
botella *bottle* (8)
botón *button* (16)
boxeo *boxing* (19)
brazo *arm* (5)
brecha *gap* (19)
breve *brief* (2)
brillar *to shine* (5)
británico/a *British* (10)
bronce *bronze* (5)
bronquitis *bronchitis* (12)
bruja *witch* (15)
bucear *to dive* (7)
buceo *diving* (3)
bueno *hello* (6)
bueno/a *good* (2); *tasty* (5)
buey *ox* (15)
bullicio *noise* (20)
buñuelo *fritter* (8)
buque *ship; boat* (18)
burla *joke* (5)
burocracia *bureaucracy* (10)
bus *bus* (3)
buscar *to look for; search* (1)
buscar en el texto *to scan* (7)
búsqueda *search* (17)

**C**

caballo *horse* (4)
cabaña *cabin* (3)
caber *to fit; hold* (13)

cabeza *head* (5)
cabo *end* (5)
cacique *chief* (11)
cada *each* (1)
cadena *chain* (3); *TV network* (15)
cadera *hip* (5)
caducidad *lapse* (12)
caer *to fall* (10)
caer bien/mal *to like/dislike someone* (20)
caer(se) *to fall down* (11)
café *coffee* (8)
cafetalero/a *coffee grower* (8)
cafetería *coffee shop* (9)
cafeto *coffee tree* (8)
caja *box* (8)
cajero/a *bank clerk; cashier* (4)
cajero automático *automatic teller machine* (19)
calabaza *pumpkin* (4)
calendario *calendar* (14)
calentamiento global *global warming* (19)
calentar (ie) *to heat* (8)
calidad *quality* (4)
cálido/a *warm* (9)
caliente *warm; hot* (8)
calificación *rating; qualification; grade* (9)
callado/a *quiet; silent* (5)
callarse *to keep/remain quiet* (13)
calle *street* (3)
calmar *to calm* (5)
calor *heat* (9)
caluroso/a *hot (weather)* (9)
cama *bed* (6)
cámara de fotos *camera* (7)
cámara de video *video camera* (7)
cámara digital *digital camera* (16)
camarero/a *waiter/waitress* (2)
camarón *shrimp* (8)
cambiar *to change* (2)
cambio *change* (4)
cambio climático *climate change* (19)
camello *camel* (4)
caminar *to walk* (5)
caminata *hike* (7)
camino *road; journey* (20)
camión *truck* (11)
camisa *shirt* (4)
camiseta *t-shirt* (4)
campamento *camp* (3)
campaña *campaign* (12)
campeonato *championship* (5)
campesino/a *peasant; country folk* (6)
campo *countryside* (3); *field* (7)
Canadá *Canada* (18)
canal *TV channel* (15)
cancelación *cancellation* (7)
cancelar una reservación *to cancel* (7)
cáncer *cancer* (12)
cancha *court* (9)
canción *song* (14)
candidato/a *candidate* (6)

canela *cinnamon* (8)
cañon *cannon* (11)
cañonazo *cannonshot* (11)
cansado/a *tired* (5)
cansancio *tiredness* (12)
cansarse *to get tired* (12)
cantante *singer* (1)
cantidad *quantity* (2)
caos *chaos* (9)
capacidad *ability* (6)
capa de ozono *ozone layer* (14)
capaz *capable* (16)
capitán *captain* (5)
cara *face* (5)
cara a cara *face to face* (7)
carácter *character* (14)
característica *characteristic* (5)
caracterizar *to characterize* (15)
cargar *to charge* (16)
cargo *position; job* (6)
caribeño/a *Caribbean* (8)
cariñoso/a *tender a* (5)
carne *meat* (5)
caro/a *expensive* (4)
carrera *career* (10)
carretera *road; highway* (3)
carro *car* (4)
carta *letter* (4)
cartel *poster; handbill* (4)
cartelera *movie guide* (15)
cartera *wallet* (4)
cartero/a *postal carrier* (6)
cartón *cardboard* (16)
casa *house* (6)
casado/a *married* (2)
casarse *to get married* (10)
casarse con alguien *to marry someone* (10)
cascada *waterfall* (3)
casco *helmet* (5)
casco antiguo *historic district* (9)
casero/a *domestic; homemad* (8)
casi *almost* (1)
casona *big house* (9)
castellano *Spanish* (13)
castillo *castle* (11)
catalán *Catalan* (15)
catarata *waterfall* (3)
catástrofe *catastrophe* (6)
catastrófico/a *catastrophic* (5)
católico/a *Catholic* (19)
catorce *fourteen* (1)
caucho *rubber* (15)
caudaloso *large (river)* (3)
caudillo *leader; chief; strong man* (10)
causa *cause* (5)
causar *to cause* (6)
cautivar *captivate* (12)
cayo *key* (3)
caza *hunting* (19)
cazuela *casserole; pot* (8)
cebolla *onion* (8)

cecina *beef jerky; dried beef* (8)
ceder la palabra *to give the floor* (13)
celebrar *to celebrate* (11)
celebrarse *to take place; occur* (15)
célebre *famous* (11)
celos *jealousy* (20)
celoso/a *jealous* (20)
cena *dinner* (2)
cenar *to dine* (6)
cenicero *ashtray* (8)
ceniza *ash* (20)
centenar *hundred* (8)
céntrico/a *central* (6)
centro *city center; downtown* (3)
centro comercial *shopping mall* (4)
ceramista *ceramicist* (2)
cerca de *near* (7)
cercano/a *nearby* (6)
cerdo *pork* (8)
cerebro *brain* (12)
cero *zero* (17)
cerrado/a *closed* (7); *narrow-minded* (20)
cerradura *lock* (16)
cerrajería *locksmith's shop* (18)
cerrajero/a *locksmith* (18)
cerrar *to close* (1)
cerro *mountain* (11)
certificado *certificate* (7)
certificado de nacimiento *birth certificate* (7)
cerveza *beer* (5)
cestería *basket making* (4)
champaña *champagne* (19)
champiñón *mushroom* (8)
chapado/a *plated* (6)
chaqueta *jacket* (4)
charlar *to chat* (14)
chequeo médico *medical checkup* (5)
chicle *gum* (12)
chileno/a *Chilean* (2)
chino/a *Chinese* (13)
chistoso/a *funny* (11)
chocar *to clash* (20)
chofer *chauffer* (17)
cicatriz *scar* (12)
ciclo *cycle* (19)
cien *one hundred* (2)
ciencia *science* (14)
ciencia ficción *science fiction* (15)
científico/a *scientist* (2)
cientos *hundreds* (4)
cierre *zipper* (16)
ciertamente *certainly* (14)
cierto/a *certain* (5); *true* (13)
cifra *figure* (18); *sign* (12)
cigarrera *cigar/cigarette case; cigar/cigarette maker or vendor* (4)
cigarrillo *cigarette* (12)
cigarro *cigar* (8)
cima *summit* (3)
cinco *five* (1)
cincuenta *fifty* (2)

cine *cinema; movies; movie theater* (1)
cineasta *film enthusiast; film critic* (16)
cintura *waist* (5)
cinturón *belt* (4)
circulación sanguínea *circulation of blood* (5)
circundante *surrounding* (3)
circunstancia *circumstance* (11)
cirugía *surgery* (12)
cirujano/a *surgeon* (12)
cita *appointment; date* (15)
citar *to cite* (18)
ciudad *city* (1)
ciudadanía *citizenship* (10)
ciudad universitaria *college campus* (9)
claro *of course; sure* (7)
claro que no *of course not* (7)
clase *class* (10)
clase social *social class* (19)
clásico/a *classic* (4)
clasificar *to classify* (11)
clave *key* (5)
clima *climate; weather* (6)
climático/a *climatic* (19)
coartada *alibi* (17)
cobarde *cowardly* (11)
cobardía *cowardliness* (14)
cobre *copper* (16)
coca *coca plant* (17)
cocalero/a *coca grower* (17)
coche *car* (4)
cocido *stew* (8)
cocina *cooking* (8); *kitchen* (6)
cocinar *to cook* (2)
cocinero/a *chef; cook* (2)
coco *coconut* (8)
cóctel *cocktail* (8)
codiciar *to covet* (19)
cocido/a *cooked* (12)
código *code* (1)
código genético (ADN) *genetic code (DNA)* (16)
codo *elbow* (5)
coherencia *coherence* (14)
colaborar *to collaborate* (10)
colar (ue) *to strain* (8)
colección *collection* (7)
coleccionar *to collect* (2)
colección de arte *art collection* (15)
colega *colleague* (11)
colesterol *cholesterol* (12)
colgar (ue) *to hang* (16)
colibrí *hummingbird* (3)
coliflor *cauliflower* (8)
colina *hill* (11)
collar *necklace* (4)
colocar *to place* (4)
colombiano/a *Colombian* (2)
colonia *colony* (11)
colonización *colonization; settlement* (10)
colonizador/a *colonist* (11)
colono *settler* (11)

colorido/a *colorful* (9)
columna *column* (5)
coma *comma* (13)
comandante *commander* (11)
comedor *dining room* (3)
comentar *to comment* (6)
comenzar (ie) *to begin; start* (5)
comer *to eat* (2)
comercial *business-related* (18)
comercializar *to commercialize* (16)
comerciante *merchant* (20)
comerciar *to trade; do business* (18)
comercio *commerce; trade* (18)
comercio justo *fair trade* (19)
cometer errores *to make mistakes* (13)
comida *food* (1)
comilla *quotation mark* (13)
comisaría *police station* (17)
comodidad *comfort* (9); *convenience* (17)
cómodo/a *comfortable* (3)
como era de esperar *as expected* (17)
cómo no *of course* (3)
como por ejemplo *for example; such as* (16)
compañero/a de clase *classmate* (1)
compañía *company; firm* (6)
comparación *comparison* (9)
compartir *to share* (1)
competir *to compete* (18)
complejo/a *complex* (7)
complemento *object* (8)
complicado/a *complicated* (5)
cómplice *accomplice* (17)
componer *to compose; fix* (5)
compositor *composer* (15)
comprar *to buy* (4)
compraventa *buying and selling* (10)
comprender *to understand* (7)
comprensivo/a *understanding* (20)
comprobar *to check; confirm* (18)
comprometerse *to get engaged* (10)
compromiso *commitment* (5)
compuerta *floodgate; sluice* (18)
computación *computing* (4)
computador/a *computer* (16)
computadora de bolsillo *palmtop computer* (16)
computadora portátil *laptop* (4)
comsumidor *consumer* (18)
comunicar *to inform; contact* (11)
comunidad *community* (6)
concebir *to conceive* (17)
concertar una cita *to make an appointment* (15)
conciencia *awareness* (6)
concierto *concert* (15)
concluir *to conclude* (6)
concurso *contest* (15)
condenar *to condemn* (10)
conducir *to lead; to drive* (7)
conductor *leader; driver* (10)
conectarse *to get along with* (20)

conexión *connection* (4)
confiable *dependable* (18)
confianza *confidence* (20)
confiar *to trust* (14)
congelado/a *frozen* (18)
congelarse *to freeze* (20)
congresista *member of congress* (11)
conmemorar *to commemorate* (20)
conmemorativo/a *commemorative* (18)
conmigo *with me* (9)
conmovedor/a *moving* (15)
conocer (zc) *to know / to be familiar with* (1)
conocido/a *known* (10)
conocimiento *knowledge* (13)
conquista *conquest* (10)
conquistador *conqueror* (10)
consciente *conscious* (5)
consecuencia *consequence* (19)
conseguir (i) *to achieve* (10); *to obtain* (5)
consejero/a *counselor* (5)
consejo *advice* (5)
conservación *conservation* (8)
conservador/a *conservative* (10)
conservante *preservative* (12)
conservar *to conserve* (2)
considerar *to consider* (8)
constatar *to verify* (17)
constituir *to make up* (2)
construir (irreg) *to build* (6)
consulta *(doctor's) office* (12)
consultorío/a *office* (18)
consumidor/a *consumer* (8)
consumo *consumption* (5)
contaminación *pollution* (9)
contaminar *to pollute* (9)
contar (ue) *to tell (a story)* (3)
contar (ue) con *to count on* (6)
contenedor *container* (18)
contenido *contents* (6)
contigo *with you* (9)
continuar *to continue* (11)
contra *against* (5)
contradecir (irreg.) *to contradict* (19)
contradicción *contradiction* (19)
contratar *to hire* (6)
contrato *contract* (6)
contribuir *to contribute* (2)
convaleciente *convalescent* (20)
convencer *to convince* (6)
conveniente *convenient* (5)
conversación *conversation* (2)
conversar *to converse* (8)
convertir *to convert* (15)
convertirse en *to become* (10)
convincente *convincing* (11)
convivir con *to live with* (19)
copa *drink* (15); *wine glass* (8)
copia *copy* (6)
copo *snowflake* (17)
corazón *heart* (3)
corbata *tie* (4)

cordero *lamb* (8)
cordillera *mountain range; the Andes* (3)
coreano *Korean* (13)
corregir *to correct* (10)
corregirse *to correct oneself* (13)
correr *to run* (2)
corridas de toros *running of the bulls* (19)
cortapuro *cigar cutter* (8)
cortar *to cut* (8)
cortarse el pelo *to cut one's hair* (18)
cortesía *courtesy* (6)
corto/a *short* (7)
cortometraje *short film* (15)
cosa *thing* (1)
cosecha *harvest* (6)
coser *to sew* (13)
cosméticos *cosmetics* (18)
costa *coast* (10)
costado *side* (9)
costar (ue) *to cost* (4); *to find hard to* (13)
costarricense *Costa Rican* (2)
costilla *rib* (8)
costoso/a *costly* (4)
costumbre *custom* (10); *habit* (5)
cotidianidad *daily activity* (2)
cotidiano/a *everyday* (11)
cotizar *to quote* (5)
crear *to create* (6)
creatividad *creativity* (14)
crecer (zc) *to grow* (1); *to grow up* (10)
crecimiento *growth* (9)
creer *to believe* (6)
crema *cream* (12)
criatura *creature* (20)
crisol *melting pot* (4)
crispar *to tense with pain* (20)
cristal *glass* (16)
crítica *review* (2)
criticar *to critique* (9)
cronológico/a *chronological* (10)
crucero *cruise* (3)
crudo/a *raw* (8)
cruzar *to cross* (12)
cuaderno *notebook* (17)
cuadra *block* (9)
cuadrado/a *square* (16)
cuadro *painting* (5); *table* (11)
cuál *which* (4)
cualquier *any* (1)
cuándo *when* (4)
cuánto(s) *how many; how much* (2)
cuarenta *forty* (2)
cuarto *bedroom; room* (6); *fourth* (6); *quarter* (7)
cuatro *four* (1)
cuatrocientos/as *four hundred* (4)
cubano/a *Cuban* (2)
cubrir *to cover* (5)
cuchara *spoon* (10)
cucharada *tablespoon* (12)
cuchillo *knife* (4)

cuello *neck* (5)
cuenta *check; bill* (8)
cuento *short story; tale* (7)
cuento de hada *fairy tale* (17)
cuero *leather* (4)
cuerpo *body* (5)
cuestionario *questionnaire* (6)
cueva *cave* (11)
cuidado *care* (12)
cuidar *to care for* (12)
cuidarse *to take care of oneself* (12)
culinario/a *culinary* (17)
cultivar *to grow* (8)
cultivo *growing* (5)
cultura *culture* (1)
cumbre *summit* (11)
cumpleaños *birthday* (4)
cuna *crib; birthplace* (7)
cuota *membership fees* (19)
cupo *course* (20)
cupón *coupon* (4)
cúpula *dome* (4)
currículo *résumé; CV* (6)
curso *course* (1)

**D**

dado/a/os/as *given* (20)
dado que *given that* (20)
daño *damage; harm* (12)
danza *dance (classic or traditional)* (2)
danzar *to dance* (17)
dar *to give* (1)
dar lástima *to feel sorry for someone/ something* (20)
dar miedo *to scare; frighten* (13)
dar risa *to make laugh* (14)
darse cuenta de *to realize* (10)
dar una excusa *to make an excuse* (15)
dar una vuelta *to go for a walk* (17)
dar un paseo *to take a walk* (5)
dar vergüenza *to embarrass* (13)
datar *to date* (11)
datar de *to date back to* (11)
dátil *date (fruit)* (8)
dato *date; piece of information* (10)
de acuerdo *okay* (13)
debajo de *under* (3)
debatir *to debate* (19)
deberse *to be owing to* (6)
debido a *due to* (3); *owing to* (6)
década *decade* (5)
decanato *dean* (9)
decena *ten* (17)
decepcionado/a *disappointed* (20)
decidir *to decide* (6)
décima *tenth* (2)
decir (irreg.) *to say* (1)
declaración *statement* (17)
declarar *to declare* (10)
de cualquier forma *in any case / event* (19)

de día *during the day* (7)
dedicarse *to dedicate oneself* (2)
de dónde *from where* (4)
defecto *fault; defect* (14)
defensor/a *defender* (11)
definitivamente *definitively* (14)
deforestación *deforestation* (19)
deformar *to deform* (5)
de golpe *suddenly* (15)
degustación *tasting* (8)
degustar *to taste* (8)
deificar *to deify* (10)
dejar *to leave* (6); *to permit* (8)
dejar de *to stop doing something* (12)
de la madrugada *in the early morning* (7)
de la mañana *in the morning* (7)
de la noche *in the evening* (7)
delantal *apron* (17)
delante de *in front of* (17)
de la tarde *in the afternoon* (7)
deletrear *to spell* (1)
delfín *dolphin* (7)
delfinario *dolphinarium* (15)
delgado/a *slender; thin* (2)
delicioso/a *delicious* (8)
delincuencia *crime* (9)
demanda *demand* (18)
demasiado/a *too much; too many* (5)
demencia *dementia* (20)
de modo similar *similarly* (14)
demostrar (ue) *to demonstrate* (8)
de ninguna manera *no way* (3)
de niño/a *as a child* (14)
de noche *at night* (7)
dentista *dentist* (7)
dentro de *inside* (8)
de nuevo *again* (17)
denunciar *to denounce* (10)
de parte de *on the part of* (6)
depender *to depend* (13)
dependiente/a *store clerk* (8)
deporte *sport* (1)
deportes acuáticos *water sports* (3)
deportista *sportsman/sportswoman* (2)
deportivo/a *sporty; casual* (3)
depresión *depression* (5)
deprimido/a *depressed* (5)
deprimir *to depress* (14)
deprimirse *to become depressed* (11)
de pronto *suddenly* (17)
derecha *right* (6)
derecho *law* (10)
derechos civiles *civil rights* (10)
de repente *suddenly* (11)
derivar *to derive* (11)
derramar *to spill* (20)
derrotar *to destroy* (10)
desacuerdo *disagreement* (3)
desafiar *challenge* (19)
desafortunadamente *unfortunately* (19)

desafortunado/a *unfortunate; less fortunate* (19)
desanimarse *to get discouraged* (13)
desaparecer *to disappear* (10)
desaparición *disappearance* (17)
desaprobación *disapproval* (13)
desaprobar *to disapprove* (14)
desarrollado/a *developed* (19)
desarrollar *to develop* (10) (18); *to development* (3)
desarrollar(se) *to develop* (13)
desarrollo *development* (17)
desastre *disaster* (11)
desayunar *to have breakfast* (5)
desayuno *breakfast* (5)
descansar *to rest* (3)
descanso *rest* (3)
descarga *discharge; shock* (16)
descartar *to discard* (19)
descender *to descend* (14)
descendiente *descendent* (11)
descenso de rápidos *rafting* (12)
descifrar *to decode* (16)
descomposición *decomposition* (16)
desconcertante *disconcerting; upsetting* (20)
desconectar *disconnect* (16)
desconfiado/a *distrustful; suspicious (of)* (19)
desconocido/a *stranger* (13); *unknown* (10)
desconocimiento *ignorance* (12)
describir *to describe* (7)
descubrimiento *discovery* (9)
descubrir *to discover* (7)
descuento *discount* (4)
desde *until* (5)
desde cuándo *since when* (4)
desde luego *of course* (7)
desde luego que no *of course not* (7)
desear *to desire* (11)
desechar *to discard; reject* (16)
desecho *waste* (20)
desembarcar *to disembark* (11)
desempeño *fulfillment; performance* (12)
desempleado/a *unemployed* (19)
desempleo *unemployment* (9) (19)
desenchufar *to unplug* (16)
desenfrenado/a *unbridled* (19)
deseo *wish* (9)
desfile *parade* (17)
deshacer *to unpack* (7)
deshonesto/a *dishonest* (18)
desierta *desert* (14)
desigualdad *inequality* (19)
desintegrar *to disintegrate* (10)
desmayarse *to faint* (12)
desnivel *unevenness* (3)
desodorante *deodorant* (4)
desolar *to ruin* (11)
desorden *mess* (14)
desordenado/a *disorderly; untidy* (14)
desorganizado/a *disorganized* (20)

despacho *office* (6)
despacio *slow* (1)
despectivo/a *disrespectful* (14)
despedir (i) *to fire* (6)
despedirse (i) de *to say goodbye to* (7)
despegar *to take off* (7)
despertador *alarm clock* (17)
despertarse (ie) *to wake up* (5)
despierto/a *awake* (17)
despistado/a *absent-minded* (14)
desplazamiento *displacement* (10)
desprestigiarse *to lose* (7)
después (de) *next; after; afterwards* (8)
destacar *to stand out; emphasize* (5)
destinar *to assign* (9)
destino *destination* (3); *destiny* (10)
destituir *to dismiss; remove* (10)
destreza *skill* (6)
destrucción *destruction* (19)
destruir *to destroy* (6)
desvencijado/a *rickety; falling apart* (20)
desventaja *disadvantage* (18)
detallado/a *detailed* (4)
detección *detection* (16)
detención *arrest; detention* (17); *detention* (17)
detener *to stop; detain* (11)
detener(se) *to halt* (11)
deteriorar *deteriorate* (12)
determinar *to determine* (20)
de todas maneras *in any case / event* (19)
de todos modos *in any case / event* (19)
detrás de *behind* (12)
devastador/a *devastating* (20)
devastar *devastate* (11)
de verdad *really* (11)
de vez en cuando *once in a while* (5)
devolver (ue) *to return* (6)
diagnosticar *to diagnose* (19)
dialogante *open; open-minded* (20)
diarrea *diarrhea* (12)
dibujante *draftsman* (2)
dibujar *to draw* (2)
dibujo *drawing* (2)
diciembre *December* (3)
dictador *dictator* (11)
dictadura *dictatorship* (10)
diecinueve *nineteen* (1)
dieciocho *eighteen* (1)
dieciséis *sixteen* (1)
diecisiete *seventeen* (1)
diente *tooth* (18)
dieta *diet* (8)
diez *ten* (1)
difícil *difficult* (1)
dificultad *difficulty* (8)
difundir *to spread* (8)
diga *hello* (6)
digitalización *digitalization* (19)
digitalizado/a *digitized* (16)
digitalizar *to digitize* (16)
digno/a *honorable; decent* (6)

diligencia *diligence* (11)
dimitir *to resign* (10)
dinámico/a *dynamic* (6)
dinastía *dynasty* (11)
dinero *money* (3)
dirección *address* (7)
dirigir *to direct* (10)
disco compacto *compact disc* (16)
discriminación *discrimination* (19)
disculparse *to apologize* (18)
disculpe *excuse me* (8)
discurso *speech* (10)
discutible *debatable* (14)
discutir *argue* (5)
diseñador/a *designer* (7)
diseñar *to design* (6) (14)
disfrazarse (de) *to disguise oneself as* (17)
disfrutar *to enjoy* (3)
disminución *reduction* (10)
dispensar *to excuse; pardon; grant* (20)
disponer de algo *to have something* (9)
disponible *available* (6)
dispositivo *device; mechanism* (16)
dispuesto *disposed; available; ready* (6)
distribución *distribution* (2)
distribuir *to distribute* (10)
distrito *district* (15)
diurno/a *daily* (9)
diversión *enjoyment* (8); *fun* (1)
divertido/a *fun* (1); *funny* (14)
divertirse (ie) *to enjoy oneself* (3); *to have fun* (15)
divorciado/a *divorced* (2)
divorciarse *to divorce* (10)
doblar *to bend* (5)
doce *twelve* (1)
docena *dozen* (8)
dócil *docile* (20)
documental *documentary* (15)
dólar *dollar* (16)
doler (ue) *to hurt* (11)
dolor *pain* (12)
dolor de barriga *stomachache* (12)
dolor de cabeza *headache* (12)
dolor de espalda *backache* (12)
dolor de estómago *stomachache* (12)
dolor de muelas *toothache* (12)
dolor de oídos *earache* (12)
domicilio *domicile; legal residence* (18)
dominar *to dominate* (11)
domingo *Sunday* (5)
dominicano/a *Dominican* (2)
dominio *mastery* (6)
donación *donation* (6)
dónde *where* (4)
dormir (ue) *to sleep* (2)
dormirse (ue) *to fall asleep* (5)
dormitorio *bedroom* (6)
dos *two* (1)
doscientos/as *two hundred* (4)
droga *drug* (12)

drogadicciones *drug addictions* (12)
ducharse *to shower* (5)
dudar *to doubt* (11)
dueño/a *owner* (8)
dulce *sweet; candy* (5)
dulzura *sweetness* (14)
duplicación *duplication* (16)
duración *duration* (7)
duradero/a *long-lasting* (16)
durante *during* (7)
durar *to last* (7)
dureza *hardness; harshness* (8)
duro/a *hard* (8)
DVD (reproductor de) *DVD player* (16)

**E**

echar una mano *to help; to lend a hand* (17)
echar un vistazo a *to take a quick look* (15)
ecología *ecology* (9)
ecologista *ecologist* (19)
economía *economy* (18)
económico/a *inexpensive* (16)
ecosistema *ecosystem* (12)
ecuatoriano/a *Ecuadorian* (2)
edad *agenda* (9)
edificación *edification* (3)
edificio *building* (3)
editar *to publish* (16)
editorial *publishing company* (18)
educado/a *well-mannered; well-educated* (14)
efectivamente *really; exactly* (13)
efectivo/a *effective* (5)
efecto *effect* (6)
eficiencia *efficiency* (18)
egipcio/a *Egyptian* (14)
egoísmo *egoism* (14)
egoísta *selfish* (2)
ejercer *to exert* (20)
ejercicio *exercise* (5)
ejército *military* (10)
elaborar *to elaborate* (8)
elección *choice* (9)
elecciones *elections* (10)
electricidad *electricity* (16)
electricista *electrician* (18)
eléctrico/a *electric* (16)
electrodomésticos *electronic appliance* (4)
elegante *elegant* (4)
elegir (i) *to choose* (1); *to elect* (3)
elevar *to elevate* (16)
eliminar *to eliminate* (8)
eludir *to elude* (20)
embajador/a *ambassador* (14)
embarazada *pregnant* (12)
embarcar *to embark; to board* (11)
embestido/a *ravage; havoc* (20)
embotellamiento *traffic jam* (9)
emigración *emigration* (14)
emigrante *emigrant* (7)
emigrar *to emigrate* (12)

emocionante *exciting; thrilling* (15)

emocionar *to excite; to touch* (14)

emotivo/a *emotional* (20)

empacar *to pack up* (18)

empezar (ie) *to begin; start* (6)

emplazamiento *site; location* (17)

empleado/a *employee* (6)

emplear *to employ* (5)

empleo *job; employment* (6)

emplumado/a *fledged* (11)

empobrecer *impoverish* (20)

emprender *to undertake* (20)

empresa *business; company; firm* (6)

empresarial *business-related* (18)

empresario *manager; promoter* (15)

empujar *to push* (19)

en absoluto *absolutely not* (14)

enamorado/a *lover* (9)

enamoramiento *infatuation* (20)

enamorarse de *to fall in love with* (10)

encabezar *to head; lead* (3)

encallar *to run aground* (20)

encantador/a *charming* (15)

encantar *to love; to like a lot* (3); *to please* (13)

encanto *charm* (9)

encargar *to order* (18)

encendedor *lighter* (8)

encender *to turn on* (16)

encerrar *to lock down; to lock up* (11)

enchufar *to plug in* (16)

enchufe *plug* (16)

encima *on top* (8)

en/como consecuencia *in/as a consequence* (20)

en conclusión *in conclusion* (6)

en contra *against* (19)

encontrar (ue) *to find out* (3)

encontrarse (ue) *to find oneself* (12)

en crecimiento *growing* (18)

en cualquier caso *in any case / event* (19)

en cuanto a *as for* (16); *with respect to* (13)

encuentro *meeting; conference* (15)

encuesta *survey* (3)

en efectivo *cash* (17)

en el extranjero *abroad* (1)

enemigo/a *enemy* (11)

enemistad *enmity* (20)

energía *energy* (16)

energía solar *solar energy* (16)

enero *January* (3)

enfadado/a *angry* (20)

énfasis *emphasis* (12)

enfermarse *to get sick* (12)

enfermedad *illness; sickness* (12)

enfermo/a *sick; ill* (4)

enfoque *focus* (14)

enfrentar *to confront* (5)

enfrente (de) *in front of* (17)

enfriar *to cool down* (8)

enfriarse *to get cold* (8)

enfundado/a *to sheathe; wear* (17)

enfurecer *to infuriate* (20)

engordar *to gain weight* (5)

engreído/a *conceited; vain* (14)

enlace *link* (16)

enlatado *canned* (12)

enojado/a *angry; annoyed* (20)

enojarse *to get angry* (20)

enorme *huge; enormous* (15)

en otras palabras *in other words* (5)

en primer lugar *in the first place* (6)

en punto *on the dot; sharp* (7)

en resumen *in short* (6)

enriquecer *to enrich* (13)

enrolar *to enroll* (10)

ensalada *salad* (4)

ensamblar *to join; to assemble* (18)

ensayo *essay* (13)

enseguida *at once; right away* (17)

en segundo lugar *in the second place* (6)

enseñanza *teaching* (13)

en serio *seriously* (11)

ensueño *daydream; fantasy* (15)

en suma *to sum up* (19)

entender *to understand* (1)

entenderse con *to get along with* (20)

enterarse *to find out* (17)

en tercer lugar *in the third place* (6)

entonces *so* (20); *then* (11)

entorno *setting; environment; climate* (3)

en torno a *around* (20)

entrada *entry* (6); *ticket* (15)

entrar *to enter* (19)

entre *among* (3)

entrega *delivery* (18)

entregar *to hand over; give; deliver* (10)

entrenador/a *trainer* (17)

entrenamiento *training* (5)

entrenar *to train* (5)

entre tanto *meanwhile* (17)

entretenido/a *entertaining* (15)

entretenimiento *entertainment* (9)

entrevistar *to interview* (1)

en último lugar *last* (15)

envasar *to pack* (12)

envase *container* (8)

envenenamiento *poison* (12)

en vez de *instead of* (3)

enviar *to send* (4)

envidia *envy* (14)

envidioso/a *envious; jealous* (14)

en vista de *in the face of* (7)

en voz alta *out loud* (18)

epidemia *epidemic* (10)

época *epoch; era* (10)

equilibrio *balance* (5)

equinoccio *equinox* (20)

equipaje *luggage* (7)

equipo *team* (3)

equitativo/a *fair; just* (6)

equivocarse *to be wrong* (14)

erguido/a *erect* (5)

erradicación *eradication* (19)

error *mistake* (13)

escala *scale* (10)

escalada *climbing* (18)

escalera *staircase* (5)

escanear *to scan* (12)

escáner *scanner* (16)

escapar *to escape* (10)

escaso/a *rare* (19)

escena *scene* (17)

escénico/a *scenic* (15)

escepticismo *skepticism* (19)

escéptico/a *skeptical* (19)

esclavitud *slavery* (10)

esclavo *slave* (10)

esclusa *lock* (18)

esconder *to hide* (18)

escondido/a *hidden* (11)

escozor *stinging; burning sensation* (12)

escribir *to write* (1)

escrito/a *written* (13)

escritor/a *writer* (2)

escritorio *desk* (6)

escrúpulo *scruples* (11)

escuchar *to listen* (1)

escuela *school* (7)

escultor/a *sculptor* (5)

escultura *sculpture* (2)

es decir *in other words* (1)

esencia *essence* (19)

esencialmente *essentially* (13)

esfera *face (of a clock)* (7)

esfuerzo *effort* (12)

eslogan *slogan* (12)

es más *furthermore* (15)

espacial *spatial* (10)

espaguetis *spaghetti* (8)

espalda *back* (5)

español *Spanish* (11)

Española *Hispaniola* (10)

español/a *Spaniard/Spanish* (2)

especial *special* (7)

especializarse (en) *to specialize (in)* (14)

especialmente *especially* (18)

especie *species* (6)

especificar *to specify* (20)

específico/a *specific* (11)

espectáculo *show* (15)

espectáculos *shows* (9)

especulación *speculation* (19)

espejo *mirror* (6)

esperanza *hope; expectancy* (12)

esperanza de vida *life expectancy* (19)

esperar *to wait; to hope* (4)

espina *thorn* (18)

espinaca *spinach* (8)

espinoso *thorny; difficult; dangerous* (18)

esplendoroso/a *splendour* (14)

espontáneamente *spontaneously* (13)

esposo/a *husband/wife* (2)

esquema *outline* (13); *scheme* (11)

esquiar *to ski* (5)
esquimal *Eskimo* (17)
esquina *corner* (16)
estabilidad *stability* (5)
estable *stable* (12)
establecer *to establish* (6)
estación *season* (3); *station* (16)
estacionamiento *parking; parking lot* (6)
estacionar *to park* (17)
estadía *stay* (7)
estadio *stadium* (9)
estadista *statesman* (11)
estadístico/a *statistical* (12)
estado *state* (1)
estado civil *marital status* (2)
Estados Unidos *United States* (10)
estadounidense *U.S. citizen/from the U.S.* (2)
estallar *to break out* (10)
estampilla *stamp* (14)
estándar *standard* (14)
estante/estantería *shelf* (6)
estar *to be* (1)
estar a dieta *to be on a diet* (5)
estar a punto de *to be at the point of* (7)
estar de acuerdo *to agree* (3)
estar de buen/mal humor *to be in a*
    *good/bad mood* (20)
estar de rebajas *to be on sale* (4)
estar en contra *to be against* (14)
estar enfadado/disgustado (con) *to be mad*
    *at someone* (20)
estar en forma *to be fit; be in shape* (5)
estar harto/a (de) *to be tired of; fed up with* (17)
estar harto de *to be fed up with* (20)
estar resfriado/a *to have a cold* (12)
estar sentado *to be seated* (5)
estatal *state* (12)
este *east* (3)
estelar *stellar* (15)
estéreo *stereo* (6)
estereotípico/a *stereotypical* (14)
estereotipo *stereotype* (14)
estética *aesthetic* (15)
estilo *style* (2)
estimar *to estimate* (6)
estirar *to stretch; to extend* (5)
estrategia *strategy* (13)
estratégico/a *strategic* (11)
estrecho/a *narrow* (9)
estrella *star* (5)
estrés *stress* (5)
estresado/a *stress* (20)
estricto/a *strict* (7)
estropear *to damage; to break* (18)
estropearse *to get damaged; to break down* (16)
estructura *structure* (10)
estudiante *student* (2)
estudiantil *student* (18)
estudiar *to study* (1)
estudio *studio* (6)
estupidez *stupidity* (14)

etapa *stage* (6)
eterna *eternal* (12)
ético/a *ethical* (19)
etiqueta *label* (1)
etnia *ethnic group; race* (10)
étnico/a *ethnic* (11)
europeo/a *European* (2)
euskera *Basque* (15)
eutanasia *euthanasia* (19)
evaluar *to evaluate* (8)
evitar *to avoid* (12)
exactamente *exactly* (14)
exagerado/a *exaggerated* (5)
examinar *to examine* (4)
excelente *excellent* (8)
excesivamente *excessively* (12)
exceso *excess* (5)
excluyente *exclusive* (19)
excursión *field trip* (3)
excusarse *to excuse oneself* (15)
exhalar *to exhale* (5)
existir *to exist* (8)
éxito *success* (2)
exitoso/a *successful* (14)
exótico/a *exotic* (3)
expedición *expedition* (10)
expediente *expedient; means* (6)
experiencia *experience* (6)
experto *expert* (20)
explicación *explanation* (13)
explicar *to explain* (5)
exploración del espacio *space exploration* (19)
explorador/a *explorer* (10)
exponer *to expose* (5)
exportación *exportation* (18); *exports* (18)
exportar *to export* (7)
exposición *exhibition* (15); *exposition* (5)
expresar *to express* (18)
expresividad *expressivity* (15)
exprimir *to express* (12)
expulsar *to expel* (11); *to throw out; to expel* (11)
extenderse *to extend; stretch* (14)
exterminio *extermination* (10)
extraer *to extract* (11)
extranjero/a *foreigner* (2)
extraño/a *strange; odd* (10)
extraterrestre *extraterrestrial* (11)
extrovertido/a *extrovert* (14); *outgoing* (2)

**F**

fabricación *making; production* (8)
fabricar *to make* (8)
fabuloso/a *fabulous* (3)
facción *faction* (2)
fácil *easy* (1)
facilidad *ease* (17)
facilitar *to facilitate* (9)
facturar la(s) maleta(s) *to check luggage* (7)
facultad *school* (10)
falda *skirt* (4)

fallecer *to die* (10)
faltar *to lack* (9)
fama *fame* (6)
familiar *relative* (2)
farmacia *pharmacy* (3)
farmacología *pharmacology* (14)
fase *phase* (7)
fastidiar *to bother* (13)
fatalidad *fatality* (20)
febrero *February* (3)
fecha *date* (7)
felicidad *happiness* (14)
feliz *happy* (10)
fenómeno *phenomenon* (3)
feria *fair* (15)
ferrocarril *railroad* (18)
ferviente *fervent* (11)
festejar *to celebrate* (20)
festival *contest* (1)
fibra *fiber* (4)
ficha *card* (2)
fidelidad *fidelity; loyalty* (14)
fiebre *fever* (10)
fiel *faithful; loyal* (14)
fiesta *festivity/party* (1)
fijar *to fix* (13)
fijarse en *to notice* (7)
Filipinas *Philippines* (18)
filmar *to film* (16)
filosofía *philosophy* (14)
filósofo *philosopher* (19)
filtro *filter* (12)
finalmente *finally* (2)
financiar *to fund* (18)
financiero/a *financial* (18)
finanzas *finances* (19)
fin de semana *weekend* (4)
fingir *to pretend; imagine* (14)
finlandés *Finnish* (13)
fino/a *fine* (2)
firma *signature* (10)
firmar *to sign* (10)
firmeza *firmness* (5)
físico/a *physical* (5)
flauta *flute* (4)
flexión *push-up* (5)
flexionar *to bend* (5)
flor *flower* (18)
florecer *to flourish* (9)
florería *flower shop* (4)
floristería *florist's shop* (18)
flotar *to float* (5)
fluidez *fluency* (10)
flujo *flower* (20)
folleto *prospect; brochure* (7)
fomentar *to foment* (19)
fondo *back* (17); *fund* (6)
forastero/a *outsider* (13)
formación *training; education* (6)
forma de ser *the way someone is* (20)
formar parte (de) *to be part of* (11)

formato *format* (18)
fórmula *formulario* (19)
formular *formulate* (14)
formulario *form* (17)
forrado/a *lined; bound* (4)
fortalecimiento *strengthening* (5)
fortaleza *fortress* (11)
fósforo *match* (16)
fotocopiadora *copy machine; photocopier* (16)
fotografía *picture* (1)
fotógrafo/a *photographer* (2)
frágil *fragile* (20)
francés *French* (13)
Francia *France* (12)
franela *flannel* (17)
frase *sentence* (4)
frase temática *topic sentence* (4)
frecuentemente *frequently* (12)
freír (i) *to fry* (8)
frenar *to brake* (12)
freno *brake* (16)
frente *forehead* (5)
fresa *strawberry* (8)
fresco/a *fresh* (4)
frijoles *beans* (8)
frío *cold* (9)
frito/a *fried* (8)
frontera *border* (13)
frustrarse *to get frustrated* (13)
fruta *fruit* (5)
frutero *fruit seller; fruit dish* (8)
fuego *fire* (8)
fuente *source* (8) (17)
fuera de *outside of* (6)
fuerte *strong* (5)
fuerza *strength* (20)
fugarse *to escape* (17)
fumador/a *smoker* (12)
fumar *to smoke* (5)
funcionar *to function; to work* (5)
funcionario/a *government official* (11)
fundado/a *founded* (7)
fundar *to found* (10)
fundirse *to blow* (16)
fútbol *soccer* (2)

**G**

gafas *glasses* (16)
galés/galesa *Welsh* (13)
gallego *Galician* (15)
gamba *shrimp* (8)
ganadería *livestock* (18)
ganador *winner* (4)
ganar *to earn* (6); *to win* (2)
garaje *garage* (17)
garantizar *to guarantee* (12)
gasolinera *gas station* (9)
gastar *to spend* (3)
gato *cat* (4)
gaviota *seagull* (12)

generación *generation* (10)
generar *to generate* (12)
género *genre* (14)
generosidad *generosity* (14)
generoso/a *generous* (14)
genial *extraordinary; great* (15)
genio *genius* (19)
gente *people* (1)
geografía *geography* (1)
gerente *manager* (6)
gérmen *germ* (5)
gestación *gestation* (20)
gestión *management* (10)
gesto *gesture* (13)
gigante *giant* (17)
gigantesco/a *gigantic* (7)
gimnasio *gym* (3)
girar *to turn* (16)
giro *turn* (20)
giro postal *money order* (7)
globalización *globalization* (19)
globo *globe* (20)
gobernador *governor* (10)
gobernar *to govern* (11)
gobierno *government* (11)
golfista *golf player* (5)
golpear *to hit* (17)
golpe de estado *coup d'état* (10)
gordo/a *fat* (5)
gorjear *to trill* (11)
gorra *cap* (3)
gorro *hat* (4)
grabado *etching* (11)
grabar *to record* (16)
gracias *thanks; thank you* (1)
gracioso/a *funny* (11)
grado *degree* (12)
gráfico *graphic* (12)
gramo *gram* (8)
Gran Bretaña *Great Britain* (10)
grande *big* (1)
granja *farm; country house* (18)
grano *bean* (17)
grasa *fat* (5)
gratis *free* (7)
gratuito *free* (12)
grave *severe; serious* (9)
gravedad *gravity* (11)
Grecia *Greece* (18)
griego *Greek* (13)
grifo *gas station (Perú)* (9)
gripe *flu* (5)
gris *gray* (4)
gritar *to shout* (20)
grito *yell* (20)
Groenlandia *Greenland* (10)
gruñón *grumpy* (3)
grupo *group* (1)
grupo sanguíneo *blood type* (12)
guantes *gloves* (4)
guapo/a *good-looking; handsome/pretty* (2)

guardacostas *coast guard* (14)
guardaespaldas *bodyguard* (17)
guardar *to keep* (16)
guardería *daycare; preschool* (9)
guardia de seguridad *security guard* (6)
guatemalteco/a *Guatemalan* (2)
gubernamental *government-related* (18)
guerra *war* (5)
guía *guide* (4)
guiar *to guide; direct* (4)
guión *script* (15)
guionista *scriptwriter* (20)
guisantes *pea* (8)
guiso *stew* (8)
gustar *to like; be pleasing to* (3)

**H**

haber *to have (in compound tenses)* (1)
habichuelas *green beans* (8)
habilidad *skill; cleverness* (17)
habitación *room* (3)
habitante *inhabitant* (1)
habitar *to inhabit; to dwell* (11)
hábito *habitación* (8)
hablador/a *talkative* (14)
hablante *speaker* (2)
hablar *to speak* (1)
hace calor *it is hot* (9)
hace frío *it is cold* (9)
hacer (irreg.) *to make; to do* (2)
hacer caso a *to pay attention to* (20)
hacer cola/fila *to wait in line* (7)
hacer de *to play the role of* (8)
hacer deporte *to play; to practice sports* (5)
hacer ejercicio *to exercise* (5)
hacer esquemas *to prepare outlines* (13)
hacer la(s) maleta(s) *to pack* (7)
hacer muecas *to make a face* (7)
hacer preguntas *to ask questions* (13)
hacerse (irreg.) *to become* (20)
hacerse daño *to hurt oneself* (12)
hacerse un lío *to get all mixed up* (13)
hacer una reservación *to make a reservation* (7)
hacer un regalo *to give a gift* (4)
hacer yoga *to do yoga* (5)
hace sol *it is sunny* (9)
hace viento *it is windy* (9)
hacia *toward* (7)
hacienda *estate; farm* (10)
hallar *to find* (20)
hambre *hunger* (12)
hamburguesa *hamburger* (20)
harina *flour* (8)
harto/a (de) *fed up (with)* (18)
hasta *until* (10)
hasta cuándo *until when* (4)
Hawai *Hawaii* (10)
hay *there is; there are* (1)
hebreo *Hebrew* (13)

hecho *fact* (10)
hectárea *hectare* (3)
heladería *ice cream shop* (4)
helado *ice cream* (4)
hemisferio *hemisphere* (18)
heredero/a *heir/heiress* (8)
herencia *heritage* (3)
hermano/a *brother/sister* (2)
hermosura *beauty* (14)
héroe *hero* (10)
heroína *heroine* (11)
herramienta *tool* (16)
hervir (ie) *to boil* (8)
híbrido/a *hybrid* (16)
hidratante *hydrating* (12)
hierbabuena *mint* (8)
higiénico *hygienic* (18)
hijo/a *son/daughter* (2)
hilar *to spin* (20)
hilo *thread* (16)
hincapié *emphasis; stress* (5)
hipocresía *hypocrisy* (14)
hipócrita *hypocritical* (14)
hipotecario/a *mortgage* (18)
hipótesis *hypothesis* (10)
hispano/a *Hispanic* (2)
hispanohablante *Spanish speaker* (14)
historia *history* (1)
hogar *home* (6)
hoja *leaf* (6)
hojear *to skim/glance through* (17)
hola *hello* (1)
holandés/a *Dutch* (10)
hondureño/a *Honduran* (2)
honestidad *honesty* (14)
honesto/a *honest; decent* (11)
hora *hour* (5)
horario *schedule* (5)
hormigón *concrete* (6)
hostelería *hotel management; hotel business* (18)
hotel *hotel* (3)
hoy en día *these days* (19)
huelga *strike* (20)
huella *trace; print* (2)
huevo *egg* (8)
huida *flight* (11)
huir *to escape; to run away* (11)
húmedo/a *humid* (3)
humo *smoke* (9)
huracán *hurricane* (6)

**I**

ida y vuelta *round trip* (3)
idealista *idealist* (20)
identificar *to identify* (6)
idioma *language* (1)
ídolo *idol* (15)
iglesia *church* (3)
ignorar *to be ignorant; not know* (19)
igual *same; equal* (8)

igual... de *as ... as* (9)
igualdad *equality* (19)
igual de *equally* (7)
ilegal *illegal* (20)
ilícito/a *illegal* (12)
ilustración *illustration* (20)
ilustrar *to illustrate* (16)
ilustre *illustrious* (11)
imagen *image* (3)
imaginar *to imagine* (19)
imbuido/a *imbued* (20)
imitar *to imitate* (13)
impaciencia *impatience* (14)
imperio *empire* (9)
impermeable *raincoat* (3)
implicado/a *person involved* (17)
importación *imports* (18)
importado/a *imported* (16)
importar *to matter* (12)
imposición *imposition* (19)
impresión *impression* (19)
impresionante *impressive* (15);
    *outstanding* (3)
impreso/a *printed* (18)
impresora *printer* (16)
imprevisto/a *unforeseen* (11)
imprimir *to impress* (17)
impuestos *taxes* (18)
inalámbrico/a *wireless* (16)
inauguración *inauguration* (18)
incapaz *incapable* (20)
incendio *fire* (16)
incierto/a *uncertain* (8)
inclinar *to lean* (5)
incluir *to include* (4)
incluso *even; including* (19)
incógnito/a *unknown* (11)
incómodo/a *uncomfortable* (3)
inconfundible *unmistakeable* (5)
inconsciente *unconscious* (12)
incorporar *to incorporate; unite* (8)
increíble *incredible* (3)
incrementar *to increase* (18)
incumplir *to break* (19)
independencia *independence* (10)
independiente *independent* (11)
independizar *to become independent* (10)
indicar *to indicate* (9)
índice *index* (12)
indígena *indigenous person; native* (2)
indigestión *indigestion* (12)
indignar *to anger* (14)
indudablemente *certainly* (13)
industria *industry* (18)
inequívoco/a *unmistakeable* (14)
inesperado/a *unexpected* (20)
infancia *childhood* (10)
infección *infection* (12)
infidelidad *infidelity* (14)
infierno *hell* (17)
inflamación *swelling; inflammation* (12)

influyente *influential* (4)
información *information* (5)
informal *casual* (4)
informática *computer science; computers* (6)
informe *report* (1)
infraestructura *infrastructure* (18)
infranqueable *insurmountable; unbridgeable* (17)
ingeniería *engineering* (12)
ingeniería genética *genetic engineering* (19)
ingeniero/a *engineer* (20)
ingenio *ingenuity; inventiveness* (20)
inglés/inglesa *English* (11)
ingresos *income* (6)
inhalar *to inhale* (5)
iniciar *to start* (10)
injerto *graft* (12)
injusto *injustice* (17)
inmediatamente *immediately* (11)
inmersión *immersion* (13)
inmigración *immigration* (11)
inmigrante *immigrant* (4)
inmobiliario/a *real estate–related* (18)
innovador *innovator* (2)
innovador/a *innovative* (15)
innovar *to innovate* (18)
inolvidable *unforgettable* (3)
inscribirse *to enroll* (13); *to register* (7)
inscrito/a *registered* (7)
inseguridad *insecurity* (9)
inseguro/a *insecure* (14)
insolación *sunstroke* (12)
insomnio *sleeplessness; insomnia* (12)
insoportable *unbearable; intolerable* (20)
inspirar *to inspire* (6)
instalaciones *facilities* (3) (5)
instalar *to install* (9)
instalarse *to settle down* (9)
instantaneidad *instantaneity* (17)
instante *instant* (10)
instaurar *to establish* (10)
instrumento *instrument* (2)
inteligencia *intelligence* (14)
inteligente *intelligent* (2)
intemporal *timeless* (2)
intensidad *intensity* (17)
intentar *to try; intend* (14)
intercambio *exchange* (2)
interés *hobby* (1); *interest* (11)
interesante *interesting* (1)
interesar *to interest* (3)
internar *to intern* (20)
interpelar *to question* (19)
interpretación *performance* (14)
interrogar *to question* (17)
interrogatorio *questioning* (17)
interrumpir *to interrupt* (10)
intoxicación *food poisoning* (12)
introvertido/a *introverted; shy* (14)
inundar *to inundate* (18)
invadir *to invade* (10)
inventar *to invent; to make up* (10)

invernadero *greenhouse; glasshouse* (15)
inversión *investment* (18)
inversionista *investor* (18)
inversor/a *investor* (18)
invertir (ie) *to invest* (9)
investigación *research; investigation* (16)
investigador/a *researcher* (19)
investigar *to research; investigate* (16)
invierno *winter* (3)
invitado/a *guest* (18)
invitar *to invite* (20)
involucrado/a *involved* (7)
involucrar *to involve* (13)
ir (irreg.) *to go* (2)
ir a *to be going to* (1)
ir de camping *to go camping* (7)
ir de compras *to go shopping* (4)
ir de copas *to go out for a drink* (15)
Irlanda *Ireland* (10)
ironía *irony* (15)
irse (irreg.) *to leave* (6)
irse del hotel *to check out* (7)
isla *island* (3)
isleño *islander* (10)
istmo *isthmus* (18)
Italia *Italy* (10)
itinerario *itinerary* (7)
izquierda *left* (6)

**J**

jabón *soap* (16)
jamás *never* (20)
jamón *ham* (8)
Japón *Japan* (10)
japonés *Japanese* (13)
jarabe *syrup* (12)
jarana *revelry; trick; jest* (20)
jardín *garden; yard* (3)
jaula de bateo *batting cage* (7)
jeroglífico *hieroglyphic* (14)
jonrón *home run* (7)
joven *youth* (6)
joya *jewelry* (14)
joyería *jeweler* (4)
jubilar *to retire* (19)
judías verdes *green beans* (8)
judío/a *Jewish* (13)
juego *game* (7)
juego de video *video game* (18)
jueves *Thursday* (5)
jugador/a *player* (2)
jugar (ue) *to play* (2)
jugo *juice* (8)
juguete *toy* (4)
juguetería *toy store* (4)
julio *July* (3)
junio *June* (3)
junto/a *together* (6)
justicia social *social justice* (19)
justo/a *fair; just* (18)

juvenil *juvenile* (4)
juventud *youth* (10)

**K**

kilo *kilogram* (8)

**L**

laberinto *labyrinth* (17)
lado *side* (5)
ladrillo *brick* (6)
ladrón *thief* (17)
lago *lake* (3)
lamentar *to lament; be sorry* (20)
lana *wool* (4)
lancha *motorboat* (11)
langosta *lobster* (12)
lapicera *pen* (16)
lápiz *pencil* (16)
largometraje *full-length film; feature film* (16)
lástima *shame; pity* (11)
lata *can* (8)
latino/a *Latino* (2)
latinoamericano/a *Latin American* (2)
lavadora *washing machine* (16)
lavandería *laundromat* (3)
lavar *to wash* (10)
lazo *bond* (4)
lección *lesson* (14)
leche *milk* (8)
lechuga *lettuce* (8)
lector *reader* (13)
lector de CD-Rom *CD-Rom reader* (16)
lectura *reading* (13)
leer *to read* (1)
leer por encima *to skim* (7)
legalización *legalization* (19)
legumbres *legumes* (8)
lejano/a *far* (18)
lejos de *from from* (7)
leña *wood* (3)
lengua *language* (13)
lengua extranjera *foreign language* (13)
lengua materna *mother tongue* (13)
lentamente *slowly* (12)
lentes de sol *sunglasses* (4)
lento/a *slow* (7)
león marino *sea lion* (15)
lesión *injury* (12)
lesionarse *to get hurt; to get injured* (12)
levantarse *to get up* (5)
levantar *to lift* (5)
ley *law* (3)
leyenda *legend* (11)
liberación *release* (5)
liberar *to free* (10)
libertad *freedom* (10)
libre *free* (8) (19)
librería *bookstore* (2)
libreta *notebook* (4)

libro *book* (2)
licencia de conducir *driver's license* (6)
licor *liquor* (4)
licorería *liquor store* (18)
líder *leader* (10)
lienzo *canvas* (5)
liga *league* (6)
ligado/a *linked* (5)
ligero/a *light* (12)
límite *limit* (7)
limón *lemon* (8)
limonada *lemonade* (12)
limpiar *to clean* (3)
limpio/a *lantern* (9)
lindo/a *nice* (15); *pretty* (14)
línea *line* (10)
linterna *lantern; lamp* (3)
listo/a *clever; ready; witty* (5)
literario/a *literary* (20)
litro *liter* (5)
llamada *call* (18)
llamar *to call* (3)
llamarse *to be called* (1)
llanuras *plains* (1)
llave *key* (11)
llavero *key ring; key maker* (4)
llegada *arrival* (7)
llegar *to arrive* (1)
llegar a tiempo *to arrive on time* (7)
llegar con retraso *to be delayed* (7)
llegar tarde *to arrive late; to be late* (7)
lleno/a *booked* (7)
llevar *to carry* (6); *to live (a healthy life)* (12); *to wear* (4)
llevar a cabo *to carry out* (16)
llevarse bien/(mal) con *to (not) get along with* (14)
llorar *to cry* (15)
llover (ue) *to rain* (9)
lluvia *rain* (9)
lluvioso/a *rainy* (9)
lobo marino *seal* (20)
localización *location* (7)
localizar *to locate* (1)
loco/a *crazy* (20)
lógico/a *logic* (5)
logotipo *logo* (18)
lograr *to achieve* (6)
lomo *back* (15)
loro *parrot* (3)
lo siento *sorry* (7)
lucha *fight* (11)
luchar *to fight* (6)
lucro *profit* (6)
lúdico/a *playful* (15)
luego *next; then* (8)
lugar *place* (3)
lugareño *villager* (20)
lujoso/a *luxurious* (6)
lunes *Monday* (5)
luz *light* (16)

# M

macarrones *macaroni* (8)
madera *wood* (6)
madre *mother* (2)
madrileño/a *resident of Madrid* (15)
madrugada *early morning* (7)
madrugar *to get up early* (3)
madurez *maturity* (14)
maestro/a *teacher* (2)
maíz *corn* (5)
majestuoso/a *majestic* (20)
maldad *wickedness* (14)
malecón *seafront* (9)
maleducado/a *ill-mannered* (14)
maleta *suitcase* (7)
maletín *briefcase* (17)
malo/a *bad* (4)
malograrse *to break down* (16)
malvado/a *wicked* (11)
mamífero *mammal* (7)
mañana *tomorrow* (7)
manatí *manatee* (7)
mandar *to send* (6)
mando *command* (11)
manejar *to drive* (6)
manía *mania* (14)
manifestación *demonstration* (10)
manifestar *to show* (10)
mano *hand* (5)
mantel *tablecloth* (20)
mantener *to maintain* (9)
mantequilla *butter* (8)
manto *mantle; cloak* (17)
manualidad *craft* (13)
manzana *apple* (8)
maquillarse *to put on makeup* (14)
máquina *machine* (16)
mar *sea; ocean* (3)
maravilla *marvel* (17)
maravilloso/a *marvellous; wonderful* (3)
marcador *marker* (11)
marcar *to dial* (6)
marco *frame; mark* (4)
mareado/a *dizzy* (12)
marearse *to get dizzy* (12)
mareas negras *oil spill; large oil slick* (19)
mareo *dizziness* (12)
marfil *ivory* (17)
marginación *marginalization* (19)
marginado/a *marginalized* (19)
marido *husband* (20)
marihuana *marijuana* (19)
marino *sailor* (20)
marisco *seafood* (8)
marítimo/a *maritime; sea* (7)
mármol *marble* (5)
marrón *brown* (4)
martes *Tuesday* (5)
marzo *March* (3)
más... que *more than* (9)

masaje *massage* (12)
masajista *masseuse* (18)
matar *to kill* (17)
mate *small pot* (4)
matemáticas *mathematics* (14)
máximo *maximum* (11)
mayo *May* (3)
mayordomo *butler* (17)
mayoría *majority* (3)
mayúscula *uppercase letter* (13)
medianoche *midnight* (4)
medicamiento *medication* (12)
medicina *medicine* (12)
médico *doctor* (2)
medida *measure* (8)
medioambiental *environmental* (18)
medio ambiente *environment* (9)
mediocridad *mediocrity* (14)
mediodía *noon* (7)
medios de transporte *transportation* (3)
medir (i) *to measure* (12)
meditar *to meditate* (14)
mejillón *mussel* (8)
mejor *the best* (3); *better* (9)
mejorar *to improve; to make better* (5)
melocotón *peach* (8)
memoria *memory* (16)
memorizar *to memorize* (13)
mencionar *to mention* (5)
menos *less* (1)
mensaje *message* (6)
mensajería *courier service* (18)
mensajero/a *courier* (18)
mente *mind* (5)
mentir (ie) *to lie* (19)
mentiroso/a *lying; deceptive* (20)
menú *menu* (8)
mercadeo *marketing* (18)
mercado *market; grocery store* (7)
mercancía *goods; merchandise* (18)
mercardo laboral *labor market* (7)
merecer (zc) *to merit; be worth* (15)
merendar (ie) *to have a snack* (8)
mes *month* (3)
mesa *table* (2)
mesero/a *waiter/waitress* (2)
meseta *plateau* (3)
mestizo/a *biracial; person of mixed race* (11)
meta *goal* (18)
metal *metal* (16)
método *method* (13)
metro *subway* (3)
metrópoli *metropolis* (15)
mexicano/a *Mexican* (2)
mezcla *mixture* (11)
mezclar *to mix* (5)
microondas *microwave* (16)
miedo *fear* (11)
miedoso/a *fearful; scary* (14)
miembro *member* (5)
mientras *while* (6)

mientras tanto *while* (11)
miércoles *Wednesday* (5)
migración *migration* (9)
migraña *migraine* (12)
mil *thousand* (4)
milenario *millenial* (9)
milenio *millenium* (19)
militar *military* (10)
milla *mile* (16)
millón *million* (4)
millonario/a *millionaire* (17)
minería *mining industry* (18)
mínimo *minimum* (10)
minoría *minority* (13)
minúscula *lowercase letter* (13)
mirada *glance* (15)
mirar *to look* (1)
miseria *misery* (20)
mismo/a *same* (9)
misterio *mystery* (17)
misterioso/a *mysterious* (11)
mitad *half* (1)
mítico/a *mythic* (10)
mito *myth* (2)
mobiliario *furniture* (18)
mochila *backpack* (4)
moda *fashion* (4)
moderadamente *moderately* (12)
moderar *to moderate* (5)
moderno/a *modern* (4)
modesto/a *modest* (20)
modificar *to modify* (18)
mojado/a *wet* (11)
molestar *to bother* (13)
molestarse *to get upset* (20)
molestia *discomfort* (12)
molesto/a *bothersome; tiresome* (20)
monarquía *monarchy* (15)
moneda *currency* (7)
monje/monja *monk/nun* (19)
mono *monkey* (3)
montaña *mountain* (1)
montañismo *mountain climbing* (7)
montañoso/a *mountainous* (12)
montar bicicleta *to ride a bike* (5)
montarse en el tren, avión, autobús *to get on the train, plane, bus . . .* (7)
monte *mountain* (20)
montevideano *resident of Montevideo* (16)
montón *pile; heap; mass* (16)
morado/a *purple* (4)
moreno/a *dark* (2)
morir (ue) *to die* (10)
mostaza *mustard* (8)
mostrar *to show* (1)
motivar *to motivate* (11)
moto *motorcycle* (16)
motocicleta *motorcycle* (20)
movilizado/a *mobilized* (6)
movimiento *movement* (10)

movimiento migratorio *migration movement* (19)
muchas veces *many times* (5)
mudarse *to move* (6)
muebles *furniture* (6)
muela *tooth* (12)
muerte *death* (6)
multiétnico/a *multiethnic* (19)
mundial *worldwide; international* (5)
mundialización *globalization* (19)
mundo *world* (1)
muñeco/a *doll* (16)
muro *wall* (10)
músculo *muscle* (5)
museo *museum* (6)
música *music* (2)
música en vivo *live music* (15)
músico *musician* (2)
muslo *thigh* (5)

**N**

nacer (zc) *to be born* (10)
nacimiento *birth* (1)
nación *nation* (6)
nacionalidad *nationality* (2)
nacionalizado/a *nationalized* (7)
nada *hardly* (2); *none; not any; nothing* (8)
nadar *to swim* (11)
nadie *no one* (18)
naranja *orange* (4)
narcotráfico *drug trafficking* (19)
nariz *nose* (5)
narración *narration* (11)
narrador/a *narrator* (17)
narrar *to narrate* (11)
natal *native* (9)
naturaleza *nature* (1)
navegador *browser* (16)
navegante *sailor* (6)
navegar *to sail* (3)
Navidad *Christmas* (4)
naviera *shipping company* (20)
necesario/a *necessary* (5)
necesidad *necessity* (6)
necesitar *to need* (4)
negocio *business* (6)
negrita *bold* (2)
negro/a *black* (4)
nervioso/a *nervous* (14)
nevera *refrigerator* (8)
nicaragüense *Nicaraguan* (2)
niebla *fog* (9)
nieve *snow* (9)
ni hablar *no way* (7)
niñero/a *babysitter* (18)
niñez *childhood* (10)
ningún; ninguno/a *none; not any* (8)
nivel *level* (5)
no cabe duda *no doubt* (13)
noche *night; evening* (6)

nocturno/a *nightly* (15)
nómada *nomadic* (11)
nombrar *to name* (5)
nombre *first name* (1)
no me digas *no way* (11)
no obstante *however* (19)
nordeste *northeast* (11)
noroeste *northwest* (12)
norte *north* (3)
Noruega *Norwegian* (18)
noticias *news* (1) (15)
novecientos/as *nine hundered* (4)
novedad *novelty* (18)
novedoso/a *novel; new; innovative* (18)
novela *novel* (17)
novela de aventuras *adventure story* (17)
novela de ficción *fiction novel* (17)
novela de misterio *mystery novel* (17)
novelista *novelist* (17)
noventa *ninety* (2)
noviembre *November* (3)
novio/a *boyfriend/girlfriend* (2)
nublado/a *foggy* (9)
nueve *nine* (1)
nuevo/a *new* (4)
nuez *nut* (4)
número *number* (1)
nunca *never* (5)

**O**

oaxaqueño/a *Oaxacan* (2)
obesidad *obesity* (5)
obligar *to obligate* (20)
obra *work* (5)
obra de arte *work of art* (15)
obra de teatro *(theater) play* (15)
obras públicas *public works* (9)
obrero/a *worker* (20)
observar *to observe* (6)
obtener *to obtain* (5)
ocasionar *to cause* (11)
océano *ocean* (10)
ochenta *eighty* (2)
ocho *eight* (1)
ochocientos *eight hundred* (4)
ocio *leisure* (9)
octubre *October* (3)
ocupado/a *busy* (7)
ocupar *to occupy* (11)
ocuparse (de) *to take care of* (7)
ocurrir *to happen; take place* (9)
odiar *to hate* (14)
odontología *dentistry* (12)
oeste *west* (3)
ofensiva *offensive* (11)
oferta *offer* (7); *supply* (18)
oferta cultural *entertainment* (15)
ofertas *sales* (7)
oficina *office* (6)
oficinista *office clerk* (6)

ofrecer (zc) *to offer* (1)
oído *ear* (12)
oír *to hear* (17)
ojo *eye* (5)
óleo *oil painting* (5)
olor *smell* (9)
olvidar *to forget* (4)
olvidarse de *to forget* (13)
ómnibus *bus* (3)
once *eleven* (1)
ónix *onyx* (4)
operación *surgery* (12)
operar *to operate on* (12)
operarse (de) *to have surgery* (12)
opinar *to express an opinion* (19)
opinión *opinion* (19)
oportunidad *opportunity* (6)
optimista *optimist* (14)
óptimo/a *optimal* (18)
opuesto/a *opposite* (18)
oración *sentence; oration; prayer* (5)
oralmente *orally* (13)
orden *order* (4)
ordenado/a *orderly* (14)
ordenador *computer* (15)
oreja *ear* (5)
organización no gubernamental (ONG) *nongovernmental organization (NGO)* (6)
organizado/a *organized* (6)
organizar *to organize* (2)
orgulloso/a *proud* (14)
orientación *direction* (17)
oriente *east* (7)
origen *origin* (2)
originario/a *native* (17)
orilla *bank* (3)
oro *gold* (11)
ortografía *spelling* (6)
oscilar *to oscillate* (18)
oscuridad *obscurity* (17)
oscuro/a *dark* (11)
o sea *that is to say* (14)
oso *bear* (3)
oso hormiguero *anteater* (3)
otoño *fall* (3)
ovacionar de pie *to give a standing ovation* (10)
ovalado/a *oval-shaped* (11)
oveja *sheep* (4)

**P**

pabellón *pavilion; canopy; banner* (15)
paciencia *patience* (6)
paciente *patient* (6)
padecer (zc) *to suffer* (12)
padre *father* (2)
padres *parents* (2)
pagar *to pay* (4)
página *page* (10)
país *country* (1)

paisaje *landscape* (1)

país en vías de desarrollo *developing country* (19)

pájaro *bird* (7)

paje *page; valet; attendant* (4)

palabra *word* (11)

paladar *palate; taste* (8)

pan *bread* (8)

panadería *bakery* (18)

panameño/a *Panamanian* (2)

pánico *panic* (11)

paño *cloth* (12)

pantalla *monitor* (16); *screen* (1)

pantalones *pants* (4)

pañuelo *handkerchief* (4)

Papá Noel *Father Christmas* (4)

papa / patata *potato* (8)

papas fritas *French fries* (4)

papel *paper* (16); *role* (14)

paquete *pack; package* (8)

paraguas *umbrella* (8)

paraguayo/a *Paraguayan* (2)

paraíso *paradise* (3)

paralelo *parallel* (20)

paralizar *to paralyze* (20)

parámetro *parameter* (12)

parapente *paragliding* (7)

para que *for what purpose* (4)

parar *to stop* (8)

parche *patch* (12)

parecer *to appear* (5)

pared *wall* (3)

pareja *pair* (1)

parrilla *grill* (3), (8)

parque *park* (3)

parque de atracciones/diversiones *amusement park* (15)

párrafo *paragraph* (4)

participar *to participate* (1)

partido *game; match* (3)

partido de fútbol *soccer game* (15)

partir *to depart* (10)

pasado *past* (11)

pasado mañana *day after tomorrow* (7)

pasantía *internship* (7)

pasaporte *passport* (7)

pasar *to happen* (19); *to spend* (6)

pasarela *gangplank* (15)

pasar lista *to take attendance* (1)

pasarlo bien *to have a good time* (4)

pasarlo mal *not to have a good time* (4)

pasar vergüenza *to be embarrassed* (20)

pase *come in* (8)

pasear *to take a walk* (3)

pasillo *corridor; hallway* (6)

pasión *passion* (5)

pastel *cake* (4)

pastelería *pastry shop* (4)

pastilla *pill* (12)

pasto *pasture* (10)

pastoreo *grazing* (10)

patentar *to patent* (16)

patología *pathology* (12)

patria *homeland* (10)

pavo *turkey* (8)

paz *peace* (10)

peaje *toll* (18)

peatón *pedestrian* (9)

pecado *sin* (20)

pecho *breast; chest* (12)

pedantería *pedantry* (14)

pedazo *piece* (8)

pedido *order* (18)

pedir *to order (in a restaurant)* (8)

peinar *to comb* (17)

pelar *to peel* (8)

pelearse *to fight; to have an argument* (20)

película *film* (2)

película de acción *action movie* (15)

película del oeste *western* (15)

película policíaca *detective movie* (15)

película de terror *horror movie* (15)

peligro *danger* (7)

peligroso/a *dangerous* (3)

pelo *hair* (5)

pelota *ball* (4)

peluquería *hairdresser; barber* (3)

pena *grief; sadness; sorrow* (11)

pendiente *earring* (4)

penetrar *to penetrate* (11)

pensamiento *thought* (10)

pensar (en) *to think (about)* (2)

pensión *lodging house* (7)

peor *worse,* (8)*; the worst* (5)

pepino *cucumber* (8)

pepita *seed* (11)

pequeño/a *small* (1)

pera *pear* (8)

pérdida *loss* (10)

perdonar *to pardon* (20)

peregrinación *pilgrimage* (9)

perezoso/a *lazy* (2)

perfeccionar *to perfect* (13)

perfil *profile* (20)

perforación *drilling* (20)

perfumería *perfume store* (4)

periódico *newspaper* (3)

periodista *journalist* (2)

período *period* (11)

permiso *permission* (12)

permiso de conducir *driver's license* (7)

permiso de trabajo *work permit* (7)

permitir *to permit* (6)

pero *but* (1)

persiana *blind; shutter* (16)

personaje *character* (3)

personalidad *personality* (2)

personas sin hogar sin techo *homeless* (19)

persuadir *to persuade* (20)

pertenecer (zc) *to belong* (10)

pertenencia *belonging* (6)

peruano/a *Peruvian* (2)

pesado/a *boring; slow; tedious* (15); *heavy* (16)

pesar *to weigh* (12)

pescadería *fishmonger; fish market* (8)

pescado *fish* (5)

pesimista *pessimistic* (14)

peso *weight* (5)

pesticida *pesticide* (20)

petróleo *oil; petroleum* (19)

petrolero/a *oil* (18)

pez *fish* (3)

picado/a *ground* (8)

picadura *sting; bite* (12)

picante *hot; spicy* (8)

picar *to itch; to sting* (12)

pico *peak; beak* (3)

pie *foot* (5)

piedra *rock; stone* (10)

piel *skin* (12)

pierna *leg* (5)

pila *battery* (4)

pilar *pillar* (18)

píldora *pill* (12)

pimienta *pepper (spice)* (8)

pimiento *pepper (vegetable)* (8)

piña *pineapple* (8)

pinacoteca *art gallery* (15)

pingüino *penguin* (12)

pintar *to paint* (2)

pintor/a *painter* (2)

pintura *painting* (2)

pionero/a *pioneer* (18)

piragüismo *canoeing* (15)

pirámide *pyramid* (6)

pirata *pirate* (11)

piscina *swimming pool* (3)

pista *clue* (17); *court; rink* (3)

pizca *pinch* (12)

placer *pleasure* (15)

planear *to plan* (15)

planificar *to plan* (15)

plano *map; plan* (7)

plano/a *flat* (3)

planta *floor* (4)

plástico *plastic* (16)

plata *silver* (4)

plataforma *platform* (9)

plátano *banana* (8)

plato *dish* (4)

playa *beach* (1)

plaza *square* (9)

plaza de toros *bullfighting ring* (15)

plazo *period; term; time* (19)

pleno/a *full* (9)

pluma *feather* (14); *pen* (16)

población *population* (1)

poblado/a *populated* (6)

poblador/a *settler* (10)

poblar *to populate* (20)

pobres *poor* (19)
pobreza *poverty* (6)
poco *a little bit* (1)
poder *power* (10)
poder (ue) *to be able to; can* (4)
poderoso/a *powerful* (20)
policía *policeman/woman* (6)
politeísta *polytheist* (14)
política *politics* (1)
político/a *politician* (2)
pollo *chicken* (4)
polución *pollution* (9)
poner (irreg.) *to put* (8)
poner nervioso/a *to make nervous* (13)
ponerse *to become* (20)
ponerse celoso/a *to get jealous* (20)
ponerse contento/a *to get happy* (20)
ponerse enfermo *to get sick* (12)
por aquí cerca *nearby* (3)
porcentaje *percentage* (12)
por consiguiente *therefore; consequently* (20)
por desgracia *unfortunately* (19)
por ejemplo *for example* (5)
por encima de *on top of* (5)
por eso *because of that* (4); *so* (11)
por la mañana *in the morning* (7)
por la noche *in the evening* (7)
por la tarde *in the afternoon* (7)
por lo tanto *therefore* (20)
porque *because* (1)
por supuesto *of course* (3)
portafolio *portfolio* (14)
portavoz *spokesman* (4)
portero/a *goalkeeper* (5)
portugués *Portuguese* (11)
por último *last* (2)
por vía aérea *by air* (9)
por vía fluvial *by water* (9)
posada *inn* (7)
posgrado *postgraduate* (10)
posición *position* (12)
posmoderno/a *postmodern* (14)
posponer (irreg.) *to postpone* (19)
postal *postcard* (7)
postre *dessert* (4)
postular *to run (for office)* (10)
postura *posture* (5)
potenciar *to empower* (13)
practicar *to practice* (2)
práctico/a *convenient; handy* (16)
precio *price* (4)
precioso/a *beautiful* (4); *precious* (8)
precisamente *precisely* (12)
preciso/a *precise* (11)
predecir *to predict* (14)
predicción *prediction* (14)
predominar *to predominate* (6)
preferir *to prefer* (6)
prefijo *prefix* (6)
pregunta *question* (1)
preguntar *to ask questions* (17)

preincaico/a *pre-Inca* (9)
prejuicio *prejudice* (20)
prematuro/a *premature* (20)
premiado/a *prized* (12)
premio *prize; award* (4)
premonición *premonition* (20)
prenda de vestir *garment* (4)
prender *to turn on* (16)
prensa *press* (15)
preocupado/a *worried* (20)
preocupar *to worry* (13)
preocuparse de *to worry about; care* (20)
preparar *to prepare* (8)
presencia *presence* (19)
presentador *presenter* (19)
presentar *to introduce* (1)
presentarse *to introduce oneself* (1)
presionar *to pressure; to apply pressure* (18)
presión/tensión *blood pressure* (5)
préstamo *loan* (6)
prestar *to lend* (12)
prestar atención *to pay attention* (4)
prestar un servicio *to provide a service* (18)
prestigio *prestige* (2)
presupuesto *budget* (4)
pretensión *pretension* (2)
prevenir *to prevent* (12)
prever *to foresee* (17)
previo/a *previous* (6)
primavera *spring* (3)
primer/a *first* (1)
prioridad *priority* (5)
prisionero *prisoner* (10)
privado/a *private* (11)
privilegiado/a *privileged* (19)
privilegiar *to privilege* (19)
probar *to try on* (4)
problema *problem* (2)
procesador de textos *word processor* (16)
proclamar *to proclaim* (10)
producir *to produce* (10)
producto interno bruto (PIB) *gross domestic product* (18)
productos lácteos *dairy products* (5)
profesión *profession* (2)
profesor/a *professor* (2)
profundamente *deeply* (19)
profundo/a *deep* (5); *profound* (20)
programación *programming* (15)
progresista *progressive; liberal* (10)
prohibir *to forbid* (20); *to prohibit* (19)
proliferar *to proliferate* (12)
promedio *average* (4)
promesa *promise* (19)
promover (ue) *to promote* (18)
pronombre *pronoun* (5)
propietario/a *proprietary* (6)
propina *tip* (8)
propio/a *own* (6)
proponer *to propose* (8)

proporcionar *to provide* (12)
proposición *proposition* (19)
propósito *goal* (6)
propuesta *proposal* (8)
proseguir *to continue; follow* (20)
próspero/a *prosperous* (12)
protagonista *main actor/actress* (15); *main character* (17)
protagonizar *to play the role of* (14)
protectorado *protectorate* (11)
protector solar *sunblock* (3)
proteger *to protect* (5)
protestar *to protest* (18)
protocolo *protocol* (19)
provenir *to come from* (10)
provincia *province* (8)
provocar *to provoke* (11)
próximo/a *next* (7)
proyectar *project* (14)
proyecto *project* (19)
prueba *proof; evidence* (17)
púa *spine; tooth* (16)
publicidad *advertising* (18)
público/a *public* (6)
pudín *pudding* (8)
pueblo *people; nation* (10); *town* (3)
puente *bridge* (15)
puerta *door* (6) (17)
puerto *harbor* (9); *port* (11)
puertorriqueño *Puerto Rican* (2)
puesto de trabajo *position; job* (6)
puesto que *since* (20)
pulmón *lung* (12)
pulsar *to press* (19)
pulsera *bracelet* (4)
puñado *handful* (17)
punto *point* (12)
punto de partida *starting point* (7)
puntual *punctual* (11)
pureza *purity* (14)

## Q

quedar (con) *to make an appointment with* (15)
quedarse *to be (located); be left; remain* (10); *to stay* (15)
quemadura *burn* (12)
quemar *to burn* (12)
quemarse *to get sunburned* (12)
querer (ie) *to want* (1)
queso *cheese* (8) (18)
quietud *calm; quietness* (16)
química *chemistry* (16)
quince *fifteen* (1)
quinientos/as *five hundred* (4)
quitamanchas *cleaner; stain remover* (14)
quitar *to get rid of* (12)
quizá *maybe* (7)

## R

racismo *racism* (19)
radicarse *to settle* (20)
raíz *root* (7)
ramo *bunch; branch* (18)
rápidamente *rapidly* (12)
rapidez *rapidity* (18)
rápido/a *fast* (7)
raro/a *weird; odd; strange* (16)
rascacielos *skyscraper* (9)
rato *while; time* (17)
ratón *computer mouse* (16)
rayo *ray* (11)
razón *reason* (4)
razonamiento *reasoning* (19)
reaccionar *to react* (11)
realidad *reality* (11)
realizar *to make* (17)
realizar un pedido *to order* (18)
rebajas *sales* (8)
rebanada *slice* (8)
rebasar *to exceed* (9)
rebelión *rebellion* (10)
recado *message* (6)
recaudar *to collect* (18)
recepción *reception desk* (7)
recepcionista *front-desk attendant* (6);
  *receptionist* (7)
receta *prescription* (12); *recipe* (8)
recetar *to prescribe* (12)
recibir *to receive* (4)
reciclar *to recycle* (9)
reciente *recent* (9)
recientemente *recently* (5)
reclamar *to claim* (18)
recoger *to pick up* (7)
recomendable *advisable* (5)
recomendación *recommendation* (12)
recomendar *to recommend* (18)
reconocer *to recognize* (11)
recordar *to remind* (6)
recorrer *to travel through* (11)
recoveco *turn; bend* (20)
recto/a *straight* (9)
recuperar *to recuperate* (10)
recursos *resources* (18)
recursos naturales *natural resources* (19)
red *network* (12); *the Web* (16)
redacción *composition* (13)
redactar *to edit* (10)
redondo/a *round* (16)
reducir *to reduce* (10)
referente *referent* (18)
referir *to refer* (4)
refinar *to refine* (6)
reflejar *to reflect* (11)
reflexión *reflection* (11)
refresco *soft drink; soda pop* (8)
refugiado/a *refugee* (17)
refugiarse *to take refuge* (11)

refutar *to refute* (19)
regalar *to give a gift* (4)
regalo *gift* (4)
regeneración *regeneration* (19)
régimen *diet* (12)
registro *register* (6)
regla *rule* (5)
regresar *to come back; return* (10)
regreso *return* (11)
rehén *hostage* (11)
reino *kingdom* (11)
reinversión *reinvestment* (19)
reiterar *to reiterate* (19)
reivindicación *to claim* (19)
relajación *relaxation* (5)
relajarse *to relax* (5)
relatar *to tell (a story)* (17)
relato *story; tale* (17)
rellenar *to fill out* (14)
reloj *watch* (4)
remojar *to soak; steep* (8)
remolacha *beet* (8)
rendirse *to surrender* (5)
renovable *renewable* (16)
renunciar a *to renounce; to give up* (20)
reparar *to repair; to fix* (16)
repartir *to distribute* (14)
reparto *delivery; distribution* (18)
repasar *to review* (9)
repelente *repellent* (3)
repetir *to repeat* (1)
repisa *shelf* (17)
replantearse *to rethink; reconsider* (20)
reportaje *interview; story; feature* (19)
reposo *repose* (11)
represivo/a *repressive* (11)
reproducir (zc) *to reproduce* (8)
requisito *requirement* (6)
rescribir *rewrite* (17)
reseña *review* (14)
resentirse *to resent* (18)
reservar *to reserve* (3)
resfriado *cold* (12)
resfriarse *to get a cold* (12)
residencia estudiantil *dorm* (9)
residir *to reside* (6)
resolver (ue) *to resolve* (6)
resolver un caso *to solve a case* (17)
respaldar *to back* (18)
respecto a *with respect to* (18)
respetar *to respect* (19)
respirar *to breathe* (20)
responder *to respond* (7)
responsable *responsible* (6)
respuesta *answer* (1)
restante *remaining* (13)
restaurante *restaurant* (8)
restaurar *to restore* (17)
resto *rest* (3)
restringir *to restrict* (19)
resultado *result* (13)

resumen *summary* (11)
resumir *to sum up* (6)
retirarse *to retreat; to withdraw* (11)
reto *challenge* (19)
retórico/a *rhetorical* (19)
retorno *return* (20)
retransmisión *broadcasting* (15)
retraso *delay* (7)
retratar *to portray; depict* (14)
reunión *meeting* (7)
reunir *to have; include* (14)
reunirse (con) *to meet* (7)
revelación *revelation* (20)
revelar *to reveal* (3)
revelar fotos *to develop* (7)
revestido/a *clad* (11)
revisar *to review* (2)
revisión *revision; review* (12)
revista *magazine* (4)
revolución *revolution* (8)
revolucionario/a *revolucionary* (11)
rey *king* (4)
rico/a *rich* (2); *tasty; delicious* (8)
riesgo *risk* (12)
rígido/a *rigid; inflexible* (20)
rincón *corner* (9)
río *river* (3)
riqueza *richness; wealth* (7)
risa *laughter* (14)
ritmo *rhythm* (8)
robo *robbery* (10)
rodaja *slice* (8)
rodear *to surround* (9)
rodilla *knee* (5)
rojo/a *red* (4)
rollito de primavera *spring roll* 19
rollo *film* (15)
romper *to break* (11)
romperse (algo) *to break (something)* (12)
ron *rum* (8)
roncar *to snore* (14)
ropa *clothing* (3)
ropa interior *underwear* (4)
ropero *closet; wardrobe* (17)
rosa *pink* (4)
rosca *roll (bread)* (8)
rostro *face* (2)
roto/a *broken* (16)
rueda *wheel* (16)
ruido *noise* (9)
ruidoso/a *noisy* (3)
ruina *ruin* (8)
rumbo a *bound for* (11)
ruso/a *Russian* (13)
rústico/a *rustic* (4)
ruta *route* (7)

## S

sábado *Saturday* (5)
sábana *sheet* (17)

saber (irreg.) *to know (a fact)* (1)
sabiduría *wisdom; knowledge* (15)
sabor *flavor* (8)
sacar *to take (out)* (5)
sacar conclusiones *to draw conclusions* (19)
sacerdotal *priestly* (10)
sacrificio *sacrifice* (5)
sal *salt* (8)
sala *living room* (6)
salado/a *salty* (8)
salida *departure* (7)
salir (lg) *to go out* (15)
salir a cenar *to go out for dinner* (15)
salir con *to go out with* (17)
secuestrar *to kidnap*
sospechar (de) *to suspect*
salir del avión, tren, autobús... *to get off the plane, train, bus...* (7)
salón/sala *living room* (6)
salpicado/a *flecked* (11)
saltar *to jump* (5)
salto *jump; leap; gap* (3)
salto de agua *waterfall* (3)
salud *health* (5)
saludable *healthy* (12)
saludar *to greet* (6)
salvadoreño/a *Salvadorean* (2)
salvaje *savage* (12)
salvar las apariencias *to save face* (7)
salvavidas *life preserver* (14)
sandalia *sandal* (4)
sandía *watermelon* (8)
sanitario/a *sanitary* (19)
sano/a *healthy* (5)
santuario *sanctuary* (9)
sartén *frying pan* (8)
satisfacción *satisfaction* (12)
satisfacer *to satisfy* (6)
seco/a *dry* (3)
secuencia *sequence* (5)
secuestro *kidnapping* (17)
secundario/a *secondary* (11)
seda *silk* (16)
seguido de *followed by* (9)
seguir *to continue* (6); *to follow* (2)
según *according to* (2)
segundo/a *second* (1)
seguramente *surely* (12)
seguro *insurance* (18); *safe; certain; a sure thing* (5)
seguro médico *health insurance* (12)
seis *six* (1)
seiscientos/as *six hundred* (4)
seleccionar *to select* (5)
sello *seal; stamp* (17)
selva *jungle* (3)
semáforo *traffic light* (9)
semana *week* (17)
semanal *weekly* (4)
semejante *fellow man* (20)
semestre *semester* (13)

semilla *seed* (6)
senador *senator* (10)
señalar *to signal* (12)
señal de tráfico/tránsito *traffic sign* (9)
sencillo *simple; plain; modest* (2)
sendero *path* (12)
sensatez *common sense* (14)
sensibilidad *sensitivity* (14)
sensible *sensitive* (14)
sentarse (ie) *to sit down* (5)
sentido del humor *sense of humor* (14)
sentimiento *feeling* (10)
sentir *to be sorry; feel* (11)
sentirse angustiado/a *to feel anguish/ stress* (20)
separarse *to separate* (10)
septiembre *September* (3)
sequía *drought* (19)
ser (irreg.) *to be* (1)
ser aficionado a *to be a regular of; be a fan of* (15)
ser humano *human being* (16)
serie *TV series* (15)
seriedad *seriousness* (14)
serio/a *reliable; serious* (2)
ser un rollo *to be very boring* (15)
servicio *service* (3)
servicio a domicilio *home delivery* (18)
servicio de emergencias *emergency room* (12)
servidumbre *servitude* (19)
servilleta *napkin* (4)
servir (i) *to serve* (5)
sesenta *sixty* (2)
sesión *session* (17)
setecientos *seven hundred* (4)
setenta *seventy* (2)
seudónimo *pseudonym* (20)
sí *of course* (7); *hello* (6)
si *if* (2)
SIDA *AIDS* (19)
siempre *always* (5)
sierra *mountains* (9)
siete *seven* (1)
siglo *century* (10)
significado *meaning* (11)
significar *to mean* (1)
siguiente *following* (10)
silencioso/a *silent; quiet* (13)
silla *chair* (4)
sillón *armchair* (6)
símbolo *symbol* (11)
simpatía *sympathy; warmth; charm* (11)
simpático/a *nice* (2)
sinceridad *sincerity* (14)
sincero/a *sincere; genuine; honest* (14)
sin embargo *nevertheless* (4)
sin fines de lucro *nonprofit* (13)
sino *but; but rather* (17)
sinopsis *synopsis* (20)
síntoma *symptom* (12)

sísmico/a *seismic* (6)
sistema de navegación GPS *GPS navigation system* (16)
sistema operativo *operating system* (16)
sitio *site* (3)
situación *situation* (2)
situar *to situate* (6)
soberanía *sovereignty* (10)
sobre *about* (2)
sobreexplotación *overexploitation* (20)
sobrenatural *supernatural* (14)
sobresalir *to stand out; excel* (8)
sobrevivir *to survive* (7)
sociable *friendly* (20); *sociable; friendly* (14)
sociedad *society* (10)
sofá *sofa* (6)
sofisticado/a *sophisticated* (6)
sojuzgar *to subdue* (19)
sol *sun* (9)
soldado *soldier* (11)
soleado/a *sunny* (9)
soledad *solitude; loneliness* (14)
soler (ue) *to usually do something* (13)
solicitante *applicant* (6)
solicitar *to apply for* (6)
solicitar una visa *to apply for a visa* (7)
solicitar un servicio *to request a service* (18)
solicitud *application* (7)
solidaridad *solidarity* (14)
sólido/a *solid* (7)
solitario/a *lonely* (3)
solo/a *alone* (3)
soltero/a *single* (2)
solucionar *to solve* (9)
sombra *shadow* (11)
sonar (ue) *to sound* (20)
sonido *sound* (13)
sonreír *to smile* (17)
sonrisa *smile* (15)
sopa *soup* (8)
sopera *soup tureen* (12)
soportar *to tolerate; bear; put up with* (14)
sordo/a *deaf* (17)
sorprendente *surprising* (10)
sorprender *to surprise* (15)
sorprenderse *to be surprised; amazed* (15)
sorprendido/a *surprised* (20)
sorpresa *surprise* (3)
sosiego *calm; peace; quiet* (16)
soso/a *tasteless* (8)
sospechar *to suspect* (17)
sospechoso/a *suspect* (17)
sostener *to sustain* (11)
sostenible *sustainable* (19)
step *paso* (1)
suave *soft* (9)
suavizar *to smooth* (14)
subida *rise; ascent* (3)
subir *to raise; go up* (1); *upload* (16)
sublevación *revolt; uprising* (10)
subrayar *to underline* (2)

subsuelo *underground* (14)
suceder *to happen; to follow* (10)
suceso *incident* (5)
sucio/a *dirty* (9)
sucursal *branch* (18)
sudar *to sweat* (12)
sudeste *southeast* (8)
sueco *Swedish* (13)
sueldo/salario *salary; wage* (6)
sueño *dream* (20); *sleep* (5)
suerte *luck* (11)
suéter *sweater* (4)
suficiente *enough* (8)
sufrir *to suffer* (5)
sugerencia *suggestion* (19)
sugerir *to suggest* (17)
sumar *to add; add up; amount to* (19)
sumergir *to dip* (8)
sumido/a *absorbed* (11)
superar *to overcome* (14); *to surpass; excel* (16)
superficie *surface* (7)
superfluo/a *superfluous* (19)
supermercado *supermarket* (4)
superpoblado/a *overpopulated* (9)
supervivencia *survival* (12)
suponer *to suppose* (17)
sureste *southeast* (3)
surgir *to emerge* (18)
suroeste *southwest* (2)
surtido *stock; supply* (18)
suscribir *to sign; endorse* (10)
sustentar *to sustain; support; feed; nourish* (20)
sustituir *to substitute* (19)
susto *fright* (11)

**T**

tabaco *tobacco* (8)
tabaquera *tobacco pouch* (8)
taberna *bar* (15)
tabla *table* (12)
tacaño/a *stingy* (20)
tacón *heel* (4)
táctica *tactic* (10)
tala de árboles *tree-felling* (19)
talento *talent* (14)
tales como *such as* (5)
talla *size* (4)
tallado/a *carved* (9)
taller *workshop; car repair* (18)
tal vez *maybe* (15)
tamaño *size* (5)
también *also* (1)
tampoco *neither* (3)
tan... como *as... as* (9)
tanto... como *as... as* (9)
tapiz *tapestry* (4)
taquilla *box office* (15)
tardar *to be late* (11)
tarde *late* (7)
tarea *task/homework* (1)

tarifa *tariff* (16)
tarjeta de crédito *credit card* (4)
tasa *rate* (12)
tasa de natalidad *birth rate* (1)
tasajo *dried beef* (8)
tatuaje *tattoo* (18)
taxi *cab* (7)
taxista *taxi driver* (6)
taza *cup* (8)
té *tea* (8)
teatro *theater* (2)
tecla *key* (16)
teclado *keyboard* (16)
técnica *technique* (5)
tecnológico/a *technological* (19)
tejedor/a *weaver* (20)
tejer *to weave; to knit* (4)
tela *cloth* (4)
telaraña *spider web* (14)
tele *television* (11)
telediario *news* (15)
teléfono *phone* (1)
teléfono celular/móvil *cell phone* (16)
telenovela *soap opera* (15)
televisor *television* (6)
tema *topic* (1)
templado/a *cool (weather)* (9)
templo *temple* (6)
temporada *season* (15)
temprano *early* (7)
tenacidad *tenacity* (14)
tendencia *trend* (1)
tender (ie) a *to tend to* (5)
tener (ie) *to have* (1); *to have a good time* (4)
tener algo en común *to have something in common* (14)
tener celos (de) *to be jealous (of)* (20)
tener curiosidad *to be curious* (13)
tener en cuenta *to keep in mind* (2)
tener exceso de peso *to be overweight* (12)
tener éxito *to be successful* (5)
tener lugar *to take place* (15)
tener miedo (a/de) *to be afraid (of) (about)* (20)
tener que *to have to* (2)
tener razón *to be right* (3)
tener un accidente *to have an accident* (12)
tenis *tennis* (4)
tenista *tennis player* (5)
tensión *blood pressure* (5) (12)
teoría *theory* (17)
tercer; tercero/a *third* (2)
tercio *third* (9)
terminación *ending* (2)
terminar *to end* (8)
termómetro *thermometer* (17)
ternura *tenderness* (14)
terraza *outdoor seating* (15)
terremoto *earthquake* (6)
territorio *territory* (10)
tesis *thesis* (19)

tesoro *treasure* (11)
testarudo *stubborn* (14)
testigo *witness* (17)
tetrapléjico *quadriplegic* (15)
texto *text* (2)
tiburón *shark* (12)
tienda de campaña *tent* (7)
tienda de deportes *sports store* (4)
tienda de juguetes *toy store* (4)
tienda de regalos *gift store* (4)
tienda de ropa *clothing store* (4)
tierno/a *tender; soft* (8)
tierra *land; earth* (11)
tímido/a *shy* (2)
tintorería *dry cleaner* (18)
típico/a *typical* (8)
tirar *to throw; throw away* (17)
titular *headline* (19)
título *degree* (6)
tocar *to touch* (5)
tocar (instruments) *to play* (2)
tocino *bacon* (8)
todavía *still* (2)
tomar *to take* (3)
tomar (alcohol) *to drink (alcohol)* (5)
tomar el sol *to sunbathe* (3)
tomar en cuenta *to take into account* (19)
tomar fotos *to take pictures* (7)
tomar notas *to take notes* (2)
tomar prestado/a *to borrow* (20)
tomar una decisión *to make a decision* (18)
tomar unas copas *to have a drink* (15)
tomate *tomato* (8)
tonificación *toning* (5)
tormenta *storm* (6)
torta *cake* (18)
tortuga *turtle* (3)
tos *cough* (12)
toser *to cough* (12)
toxina *release* (5)
trabajador/a *hardworking* (20); *worker* (18)
trabajar *to work* (1)
trabajo *position; job* (6)
trabajo en equipo *team work* (6)
trabajo escrito *essay; paper* (13)
tradición *tradition* (1)
traducción *translation* (13)
traductor/a *translator* (6)
traer *to bring* (4)
tráfico *traffic* (9)
tragar *to swallow* (12)
traición *betrayal* (20)
traje *suit* (5)
traje de baño *bathing suit* (4)
tranquilidad *calm; peacefulness* (5)
tranquilo/a *calm; quiet* (3)
transcendencia *transcendence* (18)
transformarse *to transform oneself/itself* (20)
transitar *to go through* (20)
transmitir *to transmit* (17)
transportar *to transport* (5)

transtorno *disorder; disturbance* (5)
trasbordador *ferry* (10)
trasero/a *rear* (17)
trasladarse *to move* (10)
trastorno alimenticio *eating disorder* (12)
tratado *treaty* (10)
tratamiento *treatment* (5)
tratar de *to try* (11)
travesía *crossing* (11)
trayecto *journey; route; path* (17)
trayectoria *trajectory* (14)
trece *thirteen* (1)
treinta *thirty* (2)
treinta y dos *thirty-two* (2)
treinta y uno *thirty-one* (2)
tren *train* (3)
tres *three* (1)
trescientos/as *three hundred* (4)
triángulo *triangle* (15)
tribu *tribe* (10)
trimestre *trimester* (13)
triste *sad* (14)
tristeza *sadness* (14)
triunfar *to triumph* (7)
triunfo *triumph* (11)
tronco *trunk* (5)
tropezar (ie) con *to run into* (14)
trozo *piece; fragment; passage* (8)
tumba *tomb* (6)
tumbarse *to lie down* (12)
turco *Turkish* (13)
turismo *tourism* (3)
turrón *type of Christmas candy* (4)

**U**

ubicación *location* (3)
únicamente *only* (12)
único/a *unique* (12)
Unión Europea *European Union* (10)
Unión Soviética *Soviet Union* (10)
unirse a *to join* (10)
universidad *college; university* (2)
uno *one* (1)
unos/as *some* (2)
urbanización *housing development* (9)
urgencia *emergency* (12)
uruguayo/a *Uruguayan* (2)
uso *use* (11)
usuario/a *user* (18)
utensilio *utensil* (6)
útil *useful* (8)
utilizar *to use* (18)
uva *grape* (8)

**V**

vaca *cow* (10)
vacaciones *vacation* (1)

vacío/a *empty* (7)
vacuna *vaccine* (16)
valentía *courage* (14)
valer *to be worth* (4)
valiente *brave* (11)
valioso/a *valuable* (19)
valle *valley* (9)
valor *value* (6)
vanidad *vanity* (14)
vascuense *Basque* (13)
vasija *vase* (4)
vaso *glass* (12)
vecino/a *neighbor* (2)
vegetales *vegetables* (8)
vehículo cartero/a (6)
veinte *twenty* (1)
veinticinco *twenty-five* (2)
veinticuatro *twenty-four* (2)
veintidós *twenty-two* (2)
veintinueve *twenty-nine* (2)
veintiocho *twenty-eight* (2)
veintiséis *twenty-six* (2)
veintisiete *twenty-seven* (2)
veintitrés *twenty-three* (2)
veintiuno *twenty-one* (2)
vejez *old age* (10)
vela *sailing* (3)
vello no deseado *unwanted hair* (12)
velocidad *velocity* (16)
vencer *to overcome; defeat; win* (20)
vendedor/a *sales associate* (4)
vender *to sell* (4)
venezolano/a *Venezuelan* (2)
venir *to come* (6)
ventaja *advantage* (9)
ventana *window* (6)
ver *to see* (2)
verano *summer* (3)
verdad *true; right* (9)
verdadero/a *true* (1)
verde *green* (4)
verdor *greenness* (11)
verdura *vegetable* (5)
vergüenza *shame; embarrassment* (13)
verter *to pour* (8)
vestíbulo *lobby; foyer* (17)
vestido *dress* (4)
vestimenta *clothes* (14)
vez *time; instant* (8)
viajar *to travel* (2)
viaje *trip* (1)
viajero/a *traveler* (11)
viajes espaciales *space travels* (19)
vianda *meat* (8)
vicio *vice* (14)
vida *life* (10)
vida nocturna *nightlife* (9)
vidrio *glass* (16)
viento *wind* (9)

viernes *Friday* (5)
vigilar *to watch* (5)
vincular (a) *to link* (17)
viñeta *vignette* (6)
vino *wine* (8)
vinoteca *collection of wines* (4)
violación *violation* (19)
violencia *violence* (9)
violeta *purple* (4)
virtud *virtue* (14)
viruela *smallpox* (10)
visa/visado *visa* (7)
visitante *visitor* (7)
visitar *to visit* (2) (3)
víspera de Navidad *Christmas Eve* (8)
viudo/a *widower/widow* (2)
vivienda *housing* (6)
viviente *living* (8)
vivir *to live* (2)
volar (ue) *to fly* (7)
volcán *volcano* (6)
voltio *volt* (16)
volumen *volume* (5)
voluntad *will* (12)
voluptuosidad *voluptuosity* (5)
volver (ue) *to return* (7)
volverse (ue) *to become* (20)
vomitar *to vomit* (12)
vómito *vomit* (12)
vorágine *whirl* (19)
votación *voting* (5)
voto *vote* (17)
voz *voice* (11)
vuelo *flight* (7)
vuelta *walk* (15)

**X**

xenofobia *xenophobia* (19)

**Y**

ya *already* (4)
yacimiento *site* (9)
ya no *no longer* (19)
ya que *since; as* (3)
yogur *yogurt* (8)
yuca *yucca* (8)

**Z**

zanahoria *carrot* (8)
zapatería *shoe store* (4)
zapato *shoe* (3)
zona peatonal *pedestrian zone* (9)
zona verde *green zone* (9)

# ENGLISH TO SPANISH VOCABULARY

## A

abandon *abandonar* (11)
ability *capacidad* (6)
abolition *abolición* (10)
about *sobre* (2); *alrededor* (10)
abroad *en el extranjero* (1)
absence *ausencia* (7)
absent-minded *despistado/a* (14)
absolutely not *en absoluto* (14)
absorbed *sumido/a* (11)
absurd *absurdo* (14)
abundance *abundancia* (17)
abuse *abusar, abuso* (20)
access *acceder* (3)
accident *accidente* (10)
acclaim *aclamar* (17)
accomplice *cómplice* (17)
according to *según* (2)
accumulate *acumular* (16)
accumulation *acumulación* (20)
achieve *conseguir (i)* (10); *lograr* (6)
acquire *adquirir (ie)* (4)
across *a tráves de* (5)
act *actuar* (14)
acting *actuación* (15)
action *acción* (11)
activity *actividad* (5)
actor *actor* (2)
actress *actriz* (2)
acute *agudo/a* (12)
ad *anuncio* (3)
add *añadir* (8); *sumar* (19)
addicted *adicto/a* (12)
addiction *adicción* (5)
address *dirección* (7)
adequate *apropiado/a* (13)
adjective *adjetivos* (1)
adjust to *ajustar* (15)
admiral *almirante* (10)
admire *admirar* (14)
adolescent *adolescente* (20)
advance *avance* (14)
advantage *ventaja* (9)
adventure story *novela de aventuras* (17)
adventurous *aventurero/a* (11)
advertising *publicidad* (18)
advice *consejo* (5)
advisable *aconsejable* (20); *recomendable* (5)
advisor *asesor/a* (10)
aesthetic *estética* (15)
affair *asunto* (19)
affect *afectar* (11)
affirm *afirmar* (8)
affluence *afluencia* (20)
affordable *asequible* (12)
after *después (de)* (8)
afterwards *después (de)* (8)

again *de nuevo* (17)
against *contra* (5); *en contra* (19)
agenda *edad* (9)
agile *ágil* (5)
agree *estar de acuerdo* (3)
agreeable *agradable* (5)
agreement *acuerdo* (10)
agricultural *agrícola* (9); *agropecuario/a* (18)
agriculture *agricultura* (18)
AIDS *SIDA* (19)
air *aire* (9)
air conditioning *aire acondicionado* (3)
airport *aeropuerto* (1)
alarm clock *despertador* (17)
alibi *coartada* (17)
alien *ajeno/a* (7)
allergic *alérgico/a* (12)
allergy *alergia* (12)
alliance *alianza* (11)
almost *casi* (1)
alone *solo/a* (3)
already *ya* (4)
also *también* (1)
although *aunque* (18)
always *siempre* (5)
amazed *abobado/a* (17)
ambitious *ambicioso/a* (11)
among *entre* (3)
amount to *sumar* (19)
amphitheater *anfiteatro* (7)
ample *amplio/a* (6)
amusement park *parque de atracciones/diversiones* (15)
ancestor *antepasado* (11)
ancestry *ascendencia* (2)
anecdote *anécdota* (11)
anger *indignar* (14)
angry *enfadado/a* (20)
anguish *angustia* (20)
angular *anguloso/a* (11)
animation *animación* (15)
anise *anís* (8)
annexation *anexión* (10)
annihilate *aniquilar* (16)
announce *anunciar* (10)
annoy *enojado/a* (20)
answer *respuesta* (1)
anteater *oso hormiguero* (3)
anthropologist *antropólogo/a* (10)
anticipate *anticipar* (18)
antiquated *anticuado/a* (18)
antique *antigüedad* (4)
anti-theft *antirobo* (14)
anxiety *ansiedad* (5)
any *cualquier* (1)
apartment *apartamento* (3)
apologize *disculparse* (18)

appear *parecer* (5)
appearance *apariencia* (14)
appetizer *aperitivo* (8)
applaud *aclamar* (17)
apple *manzana* (8)
applicant *solicitante* (6)
application *aplicación* (16); *solicitud* (7)
apply *aplicar* (9)
apply for *solicitar* (6)
apply pressure *presionar* (18)
appointment *cita* (15)
appreciate *apreciar* (7)
appreciation *apreciación* (13)
approach *acercamiento* (3)
appropriate *adecuado/a* (4)
approve *aprobar* (14)
approximately *aproximadamente* (2)
April *abril* (3)
apron *delantal* (17)
aquarium *acuario* (15)
arabic *árabe* (13)
archeological *arqueológico/a* (8)
archipelago *archipiélago* (11)
architect *arquitecto* (2)
architecture *arquitectura* (2)
Argentinian *argentino/a* (2)
argue *discutir* (5)
arithmetic *aritmética* (9)
arm *brazo* (5)
armchair *sillón* (6)
around *alrededor* (10); *en torno a* (20)
arrest *detención* (17)
arrival *llegada* (7)
arrive *llegar* (1)
art *arte* (2)
art collection *colección de arte* (15)
art gallery *pinacoteca* (15)
artisan work *artesanía* (4)
artist *artista* (2)
as... as *igual... de, tan... como, tanto... como* (9)
as a child *de niño/a* (14)
ascend *ascender* (9)
ascent *ascenso* (5); *subida* (3)
as expected *como era de esperar* (17)
as for *en cuanto a* (16)
ash *ceniza* (20)
ashamed *avergonzado/a* (17)
ashtray *cenicero* (8)
ask questions *hacer preguntas* (13); *preguntar* (17)
assassination *asesinato* (10)
assault *atropellar* (20)
assemble *ensamblar* (18)
assembly *asamblea* (10)
assign *destinar* (9)
assistance *asistencia* (19)
assistant *asistente* (6)
associate *asociar* (20)

assure *asegurar* (12)

asthma *asma* (12)

astonished *boquiabierto/a* (14)

asylum *asilo* (17)

at least *al menos* (5)

atmosphere *ambiente* (8); *atmósfera* (16)

at night *de noche* (7)

atom *átomo* (20)

at once *enseguida* (17)

attack *atacar* (11); *ataque* (10)

attend *acudir (a)* (15); *asistir* (2)

attendant *paje* (4)

attentively *atentamente* (13)

at the beginning of *a principios de* (20)

at the same time *al mismo tiempo* (15)

attract *atraer(se)* (4)

attraction *atracción* (8)

attractive *atractivo/a* (9)

August *agosto* (3)

austere *austero/a* (2)

author *autor/a* (11)

authoritarian *autoritario/a* (14)

authority *autoridad* (17)

authorize *autorizar* (19)

automate *automatizar* (16)

available *disponible, dispuesto* (6)

avalanche *avalancha* (8)

avaricious *avaro/a* (14)

average *promedio* (4)

aviary *aviario* (15)

avocado *aguacate* (8)

avoid *evitar* (12)

awake *despierto/a* (17)

award *premio* (4)

awareness *conciencia* (6)

**B**

babysitter *niñero/a* (18)

back *espalda* (5); *fondo* (17); *respaldar* (18)

backache *dolor de espalda* (12)

backpack *mochila* (4)

bacon *tocino* (8)

bad *malo/a* (4)

bakery *panadería* (18)

balance *equilibrio* (5)

ball *pelota* (4)

banana *plátano* (8)

bank *banco* (3); *orilla* (3)

bank clerk *cajero/a* (4)

banker *banquero/a* (19)

banking *banca* (18)

banner *pabellón* (15)

baptize *bautizar* (11)

bar *barra* (12); *taberna* (15)

barber *peluquería* (3)

Baroque *barroco/a* (14)

barrier *barrera* (14)

baseball *béisbol* (5)

basketball *baloncesto* (3)

basket making *cestería* (4)

Basque *euskera* (15); *vascuense* (13)

bathing suit *traje de baño* (4)

bathroom *baño* (6)

battery *batería* (16); *pila* (4)

batting cage *jaula de bateo* (7)

battle *batalla* (11)

be *estar* (1); *ser (irreg.)* (1)

be (located) *quedarse* (10)

be able to *poder (ue)* (4)

beach *playa* (1)

be a fan of *ser aficionado a* (15)

be afraid (of) (about) *tener miedo (a/de)* (20)

be against *estar en contra* (14)

beak *pico* (3)

bean *grano* (17)

beans *frijoles* (8)

bear *oso* (3); *soportar* (14)

beat *batir* (8)

be at the point of *estar a punto de* (7)

beautiful *bello/a* (3); *bonito/a* (1); *precioso/a* (4)

beauty *belleza* (3); *hermosura* (14)

be born *nacer* (10)

be called *llamarse* (1)

because *porque* (1)

because of that *por eso* (4)

become *convertirse en* (10); *hacerse (irreg.)* (20); *ponerse (irreg.)* (20); *volverse (ue)* (20)

become accustomed *acostumbrarse* (17)

become depressed *deprimirse* (11)

become independent *independizar* (10)

be curious *tener curiosidad* (13)

bed *cama* (6)

be delayed *llegar con retraso* (7)

bedroom *cuarto* (6); *dormitorio* (6)

bee *abeja* (12)

beef jerky *cecina* (8)

be embarrassed *pasar vergüenza* (20)

beer *cerveza* (4)

beet *remolacha* (8)

be fed up with *estar harto de* (20)

be fit *estar en forma* (5)

before *antes (de)* (3)

begin *comenzar (ie)* (5); *empezar (ie)* (6)

be going to *ir a* (1)

behind *detrás de* (12)

be ignorant *ignorar* (19)

be in a good/bad mood *estar de buen/mal humor* (20)

be in shape *estar en forma* (5)

be jealous (of) *tener celos (de)* (20)

be late *llegar tarde* (7); *tardar* (11)

believe *creer* (6)

belong *pertenecer (zc)* (10)

belonging *pertenencia* (6)

below *abajo* (5); *bajo/a* (6)

belt *cinturón* (4)

be mad at someone *estar enfadado/disgustado (con)* (20)

bend *doblar* (5); *flexionar* (5); *recoveco* (20)

beneficial *beneficioso/a* (12)

benefit *beneficiar* (18)

benefit from *aprovechar* (13)

be on a diet *estar a dieta* (5)

be on sale *estar de rebajas* (4)

be overweight *tener exceso de peso* (12)

be owing to *deberse* (6)

be part of *formar parte (de)* (11)

be pleasing to *gustar* (3)

be present at *asistir* (2)

be right *tener razón* (3)

be seated *estar sentado* (5)

besides *además* (4)

be sorry *lamentar* (20); *sentir* (11)

be successful *tener éxito* (5)

be surprised *sorprenderse* (15)

be tired of *estar harto/a (de)* (17)

betrayal *traición* (20)

better *mejor* (9)

be used up *agotarse* (19)

be very boring *ser un rollo* (15)

be worth *merecer (zc)* (15); *valer* (4)

be wrong *equivocarse* (14)

bicycle *bicicleta* (3)

big *grande* (1)

big house *casona* (9)

bilingual *bilingüe* (6)

bill *cuenta* (8)

biodiversity *biodiversidad* (12)

biography *biografía* (10)

biologist *biólogo/a* (16)

biometric *biométrico/a* (19)

biracial *mestizo/a* (11)

bird *ave* (6); *pájaro* (7)

birth *nacimiento* (1)

birth certificate *certificado de nacimiento* (7)

birthday *cumpleaños* (4)

birthplace *cuna, lugar de nacimiento* (7)

birth rate *tasa de natalidad* (1)

bite *picadura* (12)

bitterness *amargura* (14)

black *negro/a* (4)

blind *persiana* (16)

block *cuadra* (9)

blood pressure *presión/tensión* (5)

blood type *grupo sanguíneo* (12)

blouse *blusa* (4)

blow *fundirse* (16)

blue *azul* (4)

board *embarcar* (11)

boat *barco* (3); *buque* (18)

body *cuerpo* (5)

bodyguard *guardaespaldas* (17)

boil *hervir (ie)* (8)

bold *negrita* (2)

Bolivian *boliviano/a* (2)

bond *lazo* (4)

book *libro* (2)

booked *lleno/a* (7)

bookstore *librería* (2)

boot *bota* (4)

border *frontera* (13)

boring *aburrido/a* (1) (7); *pesado/a* (15)
borrow *tomar prestado/a* (20)
both *ambos* (13)
bother *fastidiar; molestar* (13)
bothersome *molesto/a* (20)
bottle *botella* (8)
bottle opener *abrebotellas* (8)
bound *forrado/a* (4)
bound for *rumbo a* (11)
box *caja* (8)
boxing *boxeo* (19)
box office *taquilla* (15)
boyfriend/girlfriend *novio/a* (2)
bracelet *pulsera* (4)
brain *cerebro* (12)
brake *frenar* (12); *freno* (16)
branch *ramo* (18); *sucursal* (18)
brandy *aguardiente* (5)
brave *valiente* (11)
bread *pan* (8)
break *romper* (11)
break (something) *romperse (algo)* (12)
break down *averiarse* (16); *estropearse* (16); *malograrse* (16)
breakfast *ayunas* (12); *desayuno* (5)
break out *estallar* (10)
breast *pecho* (12)
breathe *respirar* (20)
brick *ladrillo* (6)
bridge *puente* (15)
brief *breve* (2)
briefcase *maletín* (17)
bring *traer* (4)
British *británico/a* (10)
broadcasting *retransmisión* (15)
brochure *folleto* (7)
broken *roto/a* (16)
bronchitis *bronquitis* (12)
bronze *bronce* (5)
brother/sister *hermano/a* (2)
brown *marrón* (4)
browser *navegador* (16)
budget *presupuesto* (4)
build *construir (irreg.)* (6)
builder *albañil* (6)
building *edificio* (3)
bulletproof *antibalas* (14)
bullfighting ring *plaza de toros* (15)
bunch *ramo* (18)
bureaucracy *burocracia* (10)
burn *quemadura* (12); *quemar* (12); *arder* (17)
burning sensation *escozor* (12)
bus *autobús; bus; ómnibus* (3)
business *empresa* (6); *negocio* (6)
business-related *comercial; empresarial* (18)
busy *ocupado/a* (7)
but *pero* (1); *sino* (17)
butler *mayordomo* (17)
butter *mantequilla* (8)
button *botón* (16)

buy *comprar* (4)
buying and selling *compraventa* (10)
by air *por vía aérea* (9)
by foot *a pie* (11)
by the way *a propósito* (17)
by water *por vía fluvial* (9)

## C

cab *taxi* (7)
cabin *cabaña* (3)
cake *pastel* (4); *torta* (18)
calendar *calendario* (14)
call *llamada* (18); *llamar* (3)
calm *calmar* (5); *tranquilidad* (5); *tranquilo/a* (3)
camel *camello* (4)
camera *cámara de fotos* (7)
camp *campamento* (3)
campaign *campaña* (12)
can *lata* (8)
can (be able to) *poder (ue)* (4)
Canada *Canadá* (18)
cancel *cancelar* (7)
cancellation *cancelación* (7)
cancer *cáncer* (12)
candidate *candidato/a* (6)
candy *bombón* (18); *dulce* (5)
canned *enlatado* (12)
cannon *cañón* (11)
cannonshot *cañonazo* (11)
canoeing *piragüismo* (15)
can opener *abrelatas* (8)
canopy *pabellón* (15)
canvas *lienzo* (5)
cap *gorra* (3)
capable *capaz* (16)
captain *capitán* (5)
captivate *cautivar* (12)
car *carro* (4); *coche* (4); *automóvil* (6)
card *ficha* (2)
cardboard *cartón* (16)
care *cuidado* (12); *preocuparse de* (20)
career *carrera* (10)
care for *cuidar* (12)
Caribbean *caribeño/a* (8)
car repair *taller* (18)
carrot *zanahoria* (8)
carry *llevar* (6)
carry out *llevar a cabo* (16)
cartero/a *vehículo* (6)
carved *tallado/a* (9)
cash *en efectivo* (17)
cashier *cajero/a* (4)
cash register *cajero automático* (19)
casserole *cazuela* (8)
castle *castillo* (11)
casual *deportivo/a* (3); *informal* (4)
Catalan *catalán* (15)
catarata *waterfall* (4)
catastrophe *catástrofe* (6)

catastrophic *catastrófico/a* (5)
Catholic *católico/a* (19)
cauliflower *coliflor* (8)
cause *causa* (5); *causar* (6); *ocasionar* (11)
cave *cueva* (11)
CD-Rom reader *lector de CD-Rom* (16)
celebrate *celebrar* (11); *festejar* (20)
celery *apio* (8)
cell phone *teléfono celular/móvil* (16)
central *céntrico/a* (6)
century *siglo* (10)
ceramicist *ceramista* (2)
certain *cierto/a; seguro* (5)
certainly *ciertamente* (14)
certificate *certificado* (7)
chain *cadena* (3)
chair *silla* (4)
challenge *desafío; reto* (19)
champagne *champaña* (19)
championship *campeonato* (5)
change *cambiar* (2); *cambio* (4)
chaos *caos* (9)
character *personaje* (3); *carácter* (14)
characteristic *característica* (5)
characterize *caracterizar* (15)
charge *cargar* (16)
charm *encanto* (9); *simpatía* (11)
charming *encantador/a* (15)
chat *charlar* (14)
chauffer *chofer* (17)
cheap *barato/a* (4)
check *comprobar* (18); *cuenta* (8)
check luggage *facturar la(s) maleta(s)* (7)
check out *irse del hotel* (7)
cheese *queso* (8)
chef *cocinero/a* (2)
chemistry *química* (16)
chest *pecho* (12)
chicken *pollo* (4)
chief *cacique* (11)
childhood *infancia; niñez* (10)
Chilean *chileno/a* (2)
Chinese *chino/a* (13)
choice *elección* (9)
cholesterol *colesterol* (12)
choose *elegir (i)* (1) (3)
Christmas *Navidad* (4)
Christmas Eve *víspera de Navidad Nochebuena* (8)
chronological *cronológico/a* (10)
church *iglesia* (3)
cigar *cigarro* (8)
cigar/cigarette case *cigarrera* (4)
cigar/cigarette maker or vendor *cigarrera* (4)
cigar cutter *cortapuro* (8)
cigarette *cigarrillo* (12)
cinema *cine* (1)
cinnamon *canela* (8)
circulation of blood *circulación sanguínea* (5)
circumstance *circunstancia* (11)
cite *citar* (18)
citizenship *ciudadanía* (10)

city *ciudad* (1)
city center *centro* (3)
city hall *alcaldía* (3); *ayuntamiento* (7)
civil rights *derechos civiles* (10)
clad *revestido/a* (11)
claim *reclamar* (18); *reivindicación* (19)
clarify *aclarar* (17)
clash *chocar* (20)
class *clase* (10)
classic *clásico/a* (4)
classify *clasificar* (11)
classmate *compañero/a de clase* (1)
classroom *aula* (13)
clean *limpiar* (3); *limpio/a* (9)
cleaner *quitamanchas* (14)
clever *listo/a* (5)
cleverness *habilidad* (17)
climate *clima* (6); *entorno* (3)
climate change *cambio climático* (19)
climatic *climático/a* (19)
climb *ascender* (9)
climbing *escalada* (18)
cloak *manto* (17)
close *cerrar* (1)
closed *cerrado/a* (7)
closet *armario* (6); *ropero* (17)
cloth *paño* (12); *tela* (4)
clothes *vestimenta* (14)
clothing *ropa* (3)
clothing store *tienda de ropa* (4)
clue *pista* (17)
coast *costa* (10)
coast guard *guardacostas* (14)
coat *abrigo* (4)
coca grower *cocalero* (17)
coca plant *coca* (17)
cocktail *cóctel* (8)
coconut *coco* (8)
code *código* (1)
coffee *café* (8)
coffee grower *cafetalero/a* (8)
coffee shop *cafetería* (9)
coffee tree *cafeto* (8)
coherence *coherencia* (14)
cold (illness) *resfriado* (12)
cold (temperature) *frío* (9)
collaborate *colaborar* (10)
colleague *colega* (11)
collect *coleccionar* (2); *recaudar* (18)
collection *colección* (7)
college *universidad* (2)
college campus *ciudad universitaria* (9)
Colombian *colombiano/a* (2)
colonist *colonizador/a* (11)
colonization *colonización* (10)
colony *colonia* (11)
colorful *colorido/a* (9)
column *columna* (5)
comb *peinar* (17)
come *venir* (6)
come back *regresar* (10)

come from *provenir* (10)
come in *pase* (8)
comfort *comodidad* (9)
comfortable *cómodo/a* (3)
comma *coma* (13)
command *mando* (11)
commander *comandante* (11)
commemorate *conmemorar* (20)
commemorative *conmemorativo/a* (18)
comment *comentar* (6)
commerce *comercio* (18)
commercialize *comercializar* (16)
commitment *compromiso* (5)
common sense *sensatez* (14)
community *comunidad* (6)
compact disc *disco compacto* (16)
companions *acompañante* (7)
company *compañía* (6)
comparison *comparación* (9)
compete *competir* (18)
complex *complejo/a* (7)
complicated *complicado/a* (5)
compose *componer* (5)
composer *compositor* (15)
composition *redacción* (13)
comptentious *despectivo/a* (13)
computer *computador/a* (16); *ordenador* (15)
computer mouse *ratón* (16)
computers *informática* (6)
computer science *informática* (6)
computing *computación* (4)
conceited *engreído/a* (14)
conceive *concebir* (17)
concert *concierto* (15)
conclude *concluir* (6)
concrete *hormigón* (6)
condemn *condenar* (10)
conference *encuentro* (15)
confidence *confianza* (20)
confirm *comprobar* (18)
confront *enfrentar* (5)
connection *conexión* (4)
conqueror *conquistador* (10)
conquest *conquista* (10)
conscious *consciente* (5)
consequence *consecuencia* (19)
consequently *por consiguiente* (20)
conservation *conservación* (8)
conservative *conservador/a* (10)
conserve *conservar* (2)
consider *considerar* (8)
consultant *asesor/a* (10)
consulting service *asesoría* (18)
consumer *comsumidor* (18); *consumidor/a* (8)
consumer goods *bienes de consumo* (19)
consumption *consumo* (5)
contact *comunicar* (11)
container *contenedor* (18); *envase* (8)
contents *contenido* (6)
contest *concurso* (15); *festival* (1)
continue *seguir* (6); *continuar* (11)

contract *contrato* (6)
contradict *contradecir (irreg.)* (19)
contradiction *contradicción* (19)
contribute *contribuir* (2)
contribution *aporte* (9)
convalescent *convaleciente* (20)
convenience *comodidad* (16)
convenient *conveniente* (5); *práctico/a* (16)
conversation *conversación* (2)
converse *conversar* (8)
convert *convertir* (15)
convince *convencer* (6)
convincing *convincente* (11)
cook *cocinar* (2); *cocinero/a* (2)
cooked *codido/a* (12)
cooking *cocina* (8)
cool (weather) *templado/a* (9)
cool down *enfriar* (8)
copper *cobre* (16)
copy *copia* (6)
copy machine *fotocopiadora* (16)
corn *maíz* (5)
corner *esquina* (16); *rincón* (9)
correct *corregir* (10)
correct oneself *corregirse* (13)
corridor *pasillo* (6)
cosmetics *cosméticos* (18)
cost *costar (ue)* (4)
Costa Rican *costarricense* (2)
costly *costoso/a* (4)
cotton *algodón* (16)
cough *tos; toser* (12)
counselor *consejero/a* (5)
count on *contar (ue) con* (6)
country *país* (1)
country folk *campesino/a* (6)
country house *granja* (18)
countryside *campo* (3)
coup d'état *golpe de estado* (10)
coupon *cupón* (4)
courage *valentía* (14)
courier *mensajero/a* (18)
courier service *mensajería* (18)
course *curso* (1)
court *pista* (3); *cancha* (9)
courtesy *cortesía* (6)
cover *cubrir* (5)
covet *codiciar* (19)
cow *vaca* (10)
cowardliness *cobardía* (14)
cowardly *cobarde* (11)
craft *artesanía* (4); *manualidad* (13)
crazy *loco/a* (20)
cream *crema* (12)
create *crear* (6)
creativity *creatividad* (14)
creature *criatura* (20)
credit card *tarjeta de crédito* (4)
crib *cuna* (7)
crime *delincuencia* (9)
critique *criticar* (9)

cross *atravesar* (12); *cruzar* (12)
crossing *travesía* (11)
cruise *crucero* (3)
cry *llorar* (15)
Cuban *cubano/a* (2)
cucumber *pepino* (8)
culinary *culinario/a* (17)
culture *cultura* (1)
cup *taza* (8)
currency *moneda* (7)
currently *actualmente* (2)
custom *costumbre* (10)
cut *cortar* (8)
cut one's hair *cortarse el pelo* (18)
CV *currículo* (6)
cycle *ciclo* (19)

**D**

daily *diurno/a* (9)
daily activity *cotidianidad* (2); *a diario* (8)
dairy products *productos lácteos* (5)
damage *daño* (12); *estropear* (18)
dance *bailar* (2); *baile* (1); (classic or traditional) *danza* (2); *danzar* (17)
danger *peligro* (7)
dangerous *espinoso* (18); *peligroso/a* (3)
dare *atreverse* (19)
dark *moreno/a* (2); *oscuro/a* (11)
date *cita* (15); *datar* (11); *dato* (10); *fecha* (7)
date (fruit) *dátil* (8)
date back to *datar de* (11)
dawn *amanecer (cz)* (15)
day after tomorrow *pasado mañana* (7)
day before yesterday *anteayer, antes de ayer* (7)
daycare *guardería* (9)
daydream *ensueño* (15)
deaf *sordo/a* (17)
dean *decanato* (9)
death *muerte* (6)
debatable *discutible* (14)
debate *debatir* (19)
decade *década* (5)
December *diciembre* (3)
decent *digno/a* (6); *honesto/a* (11)
deceptive *mentiroso/a* (20)
decide *decidir* (6)
declare *declarar* (10)
decode *descifrar* (16)
decomposition *descomposión* (16)
dedicate oneself *dedicarse* (2)
deep *profundo/a* (5)
deeply *profundamente* (19)
defeat *vencer* (20)
defect *defecto* (14)
defender *defensor/a* (11)
definitively *definitivamente* (14)
deforestation *deforestación* (19)
deform *deformar* (5)
degree *grado* (12); *título* (6)
deify *deificar* (10)

delay *retraso* (7)
delete *borrar* (14)
delicious *delicioso/a* (8); *rico/a* (8)
deliver *entregar* (10)
delivery *entrega* (18); *reparto* (18)
demand *demanda* (18)
dementia *demencia* (20)
demonstrate *demostrar (ue)* (8)
demonstration *manifestación* (10)
denounce *denunciar* (10)
dentist *dentista* (7)
dentistry *odontología* (12)
deodorant *desodorante* (4)
depart *partir* (10)
departure *salida* (7)
depend *depender* (13)
dependable *confiable* (18)
depict *retratar* (14)
depress *deprimir* (14)
depressed *deprimido/a* (5)
depression *depresión* (5)
derive *derivar* (11)
descend *descender* (14)
descendent *descendiente* (11)
descent *ascendencia* (2)
describe *describir* (7)
desert *desierta* (14)
design *diseñar* (6) (14)
designer *diseñador/a* (7)
desire *desear* (11)
desk *escritorio* (6)
dessert *postre* (4)
destination *destino* (3)
destiny *destino* (10)
destroy *destruir* (6)
destruction *destrucción* (19)
detailed *detallado/a* (4)
detain *detener* (11)
detection *detección* (16)
detective movie *película policíaca* (15)
detention *detención* (17)
deteriorate *deteriorar* (12)
determine *determinar* (20)
devastate *devastar* (11)
devastating *devastador/a* (20)
develop *desarrollar* (10) *desarrollar(se)* (13); *revelar fotos* (7)
developed *desarrollado/a* (19)
developing country *país en vías de desarrollo* (19)
development *desarrollar* (3); *desarrollo* (17)
device *aparato* (16); *dispositivo* (16)
diagnose *diagnosticar* (19)
dial *marcar* (6)
diarrhea *diarrea* (12)
dictator *dictador* (11)
dictatorship *dictadura* (10)
die *morir (ue)* (10)
diet *dieta* (8); *régimen* (12)
difficult *difícil* (1); *espinoso* (18)
difficulty *dificultad* (8)

digital camera *cámara digital* (16)
digitalization *digitalización* (19)
digitize *digitalizar* (16)
digitized *digitalizado/a* (16)
diligence *diligencia* (11)
dine *cenar* (6)
dining room *comedor* (3)
dinner *cena* (2)
dip *sumergir* (8)
direct *dirigir* (10); *guiar* (4)
direction *orientación* (17)
dirty *sucio/a* (9)
disadvantage *desventaja* (18)
disagreement *desacuerdo* (3)
disappear *desaparecer* (10)
disappearance *desaparición* (17)
disappointed *decepcionado/a* (20)
disapproval *desaprobación* (13)
disapprove *desaprobar* (14)
disaster *desastre* (11)
discard *descartar* (19); *desechar* (16)
discharge *descarga* (16)
discomfort *molestia* (12)
disconcerting *desconcertante* (20)
disconnect *desconectar* (16)
discontent *descontento/a* (20)
discount *descuento* (4)
discover *descubrir* (7)
discovery *descubrimiento* (9)
discrimination *discriminación* (19)
disembark *desembarcar* (11)
disguise oneself as *disfrazarse (de)* (17)
dish *plato* (4)
dishonest *deshonesto/a* (18)
disintegrate *desintegrar* (10)
dismiss *destituir* (10)
disorder *transtorno* (5)
disorderly *desordenado/a* (14)
disorganized *desorganizado/a* (20)
displacement *desplazamiento* (10)
disposed *dispuesto* (6)
disrespectful *irrespetuoso* (14)
distant *ajeno/a* (7)
distress *angustiar* (14)
distribute *distribuir* (10); *repartir* (14)
distribution *distribución* (2); *reparto* (18)
district *distrito* (15)
distrustful *desconfiado/a* (19)
disturbance *transtorno* (5)
dive *bucear* (7)
diving *buceo* (3)
divorce *divorciarse* (10)
divorced *divorciado/a* (2)
dizziness *mareo* (12)
dizzy *mareado/a* (12)
do *hacer (irreg.)* (2)
do business *comerciar* (18)
docile *dócil* (20)
doctor *médico* (2)
doctor's office *consulta* (12)
documentary *documental* (15)

doll *muñeco/a* (16)
dollar *dólar* (16)
dolphin *delfín* (7)
dolphinarium *delfinario* (15)
dome *cúpula* (4)
domestic *casero/a* (8)
domicile *domicilio* (18)
dominate *dominar* (11)
Dominican *dominicano/a* (2)
donation *donación* (6)
door *puerta* (6) (17)
dorm *residencia estudiantil* (9)
doubt *dudar* (11)
download *bajar* (16)
downtown *centro* (3)
do yoga *hacer yoga* (5)
dozen *docena* (8)
draftsman *dibujante* (2)
draw *dibujar* (2)
draw conclusions *sacar conclusiones* (19)
drawing *dibujo* (2)
dream *sueño* (20)
dress *vestido* (4)
dried beef *cecina* (8); *tasajo* (8)
drilling *perforación* (20)
drink *beber* (5); *bebida* (5); *copa* (15)
drink (alcohol) *tomar (alcohol)* (5)
drive *conducir* (7); *manejar* (6)
driver *conductor* (10)
driver's license *licencia de conducir* (6);
  *permiso de conducir* (7)
drought *sequía* (19)
drug *droga* (12)
drug addictions *drogadicciones* (12)
drug trafficking *narcotráfico* (19)
drum *bombo* (4)
dry *seco/a* (3)
dry cleaner *tintorería* (18)
due to *debido a* (3); *a causa de* (20)
duplication *duplicación* (16)
duration *duración* (7)
during *durante* (7)
during the day *de día* (7)
Dutch *holandés/a* (10)
DVD player *DVD (reproductor de)* (16)
dwell *habitar* (11)
dynamic *dinámico/a* (6)
dynasty *dinastía* (11)

**E**

each *cada* (1)
ear *oído* (12); *oreja* (5)
earache *dolor de oídos* (12)
early *temprano* (7)
early morning *madrugada* (7)
earn *ganar* (6)
earring *pendiente* (4)
earth *tierra* (11)
earthquake *terremoto* (6)
ease *facilidad* (17)

east *este* (3); *oriente* (7)
easy *fácil* (1)
eat *comer* (2)
eating disorder *trastorno alimenticio* (12)
ecologist *ecologista* (19)
ecology *ecología* (9)
economy *economía* (18)
ecosystem *ecosistema* (12)
Ecuadorian *ecuatoriano/a* (2)
edification *edificación* (3)
editar/corregir *redactar* (10)
education *formación* (6)
effect *efecto* (6)
effective *efectivo/a* (5)
efficiency *eficiencia* (18)
effort *esfuerzo* (12)
egg *huevo* (8)
eggplant *berenjena* (8)
egoism *egoísmo* (14)
Egyptian *egipcio/a* (14)
eight *ocho* (1)
eighteen *dieciocho* (1)
eight hundred *ochocientos* (4)
eighty *ochenta* (2)
elaborate *elaborar* (8)
elbow *codo* (5)
elect *elegir (i)* (3)
elections *elecciones* (10)
electric *eléctrico/a* (16)
electrician *electricista* (18)
electricity *electricidad* (16)
electronic agenda *agenda electrónica* (16)
electronic appliance *electrodomésticos* (4)
elegant *elegante* (4)
elevate *elevar* (16)
elevator *ascensor* (6)
eleven *once* (1)
eliminate *eliminar* (8)
elude *eludir* (20)
embark *embarcar* (11)
embarrass *dar vergüenza* (13)
embarrassment *vergüenza* (13)
embassador *embajador/a* (14)
embrace *abrazar* (20)
embroidery *bordado* (20)
emerge *surgir* (18)
emergency *urgencia* (12)
emergency room *servicio de emergencias* (12)
emigrant *emigrante* (7)
emigrate *emigrar* (12)
emigration *emigración* (14)
emotional *emotivo/a* (20)
emphasis *énfasis* (12); *hincapié* (5)
emphasize *destacar* (5)
empire *imperio* (9)
employ *emplear* (5)
employee *empleado/a* (6)
employment *empleo* (6)
empower *potenciar* (13)
empty *vacío/a* (7)
encourage *animar* (12)

end *cabo* (5); *terminar* (8)
ending *terminación* (2)
endorse *suscribir* (10)
enemy *enemigo/a* (11)
energy *energía* (16)
engineer *ingeniero/a* (20)
engineering *ingeniería* (12)
English *inglés/inglesa* (11)
enjoy *disfrutar* (3)
enjoyment *diversión* (8)
enjoy oneself *divertirse (ie)* (3)
enmity *enemistad* (20)
enormous *enorme* (15)
enough *bastante* (5); *suficiente* (8)
enrich *enriquecer* (13)
enroll *enrolar* (10); *inscribirse* (13)
enter *entrar* (19)
entertaining *entretenido/a* (15)
entertainment *entretenimiento* (9); *oferta
  cultural* (15)
entry *entrada* (6)
envious *envidioso/a* (14)
environment *entorno* (3); *medio ambiente* (9)
environmental *ambiental* (9);
  *medioambiental* (18)
envy *envidia* (14)
epidemic *epidemia* (10)
epoch *época* (10)
equal *igual* (8)
equality *igualdad* (19)
equally *igual de* (7)
equinox *equinoccio* (20)
equip *aparejar* (18)
era *época* (10)
erase *borrar* (14)
erect *erguido/a* (5)
eradication *erradicación* (19)
escape *escapar* (10); *fugarse* (17); *huir* (11)
Eskimo *esquimal* (17)
especially *especialmente* (18)
essay *ensayo* (13); *trabajo escrito* (13)
essence *esencia* (19)
essentially *esencialmente* (13)
establish *establecer* (6); *instaurar* (10)
estate *hacienda* (10)
estimate *estimar* (6)
etching *grabado* (11)
eternal *eterna* (12)
ethical *ético/a* (19)
ethnic *étnico/a* (11)
ethnic group *etnia* (10)
European *europeo/a* (2)
European Union *Unión Europea* (10)
euthanasia *eutanasia* (19)
evaluate *evaluar* (8)
even *incluso* (19)
evening *noche* (6)
event *acontecimiento* (10)
everyday *cotidiano/a* (11)
evidence *prueba* (17)
exactly *efectivamente* (13); *exactamente* (14)

exaggerated *exagerado/a* (5)
examinar *examinar* (4)
exceed *rebasar* (9)
excel *sobresalir* (8); *superar* (16)
excellent *excelente* (8)
excess *exceso* (5)
excessively *excesivamente* (12)
exchange *intercambio* (2)
excite *emocionar* (14)
exciting *emocionante* (15)
exclusive *excluyente* (19)
excuse *dispensar* (20)
excuse me *disculpe* (8)
excuse oneself *excusarse* (15)
exercise *ejercicio; hacer ejercicio* (5)
exert *ejercer* (20)
exhale *exhalar* (5)
exhibition *exposición* (15)
exist *existir* (8)
exotic *exótico/a* (3)
expectancy *esperanza* (12)
expedient *expediente* (6)
expedition *expedición* (10)
expel *expulsar* (11)
expensive *caro/a* (4)
experience *experiencia* (6)
expert *experto* (20)
explain *explicar* (5)
explanation *explicación* (13)
explorer *explorador/a* (10)
export *exportar* (7)
exportation *exportación* (18)
exports *exportación* (18)
expose *exponer* (5)
exposition *exposición* (5)
express *expresar* (18); *exprimir* (12)
express an opinion *opinar* (19)
expressivity *expresividad* (15)
extend *estirar* (5); *extenderse* (14)
extension *ampliación* (18)
extermination *exterminio* (10)
extract *extraer* (11)
extraction *ascendencia* (2)
extraordinary *genial* (15)
extraterrestrial *extraterrestre* (11)
extrovert *extrovertido/a* (14)
eye *ojo* (5)
eyeglasses *anteojos* (4)

**F**

fabulous *fabuloso/a* (3)
face *cara* (5); *rostro* (2)
face (of a clock) *esfera* (7)
face down *boca abajo* (7)
face to face *cara a cara* (7)
facilitate *facilitar* (9)
facilities *instalaciones* (3) (5)
fact *hecho* (10)
faction *facción* (2)
faint *desmayarse* (12)

fair *equitativo/a* (6); *feria* (15); *justo/a* (18)
fair trade *comercio justo* (19)
fairy tale *cuento de hada* (17)
faithful *fiel* (14)
fall *caer* (10); *otoño* (3)
fall asleep *dormirse (ue)* (5)
fall down *caer(se)* (11)
falling apart *desvencijado/a* (20)
fall in love with *enamorarse de* (10)
fame *fama* (6)
famous *célebre* (11)
fan *aficionado/a* (5)
fantasy *ensueño* (15)
far *lejano/a* (18)
far from *lejos de* (7)
farm *granja* (18)
farming *agropecuario/a* (18)
fashion *moda* (4)
fast *rápido/a* (7)
fat *gordo/a* (5); *grasa* (5)
fatality *fatalidad* (20)
father *padre* (2)
Father Christmas *Papá Noel* (4)
fault *defecto* (14)
fear *miedo* (11)
fearful *miedoso/a* (14)
feather *pluma* (14)
feature *reportaje* (19)
feature film *largometraje* (16)
February *febrero* (3)
fed up (with) *harto/a (de)* (18)
fed up with *estar harto/a (de)* (17)
feed *alimentar* (5); *sustentar* (20)
feed (oneself) *alimentarse* (11)
feel *sentir* (11)
feel anguish/stress *sentirse angustiado/a* (20)
feeling *sentimiento* (10)
feel like doing *apetecer* (15)
feel sorry for someone/something *dar lástima* (20)
fellow man *semejante* (20)
ferry *trasbordador* (10)
fervent *ferviente* (11)
festivity/party *fiesta* (1)
fever *fiebre* (10)
fiber *fibra* (4)
fiction novel *novela de ficción* (17)
fidelity *fidelidad* (14)
field *campo* (7)
field trip *excursión* (3)
fifteen *quince* (1)
fifty *cincuenta* (2)
fight *lucha* (11); *luchar* (6); *pelearse* (20)
figure *cifra* (18)
file *archivo* (16)
fill out *rellenar* (14)
film *filmar* (16); *película* (2); *rollo* (15)
film critic *cineasta* (16)
film enthusiast *cineasta* (16)
filter *filtro* (12)

finally *finalmente* (2); *al final* (8)
finances *finanzas* (19)
financial *financiero/a* (18)
find *hallar* (20)
find hard to *costar (ue)* (13)
find oneself *encontrarse (ue)* (12)
find out *averiguar* (2); *encontrar (ue)* (3); *enterarse* (17)
fine *fino/a* (2)
Finnish *finlandés* (13)
fire *despedir (i)* (6); *fuego* (8); *incendio* (16)
fireman/woman *bombero/a* (6)
firm *compañía; empresa* (6)
firmness *firmeza* (5)
first *primer/a* (1)
first name *nombre* (1)
fish *pescado* (5); *pez* (3)
fish market *pescadería* (8)
fishmonger *pescadería* (8)
fit *caber* (13)
five *cinco* (1)
five hundred *quinientos/as* (4)
fix *componer* (5); *fijar* (13); *reparar* (16); *arreglar* (16)
flag *bandera* (11)
flannel *franela* (17)
flat *plano/a* (3)
flavor *sabor* (8)
flecked *salpicado/a* (11)
fledged *emplumado/a* (11)
flexible *ágil* (5)
flight *huida* (11); *vuelo* (7)
flight attendant *azafato/a* (17)
float *flotar* (5)
floodgate *compuerta* (18)
floor *planta* (4)
florist's *floristería* (18)
flour *harina* (8)
flourish *florecer* (9)
flower *flor* (18); *flujo* (20)
flower shop *florería* (4)
flu *gripe* (5)
fluency *fluidez* (10)
flute *flauta* (4)
fly *volar (ue)* (7)
focus *enfoque* (14)
fog *niebla* (9)
foggy *nublado/a* (9)
follow *seguir* (2); *suceder* (10)
followed by *seguido de* (9)
following *siguiente* (10)
foment *fomentar* (19)
food *alimentación* (18); *alimento* (8); *comida* (1)
food poisoning *intoxicación* (12)
foot *pie* (5)
forbid *prohibir* (20)
forehead *frente* (5)
foreigner *extranjero/a* (2)
foreign language *lengua extranjera* (13)
foresee *prever* (19)

forest *bosque* (3)
for example *por ejemplo* (5)
forget *olvidar* (4); *olvidarse de* (13)
form *formulario* (17)
format *formato* (18)
formulario *fórmula* (19)
formulate *formular* (14)
fortress *fortaleza* (11)
fortunate *afortunado/a* (14)
forty *cuarenta* (2)
for what purpose *para que* (4)
found *fundar* (10)
founded *fundado/a* (7)
four *cuatro* (1)
four hundred *cuatrocientos/as* (4)
fourteen *catorce* (1)
fourth *cuarto* (6)
foyer *vestíbulo* (17)
fragile *frágil* (20)
fragment *trozo* (8)
frame *marco* (4)
France *Francia* (12)
free *gratis* (7); *libre* (8); *liberar* (10);
   *gratuito* (12)
freedom *libertad* (10)
freeze *congelarse* (20)
French *francés* (13)
French fries *papas fritas* (4)
frequently *frecuentemente* (12)
fresh *fresco/a* (4)
Friday *viernes* (5)
fried *frito/a* (8)
friend *amigo/a* (2)
friendliness *amabilidad* (18)
friendly *sociable* (14)
friendship *amistad* (10)
fright *susto* (11)
frighten *asustar* (17); *dar*
   *medio* (13)
fritter *buñuelo* (8)
from where *de dónde* (4)
front-desk attendant *recepcionista* (6)
frozen *congelado/a* (18)
fruit *fruta* (5)
fruit dish *frutero* (8)
fruit seller *frutero* (8)
fry *freír (i)* (8)
frying pan *sartén* (8)
fulfillment *desempeño* (12)
full *pleno/a* (9)
full-length film *largometraje* (16)
full-time *a tiempo completo* (6)
fun *diversión; divertido/a* (1)
function *funcionar* (5)
fund *financiar* (18); *fondo* (6)
funny *chistoso/a* (11); *gracioso/a* (11);
   *divertido/a* (14)
furnish *amueblar* (6)
furnished *amueblado/a* (6)
furniture *mobiliario* (18); *muebles* (6)
furthermore *es más* (15)

**G**

gain weight *engordar* (5)
Galician *gallego* (15)
game *juego* (7); *partido* (3)
gangplank *pasarela* (15)
gap *brecha* (19); *salto* (3)
garage *garaje* (17)
garbage *basura* (9)
garden *jardín* (3)
garlic *ajo* (8)
garment *prenda de vestir* (4)
gas station *gasolinera* (9)
gas station (Perú) *grifo* (9)
generate *generar* (12)
generation *generación* (10)
generosity *generosidad* (14)
generous *generoso/a* (14)
genetic code (DNA) *código genético*
   *(ADN)* (16)
genetic engineering *ingeniería genética* (19)
genius *genio* (19)
genre *género* (14)
genuine *sincero/a* (14)
geography *geografía* (1)
germ *gérmen* (5)
German *alemán* (13)
Germany *Alemania* (18)
gestation *gestación* (20)
gesture *ademán* (17); *gesto* (13)
get a cold *resfriarse* (12)
get all mixed up *hacerse un lío* (13)
get along (poorly) with *llevarse bien/(mal)*
   *con* (14)
get along with *conectarse, entenderse con* (20)
get angry *enojarse* (20)
get bored *aburrirse* (9)
get cold *enfriarse* (8)
get damaged *estropearse* (16)
get discouraged *desanimarse* (13)
get dizzy *marearse* (12)
get engaged *comprometerse* (10)
get frustrated *frustrarse* (13)
get happy *ponerse contento/a* (20)
get hold of *agarrar* (11)
get hurt *lesionarse* (12)
get injured *lesionarse* (12)
get jealous *ponerse celoso/a* (20)
get married *casarse* (10)
get out *bajar* (13)
get ready *alistar* (17)
get rid of *quitar* (12)
get sick *enfermarse; ponerse enfermo* (12)
get sunburned *quemarse* (12)
get tired *cansarse* (12)
get up *levantarse* (5)
get up early *madrugar* (3)
get upset *molestarse* (20)
giant *gigante* (17)
gift *regalo* (4)
gift store *tienda de regalos* (4)

gigantic *gigantesco/a* (7)
give *dar* (1); *entregar* (10)
give a gift *hacer un regalo; regalar* (4)
give a standing ovation *ovacionar de pie* (10)
given *dado/a/os/as* (20)
given that *dado que* (20)
give the floor *ceder la palabra* (13)
give up *renunciar a* (20)
glance *mirada* (15)
glass *vaso* (12); *cristal* (16); *vidrio* (16)
glasses *gafas* (16)
glasshouse *invernadero* (15)
globalization *globalización; mundialización* (19)
global warming *calentamiento global* (19)
globe *globo* (20)
gloves *guantes* (4)
go *ir (irreg.)* (2)
goal *meta* (18); *propósito* (6)
goalkeeper *portero/a* (5)
go camping *acampar, ir de camping* (7)
go down *bajar* (13)
go for a walk *dar una vuelta* (17)
gold *oro* (11)
golf player *golfista* (5)
good *bien* (11); *bueno/a* (2)
good-looking *guapo/a* (2)
goodness *bondad* (14)
goods *mercancía* (18)
go out *salir (lg)* (15)
go out for a drink *ir de copas* (15)
go out for dinner *salir a cenar* (15)
go out with *salir con* (17)
go shopping *ir de compras* (4)
go through *transitar* (20)
go to bed *acostarse (ue)* (5)
go up *subir* (1)
govern *gobernar* (11)
government *gobierno* (11)
government official *funcionario/a* (11)
government-related *gubernamental* (18)
governor *gobernador* (10)
GPS navigation system *sistema de navegación*
   *GPS* (16)
grade *calificación* (9)
graft *injerto* (12)
gram *gramo* (8)
grandfather/grandmother *abuelo/a* (2)
grandparents *abuelos* (2)
grant *dispensar* (20)
grape *uva* (8)
graphic *gráfico* (12)
graphic arts *artes gráficas* (18)
gravity *gravedad* (11)
gray *gris* (4)
grazing *pastoreo* (10)
great *genial* (15)
Great Britain *Gran Bretaña* (10)
Greece *Grecia* (18)
greed *avaricia* (14)
Greek *griego* (13)
green *verde* (4)

green beans *habichuelas* (8); *judías verdes* (8)
greenhouse *invernadero* (15)
Greenland *Groenlandia* (10)
greenness *verdor* (11)
green zone *zona verde* (9)
greet *saludar* (6)
grief *pena* (11)
grill *parrilla* (3); (8)
grocery store *mercado* (7)
gross domestic product *producto interno bruto (PIB)* (18)
ground *picado/a* (8)
group *grupo* (1)
grow *crecer (zc)* (1); *cultivar* (8)
growing *cultivo* (5); *en crecimiento* (18)
growth *crecimiento* (9)
grow up *crecer (zc)* (10)
grumpy *gruñón* (3)
guarantee *garantizar* (12)
Guatemalan *guatemalteco/a* (2)
guess *adivinar* (1)
guest *invitado/a* (18)
guide *guía* (3); *guiar* (4)
gum *chicle* (12)
gym *gimnasio* (3)

**H**

habit *costumbre* (5)
habitación *hábito* (8)
hair *pelo* (5)
hairdresser *peluquería* (3)
half *mitad* (1)
hallway *pasillo* (6)
halt *detener(se)* (11)
ham *jamón* (8)
hamburger *hamburguesa* (20)
hand *mano* (5)
handbill *cartel* (4)
handful *puñado* (17)
handkerchief *pañuelo* (4)
hand over *entregar* (10)
handsome/pretty *guapo/a* (2)
handy *práctico/a* (16)
hang *colgar (ue)* (16)
happen *ocurrir* (9); *suceder* (10); *pasar* (19)
happiness *alegría* (14); *felicidad* (14)
happy *alegre* (2); *feliz* (10)
harbor *puerto* (9)
hard *duro/a* (8)
hard liquor *aguardiente* (5)
hardly *nada* (2)
hardness *dureza* (8)
hardworking *trabajador/a* (20)
harm *daño* (8)
harshness *dureza* (8)
harvest *cosecha* (6)
hat *gorro* (4)
hate *odiar* (14)
have *tener (ie)* (1)
have (in compound tenses) *haber* (1)

have a cold *estar resfriado/a* (12)
have a drink *tomar unas copas* (15)
have a good time *pasarlo bien* (4); *tener (ie)* (4)
have an accident *tener un accidente* (12)
have an argument *pelearse* (20)
have a snack *merendar (ie)* (8)
have breakfast *desayunar* (5)
have fun *divertirse (ie)* (15)
have just *acabar de* (7)
have something *disponer de algo* (9)
have something in common *tener algo en común* (14)
have surgery *operarse (de)* (12)
have to *tener que* (2)
havoc *embestido/a* (20)
Hawaii *Hawai* (10)
hazelnut *avellana* (8)
head *cabeza* (5)
headache *dolor de cabeza* (12)
headline *titular* (19)
health *salud* (5)
health insurance *seguro médico* (12)
healthy *sano/a* (5); *saludable* (12)
heap *montón* (16)
hear *oír* (17)
heart *corazón* (3)
heart attack *ataque al corazón* (12)
heat *calentar (ie)* (8); *calor* (9)
heavy *pesado/a* (16)
Hebrew *hebreo* (13)
hectare *hectárea* (3)
heel *tacón* (4)
height *altura* (12)
heir/heiress *heredero/a* (8)
hell *infierno* (17)
hello *aló* (6); *bueno* (6); *diga* (6); *hola* (1); *sí* (6)
helmet *casco* (5)
help *ayudar* (6); *echar una mano* (17)
hemisphere *hemisferio* (18)
here *acá* (12)
heritage *herencia* (3)
hero *héroe* (10)
heroine *heroína* (11)
hidden *escondido/a* (11)
hide *esconder* (18)
hieroglyphic *jeroglífico* (14)
high *alto/a* (1)
highway *autopista* (6); *carretera* (3)
hike *caminata* (7)
hill *colina* (11)
hip *cadera* (5)
hire *contratar* (6)
Hispanic *hispano/a* (2)
Hispaniola *Española* (10)
historic district *casco antiguo* (9)
history *historia* (1)
hit *golpear* (17)
hobby *interés* (1)
hold *caber* (13)

hole *agujero* (19)
home *hogar* (6)
home delivery *servicio a domicilio* (18)
homeland *patria* (10)
homeless *personas sin hogar sin techo* (19)
homemade *casero/a* (8)
home run *jonrón* (7)
Honduran *hondureño/a* (2)
honest *sincero/a* (14); *honesto/a* (11)
honesty *honestidad* (14)
honorable *digno/a* (6)
hope *esperanza* (12); *esperar* (4)
horror movie *película de terror* (15)
horse *caballo* (4)
hostage *rehén* (11)
hot *caliente* (8); *picante* (8)
hot (weather) *caluroso/a* (9)
hotel *hotel* (3)
hotel business *hostelería* (18)
hotel management *hostelería* (18)
hour *hora* (5)
house *albergar* (9); *casa* (6)
housing *vivienda* (6)
housing development *urbanización* (9)
however *no obstante* (19)
how many *cuánto(s)* (2)
how much *cuánto(s)* (2)
huge *enorme* (15)
human being *ser humano* (16)
humid *húmedo/a* (3)
hummingbird *colibrí* (3)
hundred *centenar* (8)
hundreds *cientos* (4)
hunger *hambre* (12)
hunting *caza* (19)
hurricane *huracán* (6)
hurt *doler (ue)* (11)
hurt oneself *hacerse daño* (12)
husband *marido* (20)
husband/wife *esposo/a* (2)
hybrid *híbrido/a* (16)
hydrating *hidratante* (12)
hygienic *higiénico* (18)
hypocrisy *hipocresía* (14)
hypocritical *hipócrita* (14)
hypothesis *hipótesis* (10)

**I**

ice cream *helado* (4)
ice cream shop *heladería* (4)
idealist *idealista* (20)
identify *identificar* (6)
idol *ídolo* (15)
if *si* (2)
ignorance *desconocimiento* (12)
ill *enfermo/a* (4)
illegal *ilegal* (20); *ilícito/a* (12)
ill-mannered *maleducado/a* (14)
illness *enfermedad* (12)
illustrate *ilustrar* (16)

illustration *ilustración* (20)
illustrious *ilustre* (11)
image *imagen* (3)
imagine *fingir* (14); *imaginar* (19)
imbued *imbuido/a* (20)
imitate *imitar* (13)
immediately *inmediatamente* (11)
immersion *inmersión* (13)
immigrant *inmigrante* (4)
immigration *inmigración* (11)
impatience *impaciencia* (14)
imported *importado/a* (16)
imports *importación* (18)
imposition *imposición* (19)
impoverish *empobrecer* (20)
impress *imprimir* (17)
impression *impresión* (19)
impressive *impresionante* (15)
improve *mejorar* (5)
in a hurry *apurado/a* (5)
in any case / event *de cualquier forma; de todas maneras; de todos modos; en cualquier caso* (19)
in/as a consequence *en/como consecuencia* (20)
inauguration *inauguración* (18)
incapable *incapaz* (20)
incident *suceso* (5)
include *abarcar* (11); *incluir* (4); *reunir* (14)
including *incluso* (19)
income *ingresos* (6)
in conclusion *en conclusión* (6)
in contrast to *a diferencia de* (7)
incorporate *incorporar* (8)
increase *aumentar* (10); *aumento* (18); *incrementar* (18)
incredible *increíble* (3)
independence *independencia* (10)
independent *independiente* (11)
index *índice* (12)
indicate *indicar* (9)
indigenous *autóctono/a* (11)
indigenous person *indígena* (2)
indigestion *indigestión* (12)
industry *industria* (18)
inequality *desigualdad* (19)
inexpensive *económico/a* (16)
infatuation *enamoramiento* (20)
in favor of *a favor* (19)
infection *infección* (12)
infidelity *infidelidad* (14)
inflammation *inflamación* (12)
inflexible *rígido/a* (20)
influential *influyente* (4)
inform *avisar* (16); *comunicar* (11)
information *información* (5)
infrastructure *infraestructura* (18)
in front of *delante de* (17); *enfrente (de)* (17)
infuriate *enfurecer* (20)
ingenuity *ingenio* (20)
inhabit *habitar* (11)

inhabitant *habitante* (1)
inhale *inhalar* (5)
injury *lesión* (12)
injustice *injusto* (17)
inn *posada* (7)
innovate *innovar* (18)
innovative *innovador/a* (15); *novedoso/a* (18)
innovator *innovador* (2)
in other words *en otras palabras* (5); *es decir* (1)
insecure *inseguro/a* (14)
insecurity *inseguridad* (9)
in short *en resumen* (6)
inside *dentro de* (8)
insomnia *insomnio* (12)
inspire *inspirar* (6)
install *instalar* (9)
instant *instante* (10); *vez* (8)
instantaneity *instantaneidad* (17)
instead of *en vez de* (3)
instrument *instrumento* (2)
insurance *seguro* (18)
insurmountable *infranqueable* (17)
intelligence *inteligencia* (14)
intelligent *inteligente* (2)
intend *intentar* (14)
intensity *intensidad* (17)
interest *afición* (2); *interesar* (3); *interés* (11)
interesting *interesante* (1)
intern *internar* (20)
international *mundial* (5)
internship *pasantía* (7)
interrupt *interrumpir* (10)
interview *entrevistar* (1); *reportaje* (19)
in the afternoon *de la tarde; por la tarde* (7)
in the early morning *de la madrugada* (7)
in the evening *de la noche; por la noche* (7)
in the face of *en vista de* (7)
in the first place *en primer lugar* (6)
in the morning *de la mañana; por la mañana* (7)
in the second place *en segundo lugar* (6)
in the third place *en tercer lugar* (6)
intolerable *insoportable* (20)
introduce *presentar* (1)
introduce oneself *presentarse* (1)
introverted *introvertido/a* (14)
inundate *inundar* (18)
invade *invadir* (10)
invent *inventar* (10)
inventiveness *ingenio* (20)
invest *invertir (ie)* (9)
investigate *investigar* (16)
investigation *investigación* (16)
investment *inversión* (18)
investor *inversionista* (18); *inversor/a* (18)
invite *invitar* (20)
involve *involucrar* (13)
involved *involucrado/a* (7)
Ireland *Irlanda* (10)
irony *ironía* (15)

island *isla* (3)
islander *isleño* (10)
isolated *aislado/a* (3)
isthmus *istmo* (18)
Italy *Italia* (10)
itch *picar* (12)
itinerary *itinerario* (7)
it is cold *hace frío* (9)
it is hot *hace calor* (9)
it is sunny *hace sol* (9)
it is windy *hace viento* (9)

**J**

jacket *chaqueta* (4)
January *enero* (3)
Japan *Japón* (10)
Japanese *japonés* (13)
jealous *celoso/a* (20); *envidioso/a* (14)
jealousy *celos* (20)
jest *jarana* (20)
jeweler *joyería* (4)
jewelry *joya* (14)
Jewish *judío/a* (13)
job *cargo* (6); *empleo* (6); *puesto de trabajo* (6); *trabajo* (6)
join *ensamblar* (18); *unirse a* (10)
joke *burla* (5)
journalist *periodista* (2)
journey *camino* (20); *trayecto* (17)
juice *jugo* (8)
July *julio* (3)
jump *saltar* (5); *salto* (3)
June *junio* (3)
jungle *selva* (3)
junk food *basura* (5)
just *equitativo/a* (6); *justo/a* (18)
juvenile *juvenil* (4)

**K**

keep *guardar* (16)
keep in mind *tener en cuenta* (2)
keep/remain quiet *callarse* (13)
key *cayo* (3); *clave* (5); *llave* (11); *tecla* (16)
keyboard *teclado* (16)
key maker *llavero* (4)
key ring *llavero* (4)
kidnap *secuestrar* (17)
kidnapping *secuestro* (17)
kill *matar* (17)
killing *asesinato* (10)
kilogram *kilo* (8)
kind *amable* (2)
king *rey* (4)
kingdom *reino* (11)
kiss *besar* (14)
kitchen *cocina* (6)
knee *rodilla* (5)
knife *cuchillo* (4)
knock down *atropellar* (20)

know (be familiar with) *conocer (zc)* (1)
know (a fact) *saber (irreg.)* (1)
knowledge *conocimiento* (13); *sabiduría* (15)
known *conocido/a* (10)
Korean *coreano* (13)

**L**

label *etiqueta* (1)
labor market *mercado laboral* (7)
labyrinth *laberinto* (17)
lack *faltar* (9)
lake *lago* (3)
lamb *cordero* (8)
lament *lamentar* (20)
lamp *linterna* (3)
land *aterrizar* (7); *tierra* (11)
landscape *paisaje* (1)
language *idioma* (1); *lengua* (13)
lapse *caducidad* (12)
laptop *computadora portátil* (4)
large (river) *caudaloso* (3)
large oil slick *mareas negras* (19)
last *por último* (2); *durar* (7); *en último
    lugar* (15)
last name *apellido* (1)
last night *anoche* (10)
late *tarde* (7)
lantern *linterna* (3)
Latin American *latinoamericano/a* (2)
Latino *latino/a* (2)
laughter *risa* (14)
laundromat *lavandería* (3)
law *ley* (3); *derecho* (10)
lawyer *abogado/a* (2)
lazy *perezoso/a* (2)
lead *conducir* (7)
leader *líder* (10)
leaf *hoja* (6)
league *liga* (6)
lean *inclinar* (5)
leap *salto* (3)
learn *aprender* (1)
learner *aprendiz* (13)
learning *aprendizaje* (13)
leather *cuero* (4)
leave *dejar, irse (irreg.)* (6)
left *izquierda* (6)
leg *pierna* (5)
legalization *legalización* (19)
legal residence *domicilio* (18)
legend *leyenda* (11)
legumes *legumbres* (8)
leisure *ocio* (9)
lemon *limón* (8)
lemonade *limonada* (12)
lend *prestar* (12)
lend a hand *echar una mano* (17)
less *menos* (1)
less fortunate *desafortunado/a* (19)
lesson *lección* (14)

letter *carta* (4)
lettuce *lechuga* (8)
level *nivel* (5)
liberal *progresista* (10)
library *biblioteca* (2)
lie *mentir (ie)* (19)
lie down *tumbarse* (12)
life *vida* (10)
life expectancy *esperanza de vida* (19)
life preserver *salvavidas* (14)
lift *leventar* (5)
light *ligero/a* (12); *luz* (16)
lightbulb *bombilla* (4)
lighter *encendedor* (8)
like *gustar* (3)
like a lot *amar* (20); *encantar* (3)
like/dislike someone *caer bien/mal* (20)
likewise *asimismo* (14)
limit *límite* (7)
line *línea* (10)
lined *forrado/a* (4)
link *vincular* (8); *vínculo* (8); *enlace* (16);
    *vincular (a)* (17)
linked *ligado/a* (5)
liquor *aguardiente* (5); *licor* (4)
liquor store *licorería* (18)
listen *escuchar* (1)
liter *litro* (5)
literacy *alfabetización* (16)
literary *literario/a* (20)
a little bit *poco* (1)
live *vivir* (3)
live (a healthy life) *llevar* (12)
liveliness *animación* (15)
lively *animado/a* (15)
live music *música en vivo* (15)
livestock *ganadería* (18)
live with *convivir con* (19)
living *viviente* (8)
living room *salón/sala* (6)
loan *préstamo* (6)
lobby *vestíbulo* (17)
lobster *langosta* (12)
locate *localizar* (1)
location *ubicación* (3)
lock *cerradura* (16); *esclusa* (18)
lock down *encerrar* (11)
locksmith *cerrajero/a* (18)
locksmith's shop *cerrajería* (18)
lock up *encerrar* (11)
lodge *alojarse (en)* (3)
lodging *albergue* (3); *alojamiento* (3)
lodging house *pensión* (7)
logic *lógico/a* (5)
logo *logotipo* (18)
loneliness *soledad* (14)
lonely *solitario/a* (3)
long-lasting *duradero/a* (16)
look *mirar* (1)
look for *buscar* (1)
lose *perder (ie)* (6)

lose weight *adelgazar* (5)
loss *pérdida* (10)
love *amor* (10); *amar* (20)
lover *amante* (12); *enamorado/a* (9)
low *bajo/a* (6)
lowercase letter *minúscula* (13)
loyal *fiel* (14)
loyalty *fidelidad* (14)
luck *suerte* (11)
luggage *equipaje* (7)
lung *pulmón* (12)
luxurious *lujoso/a* (6)
lying *mentiroso/a* (20)

**M**

macaroni *macarrones* (8)
machine *máquina* (16)
magazine *revista* (4)
main actor/actress *protagonista* (15)
main character *protagonista* (17)
maintain *mantener* (9)
majestic *majestuoso/a* (20)
majority *mayoría* (3)
make *hacer (irreg.)* (2)
make a decision *tomar una decisión* (18)
make a face *hacer muecas* (7)
make an appointment *concertar una
    cita* (15)
make an appointment with *quedar
    (con)* (15)
make an excuse *dar una excusa* (15)
make a reservation *hacer una reservación* (7)
make better *mejorar* (5)
make laugh *dar risa* (14)
make mistakes *cometer errores* (13)
make nervous *poner nervioso/a* (13)
make onself comfortable *acomodarse* (17)
make progress *avanzar* (17)
make up *constituir* (2); *inventar* (10)
make worse *agravar* (19)
making *fabricación* (8)
mammal *mamífero* (7)
management *gestión* (10)
manager *gerente* (6)
manatee *manatí* (7)
mania *manía* (14)
mantle *manto* (17)
many times *muchas veces* (5)
map *plano* (7)
marble *marfil* (17); *mármol* (5)
March *marzo* (3)
marginalization *marginación* (19)
marginalized *marginado/a* (19)
marijuana *marihuana* (19)
marital status *estado civil* (2)
maritime *marítimo/a* (7)
mark *marco* (4)
marker *marcador* (11)
market *mercado* (7)
marketing *mercadeo* (18)

married *casado/a* (2)
marry someone *casarse con alguien* (10)
marvel *maravilla* (17)
marvellous *maravilloso/a* (3)
mass *montón* (16)
massage *masaje* (12)
masseuse *masajista* (18)
mastery *dominio* (6)
match *fósforo* (16); *partido* (3)
mathematics *matemáticas* (14)
matter *importar* (12)
maturity *madurez* (14)
maximum *máximo* (11)
May *mayo* (3)
maybe *quizá* (7); *tal vez* (15)
mayor *alcalde/esa* (9)
mean *significar* (1)
meaning *significado* (11)
means *expediente* (6)
meanwhile *entre tanto* (17)
measure *medida* (8); *medir (i)* (12)
meat *carne* (5)
mechanism *dispositivo* (16)
medical checkup *chequeo médico* (5)
medication *medicamiento* (12)
medicine *medicina* (12)
mediocrity *mediocridad* (14)
meditate *meditar* (14)
meet *reunirse (con)* (7)
meeting *reunión* (7)
melting pot *crisol* (4)
member *miembro* (5)
member of congress *congresista* (11)
membership fees *cuota* (19)
memorize *memorizar* (13)
memory *memoria* (16)
mention *mencionar* (5)
menu *menú* (8)
merchandise *mercancía* (18)
merchant *comerciante* (20)
merit *merecer (zc)* (15)
mess *desorden* (14)
message *mensaje* (6); *recado* (6)
metal *metal* (16)
method *método* (13)
metropolis *metrópoli* (15)
Mexican *mexicano/a* (2)
microwave *microondas* (16)
midnight *medianoche* (4)
migraine *migraña* (12)
migration *migración* (9)
migration movement *movimiento migratorio* (19)
mile *milla* (16)
military *ejército* (10); *militar* (10)
milk *leche* (8)
millenial *milenario* (9)
millenium *milenio* (19)
million *millón* (4)
millionaire *millonario/a* (17)
mind *mente* (5)

mineral water *agua mineral* (4)
minimum *mínimo* (10)
mining industry *minería* (18)
minority *minoría* (13)
mint *hierbabuena* (8)
mirror *espejo* (6)
miserly *avaro/a* (14)
misery *miseria* (20)
mistake *error* (13)
mix *mezclar* (5)
mixture *mezcla* (11)
mobilized *movilizado/a* (6)
moderate *moderar* (5)
moderately *moderadamente* (12)
modern *moderno/a* (4)
modest *modesto/a* (20)
modify *modificar* (18)
monarchy *monarquía* (15)
Monday *lunes* (5)
money *dinero* (3)
money order *giro postal* (7)
monitor *pantalla* (16)
monkey *mono* (3)
monk/nun *monje/monja* (19)
month *mes* (3)
moreover *además* (4)
more than *más... que* (9)
mortgage *hipotecario/a* (18)
mother *madre* (2)
mother tongue *lengua materna* (13)
motivate *motivar* (11)
motorboat *lancha* (11)
motorcycle *moto* (16); *motocicleta* (20)
mountain *montaña* (1)
mountain climbing *montañismo* (7)
mountainous *montañoso/a* (12)
mountain range *cordillera* (3)
mountains *sierra* (9)
mouth *boca* (5)
move *mudarse* (6); *trasladarse* (10)
move forward *avanzar* (17)
movement *movimiento* (10)
movie guide *cartelera* (15)
movies *cine* (1)
movie theater *cine* (1)
moving *conmovedor/a* (15)
multiethnic *multiétnico/a* (19)
murder *asesinar* (10)
muscle *músculo* (5)
museum *museo* (6)
mushroom *champiñón* (8)
music *música* (2)
musician *músico* (2)
mussel *mejillón* (8)
mustache *bigote* (8)
mustard *mostaza* (8)
mysterious *misterioso/a* (11)
mystery *misterio* (17)
mystery novel *novela de misterio* (17)
myth *mito* (2)
mythic *mítico/a* (10)

## N

name *nombrar* (5)
napkin *servilleta* (4)
narrate *narrar* (11)
narration *narración* (11)
narrator *narrador/a* (17)
narrow *estrecho/a* (9)
narrow-minded *cerrado/a* (20)
nation *nación* (6); *pueblo* (10)
nationality *nacionalidad* (2)
nationalized *nacionalizado/a* (7)
native *indígena* (2); *natal* (9); *originario/a* (17)
natural resources *recursos naturales* (19)
nature *naturaleza* (1)
navy *armada* (11)
near *cerca de* (7)
nearby *cercano/a; por aquí cerca* (3)
necessary *necesario/a* (5)
necessity *necesidad* (6)
neck *cuello* (5)
necklace *collar* (4)
need *necesitar* (4)
neighbor *vecino/a* (2)
neighborhood *barrio* (9)
neither *tampoco* (3)
nervous *nervioso/a* (14)
network *red* (12)
never *nunca* (5); *jamás* (20)
nevertheless *sin embargo* (4)
new *nuevo/a* (4); *novedoso/a* (18)
news *noticias* (1) (15); *telediario* (15)
newspaper *periódico* (3)
next *a continuación* (8); *después (de)* (8); *luego* (8); *próximo/a* (7)
Nicaraguan *nicaragüense* (2)
nice *agradable* (2); *amable* (2); *lindo/a* (15); *simpático/a* (2)
night *noche* (6)
nightlife *vida nocturna* (9)
nightly *nocturno/a* (15)
nine *nueve* (1)
nine hundred *novecientos/as* (4)
nineteen *diecinueve* (1)
ninety *noventa* (2)
no doubt *no cabe duda* (13)
noise *bullicio* (20); *ruido* (9)
noisy *ruidoso/a* (3)
no longer *ya no* (19)
nomadic *nómada* (11)
none *ningún; ninguno/a* (8)
nongovernmental organization (NGO) *organización no gubernamental (ONG)* (6)
non-profit *sin fines de lucro* (13)
noon *mediodía* (7)
no one *nadie* (18)
north *norte* (3)
northeast *nordeste* (11)
northwest *noroeste* (12)
Norwegian *Noruega* (18)

nose *nariz* (5)
not any *nada* (8); *ningún; ninguno/a* (8)
note *anotar* (5)
notebook *cuaderno* (17)
nothing *nada* (8)
notice *advertir (ie) (de)* (12); *apreciar* (7);
  *fijarse en* (7)
not know *ignorar* (19)
not to have a good time *pasarlo mal* (4)
nourish *sustentar* (20)
novel *novedoso/a* (18); *novela* (17)
novelist *novelista* (17)
novelty *novedad* (18)
November *noviembre* (3)
now *ahora* (11)
no way *de ninguna manera* (3); *ni hablar* (7);
  *no me digas* (11)
*number número* (1)
nut *nuez* (4)

## O

Oaxacan *oaxaqueño/a* (2)
obesity *obesidad* (5)
object *complemento* (8)
obligate *obligar* (20)
obscurity *oscuridad* (17)
observe *observar* (6)
obtain *conseguir (i)*; *obtener* (5)
occupy *ocupar* (11)
occur *celebrarse* (15)
ocean *mar* (3); *océano* (10)
October *octubre* (3)
odd *extraño/a* (10); *raro/a* (16)
of course *cómo no* (3); *claro* (7); *desde luego*
  (7); *por supuesto* (3); *sí* (7)
of course not *claro que no* (7); *desde luego*
  *que no* (7)
offensive *ofensiva* (11)
offer *oferta* (18); *ofrecer (zc)* (1)
office *consultorío/a* (18); *despacho* (6);
  *oficina* (6)
office clerk *oficinista* (6)
often *a menudo* (5)
of the mind *anímico/a* (5)
oil *aceite* (8); *petróleo* (19); *petrolero/a* (18)
oil painting *óleo* (5)
oil spill *mareas negras* (19)
okay *de acuerdo* (13)
old *añejo/a* (19); *antiguo/a* (3)
old age *vejez* (10)
old-fashioned *anticuado/a* (20)
once in a while *de vez en cuando* (5)
one *uno* (1)
one hundred *cien* (2)
one-way ticket *boleto de ida* (7)
onion *cebolla* (4)
only *únicamente* (12)
on the contrary *al contrario* (14)
on the dot *en punto* (7)
on the part of *de parte de* (6)

on the verge of *a punto de* (18)
on top *encima* (8)
on top of *por encima de* (5)
onyx *ónix* (4)
open *abrir* (7); *dialogante* (20)
opening *apertura* (8)
open-minded *abierto/a* (20); *dialogante* (20)
operate on *operar* (12)
operating system *sistema operativo* (16)
opinion *opinión* (19)
opportunity *oportunidad* (6)
opposite *opuesto/a* (18)
oppress *agobiar* (20)
optimal *óptimo/a* (18)
optimist *optimista* (14)
orally *oralmente* (13)
orange *anaranjado/a* (4); *naranja* (4)
oration *oración* (5)
order *orden* (4)
order (in a restaurant) *pedir* (8)
orderly *ordenado/a* (14)
organize *organizar* (2)
organized *organizado/a* (6)
origin *origen* (2)
oscillate *oscilar* (18)
outdoor seating *terraza* (15)
outgoing *extrovertido/a* (2)
outline *esquema* (13)
out loud *en voz alta* (18)
out-of-date *anticuado/a* (18)
outpatient department *ambulatorio* (9)
outside *afuera* (16)
outside of *fuera de* (6)
outsider *forastero/a* (13)
outskirts *alrededores* (9)
outstanding *impresionante* (3)
oval-shaped *ovalado/a* (11)
overcome *superar* (14); *vencer* (20)
overexploitation *sobreexplotación* (20)
overpopulated *superpoblado/a* (9)
owing to *debido a* (6)
own *propio/a* (6)
owner *dueño/a* (8)
ox *buey* (15)
ozone layer *capa de ozono* (14)

## P

pack *envasar* (12); *hacer la(s) maleta(s)* (7);
  *paquete* (8)
package *paquete* (8)
pack up *empacar* (18)
page *página* (10); *paje* (4)
pain *dolor* (12)
paint *pintar* (2)
painter *pintor/a* (2)
painting *cuadro* (5); *pintura* (2)
pair *pareja* (1)
palate *paladar* (8)
palmtop computer *computadora de bolsillo* (16)
Panamanian *panameño/a* (2)

panic *pánico* (11)
pants *pantalones* (4)
paper *papel* (16); *trabajo escrito* (13)
parade *desfile* (17)
paradise *paraíso* (3)
paragliding *parapente* (7)
paragraph *párrafo* (4)
Paraguayan *paraguayo/a* (2)
parallel *paralelo* (20)
paralyze *paralizar* (20)
parameter *parámetro* (12)
pardon *dispensar* (20); *perdonar* (20)
parents *padres* (2)
park *estacionar* (17); *parque* (3)
parking *estacionamiento* (6)
parking lot *aparcamiento* (9);
  *estacionamiento* (6)
parrot *loro* (3)
participate *participar* (1)
part-time *a tiempo parcial* (6)
paso *step* (1)
passage *trozo* (8)
passion *pasión* (5)
passport *pasaporte* (7)
past *pasado* (11)
pastry shop *pastelería* (4)
pasture *pasto* (10)
patch *parche* (12)
patent *patentar* (16)
path *sendero* (12); *trayecto* (17)
pathology *patología* (12)
patience *paciencia* (6)
patient *paciente* (6)
pavilion *pabellón* (15)
pay *pagar* (4)
pay attention *prestar atención* (4)
pay attention to *hacer caso a* (20)
pea *guisantes* (8)
peace *paz* (10); *sosiego* (16)
peacefulness *tranquilidad* (5)
peach *melocotón* (8)
peak *pico* (3)
pear *pera* (8)
peasant *campesino/a* (6)
pedantry *pedantería* (14)
pedestrian *peatón* (9)
pedestrian zone *zona peatonal* (9)
peel *pelar* (8)
pen *bolígrafo* (12)
pen *lapicera* (16); *pluma* (16)
pencil *lápiz* (16)
penetrate *penetrar* (11)
penguin *pingüino* (12)
people *gente* (1); *pueblo* (10)
pepper (spice) *pimienta* (8)
pepper (vegetable) *pimiento* (8)
percentage *porcentaje* (12)
perfect *perfeccionar* (13)
perform *actuar* (14)
performance *actuación* (15); *desempeño*
  (12); *interpretación* (14)

perfume store *perfumería* (4)
period *período* (11); *plazo* (19)
permission *permiso* (12)
permit *dejar* (8); *permitir* (6)
personality *personalidad* (2)
persuade *persuadir* (20)
Peruvian *peruano/a* (2)
pessimistic *pesimista* (14)
pesticide *pesticida* (20)
petroleum *petróleo* (19)
pharmacology *farmacología* (14)
pharmacy *farmacia* (3)
phase *fase* (7)
phenomenon *fenómeno* (3)
Philippines *Filipinas* (18)
philosopher *filósofo* (19)
philosophy *filosofía* (14)
phone *teléfono* (1)
photocopier *fotocopiadora* (16)
photographer *fotógrafo/a* (2)
physical *físico/a* (5)
pick up *recoger* (7)
picture *fotografía* (1)
piece *pedazo* (8); *trozo* (8)
piece of information *dato* (10)
pile *montón* (16)
pilgrimage *peregrinación* (9)
pill *pastilla* (12); *píldora* (12)
pillar *pilar* (18)
pinch *pizca* (12)
pineapple *piña* (8)
pink *rosa* (4)
pioneer *pionero/a* (18)
pirate *pirata* (11)
place *lugar* (3)
place before *anteponer* (14)
plain *sencillo* (2)
plains *llanuras* (1)
plan *planear, planificar* (15)
plane *avión* (3)
plastic *plástico* (16)
plateau *meseta* (3)
plated *chapado/a* (6)
platform *plataforma* (9)
play *hacer deporte* (5); *jugar (ue)* (2);
    (instruments) *tocar* (2)
play (theater) *obra de teatro* (15)
player *jugador/a* (2)
playful *lúdico/a* (15)
play the role of *hacer de* (8); *protagonizar* (14)
pleasant *agradable* (2)
please *encantar* (13)
pleasure *placer* (15)
plot *argumento* (15)
plug *enchufe* (16)
plug in *enchufar* (16)
pocket *bolsillo* (10)
point *apuntar* (18); *punto* (12)
poison *envenenamiento* (12)
policeman/woman *policía* (6)
police station *comisaría* (17)

politician *político/a* (2)
politics *política* (1)
pollute *contaminar* (9)
pollution *contaminación* (9); *polución* (9)
polytheist *politeísta* (14)
poor *pobres* (19)
populate *poblar* (20)
populated *poblado/a* (6)
population *población* (1)
pork *cerdo* (8)
port *puerto* (11)
portfolio *portafolio* (14)
portray *retratar* (14)
Portuguese *portugués* (11)
position *cargo* (6); *puesto de trabajo* (6);
    *posición* (12)
postal carrier *cartero/a* (6)
postcard *postal* (7)
poster *cartel* (4)
postgraduate *posgrado* (10)
postmodern *posmoderno/a* (14)
postpone *posponer (irreg.)* (19)
posture *postura* (5)
pot *cazuela* (8)
potato *papa / patata* (8)
pour *verter* (8)
poverty *pobreza* (6)
power *poder* (10)
powerful *poderoso/a* (20)
practice *practicar* (2)
practice sports *hacer deporte* (5)
praise *alabar* (20)
prayer *oración* (5)
precious *precioso/a* (8)
precise *preciso/a* (11)
precisely *precisamente* (12)
predict *predecir* (14)
prediction *predicción* (14)
predominate *predominar* (6)
prefer *anteponer* (14); *preferir* (6)
prefix *prefijo* (6)
pregnant *embarazada* (12)
pre-Inca *preincaico/a* (9)
prejudice *prejuicio* (20)
premature *prematuro/a* (20)
premonition *premonición* (20)
prepare *aparejar* (18); *preparar* (8)
prepare outlines *hacer esquemas* (13)
preschool *guardería* (9)
prescribe *recetar* (12)
prescription *receta* (12)
presence *presencia* (19)
presenter *presentador* (19)
preservative *conservante* (12)
press *prensa* (15); *pulsar* (19)
pressure *presionar* (18)
prestige *prestigio* (2)
pretend *fingir* (14)
pretension *pretensión* (2)
pretty *bonito/a* (1); *lindo/a* (14)
prevent *prevenir* (12)

previous *previo/a* (6)
price *precio* (4)
priestly *sacerdotal* (10)
print *huella* (2)
printed *impreso/a* (18)
printer *impresora* (16)
priority *prioridad* (5)
prisoner *prisionero* (10)
private *privado/a* (11)
privilege *privilegiar* (19)
privileged *privilegiado/a* (19)
prize *premio* (4)
prized *premiado/a* (12)
problem *problema* (2)
proclaim *proclamar* (10)
produce *producir* (10)
production *fabricación* (8)
profession *profesión* (2)
professor *profesor/a* (2)
profile *perfil* (20)
profit *lucro* (6)
profound *profundo/a* (20)
programming *programación* (15)
progress *avanzar* (17)
progressive *progresista* (10)
prohibit *prohibir* (19)
project *proyecta* (14); *proyecto* (19)
proliferate *proliferar* (12)
promise *promesa* (19)
promote *ascender* (9); *promover (ue)* (18)
promotor *empresario* (15)
pronoun *pronombre* (5)
proof *prueba* (17)
proposal *propuesta* (8)
propose *proponer* (8)
proposition *proposición* (19)
proprietary *propietario/a* (6)
prospect *folleto* (7)
prosperous *próspero/a* (12)
protect *proteger* (5)
protectorate *protectorado* (11)
protest *protestar* (18)
protocol *protocolo* (19)
proud *orgulloso/a* (14)
provide *proporcionar* (12)
provide a service *prestar un servicio* (18)
province *provincia* (8)
provoke *provocar* (11)
pseudonym *seudónimo* (20)
public *público/a* (6)
public works *obras públicas* (9)
publish *editar* (16)
publishing company *editorial* (18)
pudding *pudín* (8)
Puerto Rican *puertorriqueño* (2)
pull out *arrancar* (17)
pumpkin *calabaza* (4)
punctual *puntual* (11)
purity *pureza* (14)
purple *morado/a* (4); *violeta* (4)
purse *bolso* (4)

push *empujar* (19)
push-up *flexión* (5)
put *poner (irreg.)* (8)
put down *agobiar* (20)
put on makeup *maquillarse* (14)
put up with *aguantar a* (20)
pyramid *pirámide* (6)

## Q

quadriplegic *tetrapléjico* (15)
qualification *calificación* (9)
quality *calidad* (4)
quantity *cantidad* (2)
quarter *cuarto* (7)
question *pregunta* (1); *interrogar* (17); *interpelar* (19)
questioning *interrogatorio* (17)
questionnaire *cuestionario* (6)
quiet *tranquilo/a* (3); *callado/a* (5); *silencioso/a* (13); *sosiego/a* (16)
quite a lot *bastante* (8)
quotation mark *comilla* (13)
quote *cotizar* (5)

## R

race *etnia* (10)
racism *racismo* (19)
rafting *descenso de rápidos* (12)
railroad *ferrocarril* (18)
rain *llover (ue)* (9); *lluvia* (9)
raincoat *impermeable* (3)
rainy *lluvioso/a* (9)
raise *subir* (1)
rapidity *rapidez* (18)
rapidly *rápidamente* (12)
rare *escaso/a* (19)
rate *tasa* (12)
rating *calificación* (9)
ravage *embestido/a* (20)
raw *crudo/a* (8)
ray *rayo* (11)
reach *alcance* (16); *alcanzar* (7)
react *reaccionar* (11)
read *leer* (1)
reader *lector* (13)
reading *lectura* (13)
ready *listo/a* (5); *dispuesto* (6); *a punto* (18)
real estate–related *inmobiliario/a* (18)
reality *realidad* (11)
realize *darse cuenta de* (10)
really *de verdad* (11); *efectivamente* (13)
rear *trasero/a* (17)
reason *razón* (4)
reasoning *razonamiento* (19)
rebellion *rebelión* (10)
receive *recibir* (4)
recent *reciente* (9)
recently *recientemente* (5)
reception desk *recepción* (7)

receptionist *recepcionista* (7)
recipe *receta* (8)
recognize *reconocer* (11)
recommend *recomendar* (18)
recommendation *recomendación* (12)
reconsider *replantearse* (20)
record *grabar* (16)
recuperate *recuperar* (10)
recycle *reciclar* (9)
red *rojo/a* (4)
reduce *reducir* (10)
reduction *disminución* (10)
refect *desechar* (16)
refer *referir* (4)
referent *referente* (18)
refine *refinar* (6)
reflect *reflejar* (11)
reflection *reflexión* (11)
refrigerator *nevera* (8)
refugee *refugiado/a* (17)
refute *refutar* (19)
regeneration *regeneración* (19)
register *inscribirse* (7); *registro* (6)
registered *inscrito/a* (7)
regret *arrepentirse (ie)* (15)
reinvestment *reinversión* (19)
reiterate *reiterar* (19)
relative *familiar* (2)
relax *relajarse* (5)
relaxation *relajación* (5)
release *liberación* (5); *toxina* (5)
reliable *serio/a* (2)
remain *quedarse* (10)
remaining *restante* (13)
remember *acordarse (ue) de* (13)
remind *recordar* (6)
removal *borrado* (12)
remove *destituir* (10)
renewable *renovable* (16)
renounce *renunciar a* (20)
rent *alquilar* (3); *alquiler* (6)
repair *arreglar, reparar* (16)
repeat *repetir* (1)
repellent *repelente* (3)
report *informe* (1)
repose *reposo* (11)
repressive *represivo/a* (11)
reproduce *reproducir (zc)* (8)
request a service *solicitar un servicio* (18)
requirement *requisito* (6)
research *investigación* (16); *investigar* (16)
researcher *investigador/a* (19)
resent *resentirse* (18)
reserve *reservar* (3)
reside *residir* (6)
resident of Madrid *madrileño/a* (15)
resident of Montevideo *montevideano* (16)
resign *dimitir* (10)
resolve *resolver (ue)* (6)
resources *recursos* (18)
respect *respetar* (19)

respond *responder* (7)
responsible *responsable* (6)
rest *descansar* (3); *resto* (3); *descanso* (5)
restaurant *restaurante* (8)
restore *restaurar* (17)
restrict *restringir* (19)
result *resultado* (13)
resume *currículo* (6)
rethink *replantearse* (20)
retire *jubilar* (19)
retreat *retirarse* (11)
return *devolver (ue)* (6); *volver (ue)*; (7) *regresar* (10); *regreso* (11); *retorno* (20)
reveal *revelar* (3)
revelation *revelación* (20)
revelry *jarana* (20)
review *revisar* (2); *crítica* (2); *repasar* (9); *revisión* (12); *reseña* (14)
revision *revisión* (12)
revolt *sublevación* (10)
revolucionary *revolucionario/a* (11)
revolution *revolución* (8)
rewrite *rescribir* (17)
rhetorical *retórico/a* (19)
rhythm *ritmo* (8)
rib *costilla* (8)
rice *arroz* (8)
rich *rico/a* (2)
richness *riqueza* (7)
rickety *desvencijado/a* (20)
ride a bike *montar bicicleta* (5)
right *derecha* (6); *verdad* (9)
right away *enseguida* (17)
rigid *rígido/a* (20)
ring *anillo* (8)
rink *pista* (3)
rise *subida* (3)
risk *riesgo* (12)
river *río* (3)
road *carretera* (3); *camino* (20)
roast *asado* (8); *asar* (8)
roasted *asado/a* (8)
robbery *robo* (10)
rock *piedra* (10)
role *papel* (14)
roll (bread) *rosca* (8)
room *cuarto* (6); *habitación* (3)
root *raíz* (7)
round *redondo/a* (16)
round trip *ida y vuelta* (3)
round-trip ticket *boleto de ida y vuelta* (7)
route *ruta* (7); *trayecto* (17)
rubber *caucho* (15)
ruin *desolar* (11); *ruina* (8)
rule *regla* (5)
rum *ron* (8)
run *correr* (2)
run (for office) *postular* (10)
run aground *encallar* (20)
run away *huir* (11)
run into *tropezar (ie) con* (14)

running of the bulls *corridas de toros* (19)
run out *agotarse* (19)
Russian *ruso/a* (13)
rustic *rústico/a* (4)

**S**

sacrifice *sacrificio* (5)
sad *triste* (14)
sadness *pena* (11); *tristeza* (14)
safe *seguro* (5)
sail *navegar* (3)
sailing *vela* (3)
sailor *marino* (20); *navegante* (6)
salad *ensalada* (4)
salary *salario; sueldo* (6)
sales *ofertas* (7); *rebajas* (4)
sales associate *vendedor/a* (4)
salt *sal* (8)
salty *salado/a* (8)
Salvadorean *salvadoreño/a* (2)
same *igual* (8); *mismo/a* (9)
sanctuary *santuario* (9)
sandal *sandalia* (4)
sanitary *sanitario/a* (19)
satellite dish *antena parabólica* (7)
satisfaction *satisfacción* (12)
satisfy *satisfacer* (6)
Saturday *sábado* (5)
savage *salvaje* (12)
save *ahorrar* (4)
save face *salvar las apariencias* (7)
savings *ahorro* (16)
say *decir (irreg.)* (1)
say goodbye to *despedirse (i) de* (7)
scale *escala* (10)
scan *buscar en el texto* (7); *escanear* (12)
scanner *escáner* (16)
scar *cicatriz* (12)
scare *dar miedo* (13)
scared *asustado/a* (20)
scary *miedoso/a* (14)
scene *escena* (17)
scenic *escénico/a* (15)
schedule *horario* (5)
scheme *esquema* (11)
scholarship *beca* (11)
school *escuela* (7); *facultad* (10)
science *ciencia* (14)
science fiction *ciencia ficción* (15)
scientific advance *adelanto científico* (19)
scientist *científico/a* (2)
scope *alcance* (16)
screen *pantalla* (1)
script *guión* (15)
scriptwriter *guionista* (20)
scruples *escrúpulo* (11)
sculptor *escultor/a* (5)
sculpture *escultura* (2)
sea *mar* (3); *marítimo/a* (7)
seafood *marisco* (8)

seafront *malecón* (9)
sea gull *gaviota* (12)
seal (animal) *lobo marino* (20)
sea lion *león marino* (15)
search *buscar* (1); *búsqueda* (17)
season *estación* (3); *temporada* (15)
seat *asiento* (14)
second *segundo/a* (1)
secondary *secundario/a* (11)
security guard *guardia de seguridad* (6)
see *ver* (2)
seed *pepita* (11); *semilla* (6)
seismic *sísmico/a* (6)
select *seleccionar* (5)
self-assessment *autoevaluación* (13)
selfish *egoísta* (2)
sell *vender* (4)
semester *semestre* (13)
senator *senador* (10)
send *enviar* (4); *mandar* (6)
sense of humor *sentido del humor* (14)
sensitive *sensible* (14)
sensitivity *sensibilidad* (14)
sentence *frase* (4); *oración* (5)
separate *separarse* (10)
September *septiembre* (3)
sequence *secuencia* (5)
serious *grave* (9); *serio/a* (2)
seriously *en serio* (11)
seriousness *seriedad* (14)
serve *servir (i)* (5)
service *servicio* (3)
servitude *servidumbre* (19)
session *sesión* (17)
setting *entorno* (3)
settle *radicarse* (20)
settle down *instalarse* (9)
settlement *asentamiento* (6); *colonización* (10)
settler *poblador/a* (10); *colono* (11)
seven *siete* (1)
seven hundred *setecientos* (4)
seventeen *diecisiete* (1)
seventy *setenta* (2)
severe *grave* (9)
sew *coser* (13)
shadow *sombra* (11)
shame *lástima* (11); *vergüenza* (13)
share *compartir* (1)
shark *tiburón* (12)
sharp *en punto* (7)
sheathe *enfundado/a* (17)
sheep *oveja* (4)
sheet *sábana* (17)
shelf *estante estantería* (6); *repisa* (17)
shine *brillar* (5)
ship *barco* (3); *buque* (18)
shipping company *naviera* (20)
shirt *camisa* (4)
shock *descarga* (16)
shoe *zapato* (3)
shoe store *zapatería* (4)

shopping mall *centro comercial* (4)
short *corto/a* (7)
short film *cortometraje* (15)
short story *cuento* (7)
shout *gritar* (20)
show *mostrar* (1); *manifestar* (10); *espectáculo* (15)
shower *ducharse* (5)
shows *espectáculos* (9)
shrimp *camarón* (8); *gamba* (8)
shy *tímido/a* (2); *introvertido/a* (14)
sick *enfermo/a* (4)
sickness *enfermedad* (12)
side *costado* (9); *lado* (5)
sign *firmar* (10); *suscribir* (10); *cifra* (12)
signal *señalar* (12)
signature *firma* (10)
silent *callado/a* (5); *silencioso/a* (13)
silk *seda* (16)
silver *plata* (4)
similarly *de modo similar* (14)
simple *sencillo* (2)
sin *pecado* (20)
since *ya que* (3); *puesto que* (20)
sincere *sincero/a* (14)
sincerity *sinceridad* (14)
since when *desde cuándo* (4)
singer *cantante* (1)
single *soltero/a* (2)
sit down *sentarse (ie)* (5)
site *sitio* (3); *yacimiento* (9); *emplazamiento* (17)
situate *situar* (6)
situation *situación* (2)
six *seis* (1)
six hundred *seiscientos/as* (4)
sixteen *dieciséis* (1)
sixty *sesenta* (2)
size *talla* (4); *tamaño* (5)
skeptical *escéptico/a* (19)
skepticism *escepticismo* (19)
ski *esquiar* (5)
skill *destreza* (6); *habilidad* (17)
skim *leer por encima* (7)
skim/glance through *hojear* (17)
skin *piel* (12)
skirt *falda* (4)
skyscraper *rascacielos* (9)
slave *esclavo* (10)
slavery *esclavitud* (10)
sleep *dormir (ue)* (2); *sueño* (5)
sleeplessness *insomnio* (12)
slender *delgado/a* (2)
slice *rebanada; rodaja* (8)
slogan *eslogan* (12)
slow *despacio* (1); *lento/a* (7)
slowly *lentamente* (12)
sluice *compuerta* (18)
small *pequeño/a* (1)
small pot *mate* (4)
smallpox *viruela* (10)

smell *olor* (9)
smile *sonrisa* (15); *sonreír* (17)
smoke *fumar* (5); *humo* (9)
smoker *fumador/a* (12)
smooth *suavizar* (14)
snore *roncar* (14)
snow *nieve* (9)
snowflake *copo* (17)
so *así que* (3) ; *por eso* (11); *entonces* (20)
soak *remojar* (8)
soap *jabón* (16)
soap opera *telenovela* (15)
soccer *fútbol* (2)
soccer game *partido de fútbol* (15)
sociable *sociable* (14)
social class *clase social* (19)
social justice *justicia social* (19)
society *sociedad* (10)
sock *calcetín* (4)
soda pop *refresco* (8)
sofa *sofá* (6)
soft *blando/a* (8); *suave* (9); *tierno/a* (8)
soft drink *refresco* (8)
solar energy *energía solar* (16)
soldier *soldado* (11)
solid *sólido/a* (9)
solidarity *solidaridad* (14)
solitude *soledad* (14)
solve *solucionar* (9)
solve a case *resolver un caso* (17)
some *alguno/a* (10); *unos/as* (2)
someone *alguien* (17)
something *algo* (11)
son/daughter *hijo/a* (2)
song *canción* (14)
sophisticated *sofisticado/a* (6)
sorrow *pena* (11)
sorry *lo siento* (7)
soul *alma* (1)
sound *sonido* (13); *sonar (ue)* (20)
soundtrack *banda sonora* (15)
soup *sopa* (8)
soup tureen *sopera* (12)
source *fuente* (8) (17)
southeast *sureste* (3); *sudeste* (8)
southwest *suroeste* (3)
sovereignty *soberanía* (10)
Soviet Union *Unión Soviética* (10)
spa *balneario* (12)
space exploration *exploración del espacio* (19)
space travels *viajes espaciales* (19)
spaghetti *espaguetis* (8)
Spaniard/Spanish *español/a* (2)
Spanish *castellano* (13); *español* (11)
Spanish speaker *hispanohablante* (14)
spatial *espacial* (10)
speak *hablar* (1)
speaker *hablante* (2)
special *especial* (7)
specialize (in) *especializarse (en)* (14)

species *especie* (6)
specific *específico/a* (11)
specify *especificar* (20)
speculation *especulación* (19)
speech *discurso* (10)
speechless *boquiabierto/a* (14)
spell *deletrear* (1)
spellbound *abobado/a* (17)
spelling *ortografía* (6)
spend *gastar* (3); *pasar* (6)
spicy *picante* (8)
spider web *telaraña* (14)
spill *derramar* (20)
spin *hilar* (20)
spinach *espinaca* (8)
spine *púa* (16)
splendour *esplendoro/a* (14)
spokesman *portavoz* (4)
spontaneously *espontáneamente* (13)
spoon *cuchara* (10)
sport *deporte* (1)
sportsman/sportswoman *deportista* (2)
sports store *tienda de deportes* (4)
sporty *deportivo/a* (3)
spread *difundir* (8)
spring *primavera* (3)
spring roll *rollito de primavera* 19
square *plaza* (9); *cuadrado/a* (16)
stability *estabilidad* (5)
stable *estable* (12)
stadium *estadio* (9)
stage *etapa* (6)
stain remover *quitamanchas* (14)
staircase *escalera* (5)
stamp *sello* (17); *estampilla* (14)
standard *estándar* (14)
stand out *destacar* (5); *sobresalir* (8)
star *estrella* (5)
start *comenzar (ie)* (5); *empezar (ie)* (6); *iniciar* (10); *arrancar* (17)
starting point *punto de partida* (7)
state *estado* (1); *estatal* (12)
statement *declaración* (17)
statesman *estadista* (11)
station *estación* (16)
statistical *estadístico/a* (12)
stay *estadía* (7); *quedarse* (15)
steak *bistec* (8)
steep *remojar* (8)
stellar *estelar* (15)
stereo *estéreo* (6)
stereotype *estereotipo* (14)
stereotypical *estereotípico/a* (14)
stew *cocido* (8); *guiso* (8)
still *todavía* (2)
sting *picadura* (12); *picar* (12)
stinging *escozor* (12)
stingy *tacaño/a* (20)
stock *surtido* (18)
stock market *bolsa* (20)
stomach *barriga* (12)

stomachache *dolor de barriga; dolor de estómago* (12)
stone *piedra* (10)
stop *detener* (11); *parar* (8)
stop doing something *dejar de* (12)
storage room *almacén* (5) (18)
store *almacenar* (18)
store clerk *dependiente/a* (8)
storm *tormenta* (6)
story *relato* (17); *reportaje* (19)
straight *recto/a* (9)
strain *colar (ue)* (8)
strange *extraño/a* (10); *raro/a* (16)
stranger *desconocido/a* (13)
strategic *estratégico/a* (11)
strategy *estrategia* (13)
strawberry *fresa* (8)
stream *arroyo* (20)
street *calle* (3)
strength *fuerza* (20)
strengthening *fortalecimiento* (5)
stretch *extenderse* (14)
stress *estrés* (5)
stretch *estirar* (5)
strict *estricto/a* (7)
strike *huelga* (20)
strong *fuerte* (5)
strong man *caudillo* (10)
structure *estructura* (10)
stubborn *testarudo* (14)
student *estudiante* (2); *estudiantil* (18)
studio *estudio* (6)
study *estudiar* (1)
stupidity *estupidez* (14)
style *estilo* (2)
subdue *sojuzgar* (19)
substitute *sustituir* (19)
subway *metro* (3)
success *éxito* (2)
successful *exitoso/a* (14)
such as *como por ejemplo* (16)
suddenly *de repente* (11); *de golpe* (15); *de pronto* (17)
suffer *sufrir* (5); *padecer (zc)*
sugar *azúcar* (5)
suggest *sugerir* (17)
suggestion *sugerencia* (19)
suit *traje* (5)
suitcase *maleta* (7)
summary *resumen* (11)
summer *verano* (3)
summit *cima* (3); *cumbre* (11)
sum up *en suma* (19); *resumir* (6)
sun *sol* (9)
sunbathe *tomar el sol* (3)
sunblock *protector solar* (3)
Sunday *domingo* (1)
sunglasses *lentes de sol* (4)
sunny *soleado/a* (9)
sunset *anochecer* (15)
sunstroke *insolación* (12)

superfluous *superfluo/a* (19)
supermarket *supermercado* (4)
supernatural *sobrenatural* (14)
supply *oferta; surtido* (18)
support *apoyar, apoyo* (11)
suppose *suponer* (17)
sure *claro* (7)
surely *seguramente* (12)
surface *superficie* (7)
surgeon *cirujano/a* (12)
surgery *cirugía* (12); *operación* (12)
surpass *superar* (16)
surprise *sorprender* (15); *sorpresa* (3)
surprised *sorprendido/a* (20)
surprising *sorprendente* (10)
surrender *rendirse* (5)
surround *rodear* (9)
surrounding *circundante* (3)
surroundings *alrededores* (9)
survey *encuesta* (3)
survival *supervivencia* (12)
survive *sobrevivir* (7)
suspect *sospechar, sospechoso/a* (17)
suspicious (of) *desconfiado/a* (19)
sustain *sostener* (11)
sustainable *sostenible* (19)
swallow *tragar* (12)
sweat *sudar* (12)
sweater *suéter* (4)
Swedish *sueco* (13)
sweep along *arrastrar* (19)
sweet *dulce* (5)
sweeten *azucarar* (8)
sweetness *dulzura* (14)
swelling *inflamación* (12)
swim *nadar* (11)
swimming pool *piscina* (3)
Swiss chard *acelga* (8)
symbol *símbolo* (11)
sympathy *simpatía* (11)
symptom *síntoma* (12)
synopsis *sinopsis* (20)
syrup *almíbar* (8); *jarabe* (12)

**T**

table *mesa* (2); *cuadro* (11); *tabla* (12)
tablecloth *mantel* (20)
tablespoon *cucharada* (12)
tactic *táctica* (10)
take *tomar* (3); *agarrar* (11);
take (out) *sacar* (5)
take advantage of *aprovecharse de* (13)
take a quick look *echar un vistazo a* (15)
take attendance *pasar lista* (1)
take a walk *pasear* (3); *dar un paseo* (5)
take care of *ocuparse (de)* (7)
take care of oneself *cuidarse* (12)
take in account *tomar en cuenta* (19)
take notes *tomar notas* (2)

take off *despegar* (7)
take pictures *tomar fotos* (7)
take place *ocurrir* (9); *tener lugar* (15)
take possession of *apoderarse (de)* (11)
take refuge *refugiarse* (11)
tale *cuento* (7); *relato* (17)
talent *talento* (14)
talkative *hablador/a* (14)
tapestry *tapiz* (4)
tariff *tarifa* (16)
task/homework *tarea* (1)
taste *degustar* (8)
tasteless *soso/a* (8)
tasting *degustación* (8)
tasty *bueno/a* (5); *rico/a* (8)
tattoo *tatuaje* (18)
taxes *impuestos* (18)
taxi driver *taxista* (6)
tea *té* (8)
teacher *maestro/a* (2)
teaching *enseñanza* (13)
team *equipo* (3)
team work *trabajo en equipo* (6)
technique *técnica* (5)
technological *tecnológico/a* (19)
tedious *pesado/a* (15)
television *tele* (11); *televisor* (6)
tell (a story) *contar (ue)* (3); *relatar* (17)
temple *templo* (6)
ten *decena* (17); *diez* (1)
tenacity *tenacidad* (14)
tender *tierno/a* (8)
tender a *cariñoso/a* (5)
tenderness *ternura* (14)
tend to *tender (ie) a* (5)
tennis *tenis* (4)
tennis player *tenista* (5)
tense with pain *crispar* (20)
tent *tienda de campaña* (7)
tenth *décima* (2)
term *plazo* (19)
territory *territorio* (10)
text *texto* (2)
thank *agradecer (cz)* (15)
thanks *gracias* (1)
thank you *gracias* (1)
that is to say *o sea* (14)
theater *teatro* (2)
the best *mejor* (3)
then *entonces* (11); *luego* (8)
theory *teoría* (17)
there *allá* (4); *allí* (2)
there are *hay* (1)
therefore *así pues* (15); *por consiguiente* (20); *por lo tanto* (20)
there is *hay* (1)
thermometer *termómetro* (17)
these days *hoy en día* (19)
thesis *tesis* (19)
the way someone is *forma de ser* (20)

the Web *red* (16)
the worst *peor* (5)
thief *ladrón* (17)
thigh *muslo* (5)
thin *delgado/a* (2)
thing *cosa* (1)
think (about) *pensar (en)* (2)
thinning *adelgazamiento* (16)
third *tercer; tercero/a* (2); *tercio* (9)
thirteen *trece* (1)
thirty *treinta* (2)
thirty-one *treinta y uno* (2)
thirty-two *treinta y dos* (2)
thorn *espina* (18)
thorny *espinoso* (18)
thought *pensamiento* (10)
thousand *mil* (4)
thread *hilo* (16)
threaten *amenazar* (19)
three *tres* (1)
three hundred *trescientos/as* (4)
thrilling *emocionante* (15)
through *a tráves de* (5)
throw *arrojar* (17); *tirar* (17)
throw away *botar* (19); *tirar* (17)
throw out *expulsar* (11)
Thursday *jueves* (5)
ticket *boleto* (3); *entrada* (15)
tie *corbata* (4)
time *vez* (8); *rato* (17)
timeless *intemporal* (2)
tip *propina* (8)
tired *cansado/a* (5)
tiredness *cansancio* (12)
tiresome *molesto/a* (20)
tobacco *tabaco* (8)
tobacco pouch *tabaquera* (8)
together *junto/a* (6)
toilet *baño* (6)
tolerate *soportar* (14)
toll *peaje* (18)
tomato *tomate* (8)
tomb *tumba* (6)
tomorrow *mañana* (7)
toning *tonificación* (5)
tool *herramienta* (16)
too many, too much *demasiado/a* (5)
tooth *diente* (18)
toothache *dolor de muelas* (12)
topic *tema* (1)
topic sentence *frase temática* (4)
to the left *a la izquierda* (6)
to the right *a la derecha* (6)
touch *tocar* (5); *emocionar* (14)
tourism *turismo* (3)
toward *hacia* (7)
town *pueblo* (3)
toy *juguete* (4)
toy store *juguetería; tienda de juguetes* (4)
trace *huella* (2)

trade *comerciar, comercio* (18)
tradition *tradición* (1)
traffic *tráfico* (9)
traffic jam *embotellamiento* (9)
traffic light *semáforo* (9)
traffic sign *señal de tráfico/tránsito* (9)
train *entrenar* (5); *tren* (3)
trainer *entrenador/a* (17)
training *entrenamiento* (5); *formación* (6)
trajectory *trayectoria* (14)
transcendence *transcendencia* (18)
transform oneself/itself *transformarse* (20)
translation *traducción* (13)
translator *traductor/a* (6)
transmit *transmitir* (17)
transport *transportar* (5)
transportation *medios de transporte* (3)
travel *viajar* (2)
traveler *viajero/a* (11)
traveling *ambulante* (18)
travel through *recorrer* (11)
tray *bandeja* (8)
treasure *tesoro* (11)
treatment *tratamiento* (5)
treaty *tratado* (10)
tree *árbol* (2)
tree-felling *tala de árboles* (19)
trend *tendencia* (1)
triangle *triángulo* (15)
tribe *tribu* (10)
trill *gorjear* (11)
trimester *trimestre* (13)
trip *viaje* (1)
triumph *triunfar* (7); *triunfo* (11)
truck *camión* (11)
true *verdadero/a* (1); *verdad* (9);
  *cierto/a* (13)
trunk *tronco* (5)
trust *confiar* (14)
try *tratar de* (11); *intentar* (14)
try on *probar* (4)
t-shirt *camiseta* (4)
Tuesday *martes* (5)
turkey *pavo* (8)
Turkish *turco* (13)
turn *girar* (16); *giro* (20); *recoveco* (20)
turn off *apagar* (16)
turn on *encender* (16); *prender* (16)
turn up *acudir (a)* (15)
turtle *tortuga* (3)
TV channel *canal* (15)
TV network *cadena* (15)
TV series *serie* (15)
twelve *doce* (1)
twenty *veinte* (1)
twenty-eight *veintiocho* (2)
twenty-five *veinticinco* (2)
twenty-four *veinticuatro* (2)
twenty-nine *veintinueve* (2)
twenty-one *veintiuno* (2)

twenty-seven *veintisiete* (2)
twenty-six *veintiséis* (2)
twenty-three *veintitrés* (2)
twenty-two *veintidós* (2)
two *dos* (1)
two hundred *doscientos/as* (4)
typical *típico/a* (8)

## U

umbrella *paraguas* (8)
unbearable *insoportable* (20)
unbridgeable *infranqueable* (17)
unbridled *desenfrenado/a* (19)
uncertain *incierto/a* (8)
uncomfortable *incómodo/a* (3)
unconscious *inconsciente* (12)
under *debajo de* (3)
underground *subsuelo* (14)
underline *subrayar* (2)
understand *comprender* (7); *entender* (1)
understanding *comprensivo/a* (20)
undertake *emprender* (20)
underwear *ropa interior* (4)
unemployed *desempleado/a* (19)
unemployment *desempleo* (9) (19)
unevenness *desnivel* (3)
unexpected *inesperado/a* (20)
unforeseen *imprevisto/a* (11)
unforgettable *inolvidable* (3)
unfortunate *desafortunado/a* (19)
unfortunately *desafortunadamente, por
  desgracia* (19)
unfriendly *antipático/a* (2)
unique *único/a* (12)
unite *incorporar* (8)
United States *Estados Unidos* (10)
university *universidad* (2)
unknown *desconocido/a* (10);
  *incógnito/a* (11)
unmistakeable *inconfundible* (5);
  *inequívoco/a* (14)
unpack *deshacer* (7)
unpleasant *antipático/a* (2)
unplug *desenchufar* (16)
untidy *desordenado/a* (14)
until *desde* (5); *hasta* (10)
until when *hasta cuándo* (4)
unwanted hair *vello no deseado* (12)
upload *subir* (16)
uppercase letter *mayúscula* (13)
uprising *sublevación* (10)
ups and downs *altibajos* (14)
upsetting *desconcertante* (20)
Uruguayan *uruguayo/a* (2)
U.S. citizen/from the U.S.
  *estadounidense* (2)
use *uso* (11); *utilizar* (18)
useful *útil* (8)
user *usuario/a* (18)

usually do something *soler (ue)* (13)
utensil *utensilio* (6)

## V

vacation *vacaciones* (1)
vaccine *vacuna* (16)
vain *engreído/a* (14)
valet *paje* (4)
valley *valle* (9)
valuable *valioso/a* (19)
value *valor* (6)
vanity *vanidad* (14)
vase *vasija* (4)
vegetable *verdura* (5)
vegetables *vegetales* (8)
velocity *velocidad* (16)
Venezuelan *venezolano/a* (2)
verify *constatar* (17)
vice *vicio* (14)
video camera *cámara de video* (7)
video game *juego de video* (18)
vignette *viñeta* (6)
villager *lugareño* (20)
violation *violación* (19)
violence *violencia* (9)
virtue *virtud* (14)
visa *visa visado* (7)
visit *visitar* (2) (3)
visitor *visitante* (7)
voice *voz* (11)
volcano *volcán* (6)
volt *voltio* (16)
volume *volumen* (5)
voluptuosity *voluptuosidad* (5)
vomit *vomitar* (12); *vómito* (12)
vote *voto* (17)
voting *votación* (5)

## W

wage *sueldo salario* (6)
waist *cintura* (5)
wait *esperar* (4)
waiter/waitress *camarero/a* (2);
  *mesero/a* (2)
wait in line *hacer cola/fila* (7)
wake up *despertarse (ie)* (5)
walk *caminar* (5); *vuelta* (15)
wall *muro* (10); *pared* (3)
wallet *cartera* (4)
want *querer (ie)* (1)
war *guerra* (5)
wardrobe *ropero* (17)
warehouse *almacén* (18); *almacenar* (18)
warm *acogedor/a* (9); *cálido/a* (9);
  *caliente* (9)
warmth *simpatía* (11)
warn *advertir (ie) (de)* (12); *avisar* (16)
warning *advertencia* (12)

wash *lavar* (10)

washing machine *lavadora* (16)

wasp *avispa* (12)

waste *desecho* (20)

watch *reloj* (4); *vigilar* (5)

water *agua* (1)

waterfall *cascada; catarata; salto de agua* (3)

watermelon *sandía* (8)

water sports *deportes acuáticos* (3)

wealth *riqueza* (7)

weapon *arma* (1)

wear *llevar* (4)

weather *clima* (6)

weave *tejer* (4)

weaver *tejedor/a* (20)

Wednesday *miércoles* (5)

week *semana* (17)

weekend *fin de semana* (4)

weekly *semanal* (4)

weigh *pesar* (12)

weight *peso* (5)

weird *raro/a* (16)

welcoming *acogedor/a* (9)

well *bien* (11)

well/badly located *bien/mal situado/a* (9)

well-being *bienestar* (2)

well-educated *educado/a* (14)

well-mannered *educado/a* (14)

Welsh *galés/galesa* (13)

west *oeste* (3)

western *película del oeste* (15)

wet *mojado/a* (11)

whale *ballena* (17)

wheel *rueda* (16)

when *cuándo* (4)

where *dónde* (4)

which *cuál* (4)

while *mientras* (6); *mientras tanto* (11); *rato* (17)

whirl *vorágine* (19)

white *blanco/a* (4)

whitish *blanquecino/a* (17)

wicked *malvado/a* (11)

wickedness *maldad* (14)

widower/widow *viudo/a* (2)

will *voluntad* (12)

win *ganar* (2); *vencer* (20)

wind *viento* (9)

window *ventana* (6)

wine *vino* (8)

wine collection *vinoteca* (4)

wine glass *copa* (8)

wine store *bodega* (4)

winner *ganador* (4)

winter *invierno* (3)

wireless *inalámbrico/a* (16)

wisdom *sabiduría* (15)

wish *deseo* (9)

witch *bruja* (15)

withdraw *retirarse* (11)

with me *conmigo* (9)

with respect to *en cuanto a* (13); *respecto a* (18)

with you *contigo* (9)

witness *testigo* (17)

witty *listo/a* (5)

wonderful *maravilloso/a* (3)

wood *leña* (3); *madera* (6)

wool *lana* (4)

word *palabra* (11)

word processor *procesador de textos* (16)

work *trabajar* (1); *funcionar* (5); *obra* (5)

worker *obrero/a* (20); *trabajador/a* (18)

work of art *obra de arte* (15)

work permit *permiso de trabajo* (7)

workshop *taller* (18)

world *mundo* (1)

world affairs *asunto de interés mundial* (19)

worldwide *mundial* (5)

worried *preocupado/a* (20)

worry *preocupar* (13)

worry about *preocuparse de* (20)

worse *peor* (5)

write *escribir* (1)

write down *apuntar* (18)

writer *escritor/a* (2)

written *escrito/a* (13)

## X

xenophobia *xenofobia* (19)

## Y

yard *jardín* (3)

year *año* (12)

yell *grito* (20)

yellow *amarillo/a* (4)

yesterday *ayer* (7)

yogurt *yogur* (8)

youth *joven* (6); *juventud* (10)

yucca *yuca* (8)

## Z

zero *cero* (17)

zipper *cierre* (16)

# CREDITS

## Text Credits

p. 301 "En el país de las maravillas," by Victor Montoya; p. 265 "Un hermoso cambio de registro," by Alex Ramirez; p. 283 "Un uruguayo desembarca en Hollywood tras destruir Montevideo con robots gigantes," by Ecoprensa S.A.; p. 319 "La ampliación del Canal de Panamá abre sus compuertas a un nuevo desarrollo económico," by Portal Universia S.A.

## Photo Credits

p. 4 (1) Ciro Cesar/La Opinion/Newscom; p. 4 (2) Ciro Cesar/La Opinion\Newscom Getty Images, Inc.; p. 4 (3) Capricornis Photographic inc.\Shutterstock; p. 4 (4) Christian Summer\iStockphoto.com; p. 4 (5) Caramaria/Lidian Neeleman/Dreamstime.com; p. 4 (6) Liem Bahneman\Shutterstock; p. 4 (7) Keith Binns\iStockphoto.com; p. 4 (8) Nick Tzolov\iStockphoto.com; p. 4 (9) iStockphoto.com; p. 7 (1) Newscom; p. 7 (2) Suljo\Dreamstime LLC -Royalty Free; p. 7 (3) AP Wide World Photos; p. 7 (4) stocklight\Shutterstock; p. 7 (6) Entertainment Press\Shutterstock lev radin\Shutterstock; p. 9 (3) Jgz\Fotolia, LLC - Royalty Free; p. 9 (2) Andrzej Gibasiewicz\iStockphoto.com; p. 9 (1) lubilub\iStockphoto.com; p. 9 (6) Rafael Ramirez Lee\Shutterstock; p. 9 (5) gary718\Shutterstock; p. 9 (4) stockcam\iStockphoto.com; p. 15 (bottom left) Carrie-Anne Gonzalez\iStockphoto.com; p. 15 (bottom right) Hazim Sahib Jalil Al-hakeem\iStockphoto.com; p. 15 (top left) Tashka/Natalia Bratslavsky/Dreamstime.com; p. 15 (top center) Therese Mckeon\iStockphoto.com; p. 15 (top right center) Emmanuel Dunand/AFP/Getty Images; p. 15 (top right) Thinkstock; p. 20 (bottom left) Reuters / B Mathur / Landov; p. 20 (bottom center) AP Wide World Photos; p. 20 (bottom right) Wikipedia, The Free Encyclopedia; p. 24 carolgaranda\Shutterstock; p. 28 NASA/Johnson Space Center; p. 28 (2) AP Photo/Eric Gay; p. 28 (3) stocklight\Shutterstock; p. 28 (4) Michael Tran/FilmMagic/Getty Images, Inc.; p. 28 (5) Getty Images; p. 28 (6) Doug Pensinger/Getty Images, Inc.; p. 28 (10) Entertainment Press\Shutterstock; p. 28 (8) Lilac Mounlain\Shutterstock; p. 28 (7) Andy Lyons/Getty Images, Inc.; p. 28 (9) Ken Inness\Shutterstock; p. 31 (left) © Lynsey Addario / CORBIS All Rights Reserved; p. 31 (right) Christopher Considine\Latin American Masters Gallery; p. 33 (left) Susan Van Etten\PhotoEdit Inc.; p. 33 (center) Robert Fried/robertfriedphotography.com; p. 33 (right) David L. Clawson; p. 20 (top left) AP/Wide World Photos; p. 20 (top center) © Reuters/CORBIS; p. 20 (top right) Getty Images, Inc.; p. 38 (1) Rafael Martin-Gaitero\Shutterstock; p. 38 (2) Jeff Luckett\iStockphoto.com; p. 38 (3) Travelcaes/Kristina Mahlau/Dreamstime.com; p. 38 (4) Getty Images/De Agostini Editore Picture Library; p. 38 (5) Patrick Keen\iStockphoto.com; p. 46 Kevin Schafer/Stone/Getty Images; p. 47 Robert Wroblewski\Shutterstock; p. 49 (top) Janne Hamalainen\Shutterstock; p. 49 (bottom) Aneese\Dreamstime LLC -Royalty Free; p. 51 (top) Silva, Juan\Getty Images Inc. - Image Bank; p. 51 (bottom) © Walt Disney Co/courtesy Everett Collection; p. 56 (top) Demetrio Carrasco © Dorling Kindersley, Courtesy of Palacio San Martin; p. 59 (left) Mlenny Photography/Alexander Hafemann/iStockphoto; p. 59 (right) Mlenny Photography/Alexander Hafemann/iStockphoto; p. 63 Cristian Lazzari\iStockphoto.com; p. 69 Newscom; p. 67 Jose Fuste Raga\AGE Fotostock America, Inc.; p. 74 (top center) Jed Jacobsohn/Getty Images, Inc.; p. 74 (bottom center) Miguel Riopa/AFP/Getty Images; p. 74 (right) Juan Mabromata/ AFP/Getty Images; p. 75 Stephen Cobum\Shutterstock; p. 77 Danilo\Shutterstock; p. 81 Travis Lindquist/Getty Images, Inc.; p. 87 (right)digitalsport-photoagency/shutterstock; p. 87 (left) Photo by Atsushi Tomura/AFLO SPORT/Newscom; p. 74 (top left) Getty Images, Inc.; p. 74 (bottom left) Getty Images, Inc.; p. 99 (left) D. Donne Bryant Stock Photography; p. 99 (center) John Mitchell\D. Donne Bryant Stock Photography; p. 99 (right) John Mitchell\D. Donne Bryant Stock Photography; p. 110 (top left) Rough Guides Dorling Kindersley; Alain Lacroix Dreamstime LLC-Royalty Free; p. 110 (top center) Rafa Irusta\Shutterstock; p. 110 (top right) Franck Boston\Shutterstock; p. 110 (center left) Marie C. Fields\Shutterstock; p. 110 (bottom left) Alexey Stiop\Shutterstock; Getty Images, Inc.; p. 121 Andreas Meyer\Shutterstock; p. 123 (top) Photographers Direct; p. 123 (center) Adam Jones, Ph.D.; p. 123 (bottom) Newscom; p. 128 (5) Paul Cowan\Fotolia, LLC - Royalty Free; p. 128 (1) Analia Valeria Urani\Shutterstock; p. 128 (3) Monkey Business Images\Shutterstock; p. 128 (4) Tony Freeman\PhotoEdit Inc.; p. 128 (2) Felipex\iStockphoto.com; p. 128 (6) Linda Whitwam © Dorling Kindersley; p. 133 robert van beets\iStockphoto.com; p. 135 Keith Kevit\Shutterstock; p. 136 ©/Latin Focus.com; p. 138 (1) Photos.com\Getty Images - Thinkstock; p. 138 (2) Regien Paassen\Shutterstock; p. 138 (3) Joel Blit\Shutterstock; p. 138 (4) Amanda Lewis\iStockphoto.com; p. 139 ©/Latin Focus.com; p. 141 (top) Clyde Westall Hensley; p. 141 (bottom) Ulf Andersen/Getty Images, Inc.; p. 146 (bottom) YinYang\iStockphoto.com; p. 146 (center) Yory Frenklakh\iStockphoto.com; p. 149 (left) ©/Latin Focus.com; p. 149 (right) Richard Lord Enterprises; p. 150 YinYang\iStockphoto.com; p. 153 Michael Jones Photography/Photographers Direct; p. 159 (top) Oscar Pinto\Fotolia, LLC -Royalty Free; p. 159 (bottom) © Arturo Fuentes/Latin Focus.com; p. 146 (top) Stephen Alvarez\National Geographic Image Collection; p. 164 (1) Yaroslav Gerzhedovich\iStockphoto.com; p. 164 (2) Comstock\Thinkstock; p. 164 (3) Photos.com\Getty Images - Thinkstock; p. 164 (4) Photos.com\Getty Images - Thinkstock; p. 164 (5) John Neubauer\PhotoEdit Inc.; p. 165 (1) Sourabhj\Dreamstime LLC - Royalty Free; p. 165 (2) Enrico69\Dreamstime LLC -Royalty Free; p. 165 (3) © Ric Ergenbright/CORBIS All Rights Reserved; p. 165 (4) Jason Speros\Shutterstock; p. 167 Getty Images, Inc.; p. 169 (right) © Topham/The Image Works; p. 169 (left) © Bettmann/CORBIS; p. 170 (1) Julien Tromeur\Fotolia, LLC - Royalty Free; p. 170 (2) Binkski\Fotolia, LLC - Royalty Free; p. 170 (3) Alexander Zhiltsov\Dreamstime LLC -Royalty Free; p. 170 (4) sweetym\iStockphoto.com; p. 170 (5) MiquelMunill\iStockphoto.com; p. 170 (6) Alena Yakusheva\Fotolia, LLC - Royalty Free; p. 177 Mark Van Overmeire\Shutterstock; p. 183 Albuquerque Seismological Lab, USGS; p. 184 (left) SuperStock, Inc.; p. 184 (right) Mireille Vautier\Picture Desk, Inc./Kobal Collection; p. 185 AP Wide World Photos; p. 187 ©/ CORBIS All Rights Reserved; p. 190 Getty

# INDEX